Approaches to Teaching the Works of Orhan Pamuk

Approaches to Teaching the Works of Orhan Pamuk

Edited by

Sevinç Türkkan

and

David Damrosch

The Modern Language Association of America

New York 2017

Library of Congress Cataloging-in-Publication Data

Names: Türkkan, Sevinç, 1977– editor. | Damrosch, David editor.
Title: Approaches to teaching the works of Orhan Pamuk / edited by Sevinç Türkkan and David Damrosch.
Description: New York : The Modern Language Association of America, 2017. | Series: Approaches to teaching world literature, ISSN 1059-1133 ; 146 | Includes bibliographical references and index.
Identifiers: LCCN 2017026389 (print) | LCCN 2017031144 (ebook) | ISBN 9781603293204 (Epub) | ISBN 9781603293211 (Kindle) | ISBN 9781603293181 (cloth : alk. paper) | ISBN 9781603293198 (pbk. : alk. paper)
Subjects: LCSH: Pamuk, Orhan, 1952—Study and teaching (Higher)
Classification: LCC PL248.P34 (ebook) | LCC PL248.P34 Z5375 2017 (print) | DDC 894/.3533—dc23
LC record available at https://lccn.loc.gov/2017026389

Published by The Modern Language Association of America
85 Broad Street, suite 500, New York, New York 10004–2434
www.mla.org

CONTENTS

PREFACE

The awarding of the Nobel Prize in Literature to Orhan Pamuk in 2006 established him as a preeminent novelist internationally and sealed his stature in Turkey as a figure of letters. Before the award, only five of his novels were available in English, German, and French translations, and his memoir *Istanbul* had only appeared in English and German. Since the award Pamuk's writing has been translated into fifty-five languages, seven million copies of his books have been sold, and his work has earned universal critical acclaim. In North America he is among the most frequently taught contemporary novelists; students and teachers alike are drawn to his works, both for their innovative aesthetic qualities and for the provocative and timely concerns they raise. His works interrogate problems of modernity and of civilizational divides in the Turkish context and integrate the Ottoman legacy formally and thematically in stylistically innovative ways. Pamuk brought Istanbul back onto the world literary map almost single-handedly.

This is the first volume in the series Approaches to Teaching World Literature that is devoted to the works of a Turkish author and only the second to focus on an author from a Muslim country. Scholars, teachers, and students will find here a multiplicity of approaches, methods, perspectives, and interpretations of Pamuk's compelling and challenging literary output. Pamuk's place in the genealogy of Turkish literature can be difficult to comprehend for the anglophone reader, partly because few works by Turkish writers, other than those by Pamuk, are available in English. Consequently, Pamuk has been made to stand as the representative of all Turkish literature or else has often been idealized as exceptional for his ability to transcend Turkishness. In world literature survey courses he sometimes represents the entirety of Middle Eastern literatures, or he is cast as either the least European writer in modern world literature courses or the most European writer in non-Western literature surveys. Few instructors are familiar with all his work (his first novel still awaits translation into English) or with the substantial scholarship on his work in Turkish. Teaching Pamuk's work in translation poses cultural and linguistic challenges. In particular, it can be difficult for teachers to know how to approach the many stylistic and thematic aspects of his novels, his subtle references to problems of Turkish modernity and to the Ottoman archive, his intriguing use of intertextual elements, and his characters' metatextual commentaries. This volume engages substantially with all these concerns.

In response to the need for critical studies, syllabi, and other teaching resources, in part 1, "Materials," we offer discussion of Pamuk's background, his relation to other writers—Turkish and international—and the critical reception of his works. In part 2, "Approaches," twenty scholars share their insights into teaching Pamuk's works, providing useful information and concrete suggestions for introducing his work in the classroom. Part 2 is organized into five sections: Historical and Cultural Contexts; Pamuk, Translation, and the Transnational Context; Teaching Pamuk beyond the East-West Divide; Teaching Pamuk in Dialogue with World Literature; and Aesthetic Representations and Visual Studies. Of course, fitting individual contributions into such neat divisions is problematic and the way they overlap across sections attests to the complexities of Pamuk's works. We hope that these overlaps promote broader, more creative perspectives on individual texts. Whether one teaches Pamuk in a world literature survey, in a course on the global novel, in a Turkish or Middle Eastern studies seminar, or in a history or visual studies class, this volume should help teachers establish a more concrete portrait of the author and his oeuvre —a portrait with all its pluralities, nuances, and complex realities.

In the time since we began assembling this volume, Pamuk has produced two new novels. Told from the perspectives of two brothers, *Kafamda Bir Tuhaflık* (2014 [*A Strangeness in My Mind*; 2015]) is a modern epic that chronicles the transformations of Istanbul and its citizens during the last decades of the twentieth century and the early twenty-first century. The style and narrative technique of this novel recall Pamuk's early literary preoccupations and suggest his mature return to the historical realism of his early novels. Published in 2016, *Kırmızı Saçlı Kadın* (*The Red-Haired Woman*; 2017) narrates the traumatic romantic experience of its young protagonist against the backdrop of a tragic crime. Though our volume doesn't include a discussion of these recent works, the section on historical and cultural contexts should serve well teachers who would venture into unexplored territory. Pamuk's career trajectory suggests that he will continue to explore the human predicament in imaginative ways, and we expect more scholarship on his works will further illuminate the unique literary landscape he has opened up for us.

FOREWORD

The Elephant in the Classroom

Orhan Pamuk

I have been teaching comparative literature at Columbia University for the past ten years. At the start of every semester, if I plan to discuss one of my own novels in class, I always tell my new students an old story about writing and teaching. It's a popular anecdote, first mentioned in Brian Boyd's wonderful biography of Vladimir Nabokov (303), told often enough that it now exists in various versions. It takes place in 1957, when Nabokov was proposed for an appointment at Harvard University as professor of Russian literature. The subject of Nabokov's possible appointment soon led to the usual arguments at faculty meetings between professors who were in favor and those who were against. At one such meeting, a professor who did want to see Nabokov join the faculty reminded his colleagues that Nabokov was one of Russia's greatest writers. The linguist Roman Jakobson, who opposed Nabokov's appointment, retorted, "Gentlemen, even if one allows that he is an important writer, are we next to invite an elephant to be Professor of Zoology?"

I remind my laughing students that the truthfulness of this tale is questionable and then turn to the real matter at hand.

"This semester, I will stand before you as an elephant, but I will also try my best to be a professor." Elephants don't know what it is that makes them elephants. Elephants just are. Similarly, novelists do not consciously dwell on what they do when they write. The things novelists mean to describe and express, the landscapes and territories they wish to cover, may be different from those elements of a text that readers and students should focus on. The author of a novel is not always in the best position to interpret it, and eventually others may become more familiar with the text than the author. Most of my bright students at Columbia were fully aware of these paradoxes, so I didn't have to spend too much time on the subject, though I did occasionally warn them: "I am going to speak now not in my capacity as a professor, but as the elephant in the classroom."

As the elephant in the classroom, I tell students that one of the reasons I wrote *My Name Is Red* was that at the age of twenty-two, I had always wanted to be a painter but had failed. With this novel I wanted to construct a narrative inspired by the contrast between what a painter envisions and the way his or her hand can sometimes move of its own accord. (This is similar to the difference between being a novelist and being a professor teaching a class on the art of the novel.) Eventually, these ideas led me to the question of what John Berger terms "ways of seeing," so I also ended up exploring the East-West dichotomy, Persian miniatures, Renaissance art, and history.

As the elephant in the classroom, I also tell my students that everything that happens to the protagonist, Ka, in the first two hundred pages of my novel *Snow* is almost exactly what I experienced myself when I first arrived in Kars in 1999 to write that book. I wanted to write a political novel that would contain an entire nation, just like those Graham Greene novels (*The Heart of the Matter*, *The Quiet American*, *Our Man in Havana*) that are set in poor and troubled Third World countries.

Though I tried to resist the temptation, I was inclined—even more so than my students—to see my own "novels of a nation" as introductions to the cultural norms and particular afflictions of Turkey, the Middle East, and the entire Muslim world. But in teaching my novels, how much emphasis should I place on Turkish history, the transformation of Istanbul, or Islam and secularism, so that the logic of my novels would be more accessible to my students? After a lifetime spent battling against political pressures on literature, devoting more classroom time to political ironies over literary nuances made me feel like a traitor. Whether I was teaching my own novels or *Anna Karenina*, *Mrs. Dalloway*, or *The Red and the Black*, I felt that by discussing politics and history, I was betraying true literature—a feeling that stayed with me like a kind of heartache.

Before I started teaching at Columbia in September 2006, I had already taught seminars and given lectures about my novels at universities outside Turkey, but I had never held a regular teaching post anywhere. No Turkish university had offered me a position, and I didn't really need the money anyway, so until the age of fifty-four, all I did for a living was write novels. However, the political pressures I was facing in Turkey made the offers I received from American universities more attractive, and I began to feel it might be worth moving abroad for a time.

Giving seminars with brilliant academics such as Andreas Huyssen, David Damrosch, and Bruce Robbins, all of whom I now consider friends, helped me overcome my apprehensions about embarking on a teaching career in middle age. Half an hour before class was due to start, I would meet with one of my professor friends in his office to establish what we were going to cover that day and to split topics between us. I enjoyed these discussions as much as the classes themselves. "I'll need to mention that the key to understanding the newspaper columns in *The Black Book* is to bear in mind that columnists in Turkey are all armchair philosophers," I would exclaim. Or perhaps: "When I was writing *My Name Is Red*, I made a floor plan of the house and garden where Shekure and her sons lived; I should make a few copies and hand them out to the class."

My experienced colleagues, smiling kindly upon my agitated eagerness, would tell me that letting a seminar follow its natural course could sometimes be more instructive, and yet I would still walk into class feeling tense and worried, and if that day's topic happened to be one of my own novels, I would feel as foolish as if I'd taken the floor to speak when I had absolutely nothing to say. Sometimes in the middle of a class I would sense how absurd it was for a man to be discussing his own novels with his own students, and I would find myself thinking that just as there was something inherently pretentious about teaching a class called the Art of the Novel so too there was about the act of writing a novel.

Adding to the uncertainty I felt was my own interest in that ever-expanding area that students and professors refer to as theory. Since I enjoyed thinking about theory more than any other writer I knew and tried to keep up with new contributions to the field of cultural studies, I would sometimes end up theorizing my own work. "In this passage, our author is aiming to explore the history of the streets and shops of Istanbul," I would tell the class. "Tombola-Bingo is an Italian game that came from Naples to Istanbul, spread through the Levantine community, and was eventually adopted by the secular Turkish middle classes as a traditional New Year's Eve entertainment," I would say. "In Islamic societies, where men and women rarely get to interact unless they are already married, boys and girls will develop an alternative language with its own special grammar of silent glances, frowns, moments of deliberate immobility, and pointed questions such as, 'Would you like another meatball?'"

I would say all this, but at the same time I would wonder if I was making too much of the undercurrents of Turkishness and Istanbul that run through my novels. On the one hand, I agreed with my colleague David Damrosch's view that, to put it simply, world literature is made up of books that have acquired new meaning in translation (*What* 5); but, on the other hand, I made every effort to ensure that when they were translated, my novels would not acquire meanings or be interpreted in ways I had never intended—that they would, in essence, remain within their Turkish context.

Ten years of teaching has shown me that staying away from theory and discovering with my students the intricacies of novels—my own and others'—helps to avoid these anxieties and contradictions. So at the start of every class, I will devote some time to poring over the pages I've set for that day. "Before we begin our discussion, let's analyze what's been happening here," I'll say. "Why do you think Ka is arranging the meeting at the Hotel Asia?" "What key events from this section should we discuss?" "What do you think is the dominant mood in these pages?"

The first thing I learned from my students was something I already knew in the back of my mind: like most educated upper-middle-class Turkish men, I too had an authoritarian streak in me, and even though I enjoyed teaching through discussion, I still believed that my real job was to tell students the "facts" about my novels. Sometimes I would get bored halfway through class and glance at the motionless hour and minute hands on the enormous clock above the blackboard. Sometimes I would marvel at a student reminding me of the nuances and oddities of a novel I'd written years ago and wonder if I'd even meant any of it.

Whenever I set theory and social context aside in favor of a close reading of novels, seeking out their subtleties and internal symmetries, I would discover just how much I had forgotten about my own books. I'd spent so much time going over *Anna Karenina* and *Demons* before class and analyzing them for my students that I had all but memorized those texts. But I couldn't bring myself to do the same kind of preparation for my own novels, and so approached every class with the feeling that I was about to give a lecture on some other writer whose work I didn't know that well and embarrass myself in front of my students.

One day, just before class was due to start, a student saw me frantically skimming through *Snow* outside the classroom. "That's what happens if you don't bother to do your reading!" he joked. He had that teasing, mischievous expression I sometimes see on students' faces when they spot little things in my novels that I hadn't even realized, or when they don't agree with the logic of a novel and point out its contradictions and ambiguities. After ten years of giving lectures on my own work, now when I catch that expression on my students' faces I have a comforting thought: "Maybe they'd rather have an elephant in the classroom than a professor."

NOTE

This essay was translated by Ekin Oklap.

Part One

MATERIALS

The Author

Orhan Pamuk was born in 1952 into an upper-class family in the affluent Istanbul neighborhood of Nişantaşı. In his memoir *Istanbul* he articulates his ambivalent feelings about belonging to a family that provided for him but also quarreled mercilessly over property and money (14–15).[1] A reluctant student, he devoted his adolescent years to painting. He attended Istanbul's Robert College, where an extensive library of world literature, mostly in English translation, supplemented his father's private library of Turkish and French books. He studied architecture at Istanbul Technical University but did not complete a degree. He then earned a degree in journalism from Istanbul University; however, he never worked as a journalist, having decided at age twenty-two to become a writer.

As a university student in the 1970s, Pamuk witnessed Marxist-Leninist revolutionists and their conservative opponents violently clash with the police on campuses across the country. He briefly joined a revolutionary group of upper-class Marxists, but his beliefs were related more to his intellectual and aesthetic aspirations than to political commitment. He turned to writing as an outlet for his frustration about his bourgeois background and disappointment in the aftermath of the 1971 military coup. As a son of a prosperous family, Pamuk enjoyed the privilege of being able to dedicate himself exclusively to writing.

Pamuk lives in Istanbul but has spent a good amount of time abroad, participating in the Iowa Writers' Workshop in 1985 and undertaking research for his novels in various major cities across the globe. As the Robert Yik-Fong Tam Professor of the Humanities at Columbia University, he teaches fall-semester courses in New York City when he is not touring the world to promote his books.

Fiction, Screenplay, and the Museum of Innocence

It is impossible to separate Pamuk's development as a novelist from the shifting political scene in Turkey. At age nineteen, Pamuk witnessed what has come to be known as "the coup by memorandum" (12 March 1971), which led to the imprisonment of many intellectuals, including writers, journalists, and scholars; at age twenty-eight, he saw Turkey's third coup in twenty years (12 September 1980). These coups—and the earlier imprisonments of writers such as Nazım Hikmet (1902–63), Kemal Tahir (1910–73), and Orhan Kemal (1914–70) for their political beliefs—left indelible marks on Pamuk.

All Pamuk's projects demonstrate high ambition, serious research, and complete dedication. His first novel, *Cevdet Bey ve Oğulları* (1982 ["Cevdet Bey and His Sons"]), a six-hundred-page work considered a classic in Turkish, narrates the dissolutions and continuities across three generations of a Nışantaşı family whose fate and struggles reflect those of the modern Turkish Republic at the turn of the twentieth century. Pamuk modeled the structure of the novel after Thomas Mann's *Buddenbrooks* (1901) and his characters after books by Jean-Paul Sartre and Albert Camus (Pamuk, *Öteki Renkler* 141). Yet Pamuk was equally engaged with his predecessors at home. *Cevdet Bey ve Oğulları* attests to his admiration for Yaşar Kamal's lyricism, even as it breaks away from the dominant trend of Anatolian realism and *köy romanı* ("village novels") (Shaw 247). Pamuk, his affinity for synthesis already evident, draws on the nineteenth-century realist novel while supplementing it with Turkish stylistic models. Pamuk recalls rummaging in his grandfather's railway journals and combing old bookstores for popular novels of the 1930s and for other material with which to build the texture of his work (*Öteki Renkler* 140). The manuscript (with the initial title "Karanlık ve Işık" ["Darkness and Light"]) won the 1979 Milliyet Publishing Award for the best unpublished work in Turkey, but the publisher declined publication because of the failing economy in Turkey. About ten years after he penned the novel, Pamuk succeeded in getting it published as *Cevdet Bey ve Oğulları*. It received enthusiastic reviews in Turkey for its historical depth and psychological subtlety and won the prestigious Orhan Kemal Novel Prize in 1983.

Pamuk's second novel, *Sessiz Ev* (1983 [*Silent House*; 2012]), was published the following year. Scholars have recognized the modernist styles of William Faulkner and Virginia Woolf in Pamuk's first experiment with multiple perspectives. Set amid the economic and social turbulence before the 1980 coup, the novel depicts the conflict between right-wing nationalists and communist extremists, and how this turbulent spirit affects the fate of a family in decline. Pamuk writes that the novel's family matriarch was partly based on his cruel, though ignorant, maternal grandmother (*Öteki Renkler* 144). Intertextually connected to his previous novel, *Silent House* includes references to Ivan Turgenev's *Fathers and Sons*, to Pamuk's brother, and to "Orhan who is supposedly writing a novel" (*Silent House* 288). The novel received the Madaralı Award in 1984 for the best Turkish novel of the year (Shaw 250), yet reviewers were unenthusiastic about Pamuk's narrative and stylistic experimentation (Özkırımlı).

In his third novel, *Beyaz Kale* (1985 [*The White Castle*; 1990]), which takes the form of an allegory, Pamuk turned his attention to Turkey's repudiated Ottoman archive to reflect on cross-cultural exchange. He read sources transliterated from Ottoman into modern Turkish, set his novel during the seventeenth-century reign of Sultan Mehmed IV, and, in a highly inventive gesture, used the motif of the doppelgänger to explore the relation between essentialist Eastern and Western identities. In Turkey Pamuk's stylistic innovations were welcomed by some critics, while others deplored what they saw as a lack of historical detail compared with his previous novels. He was also accused of plagiarism by critics who noticed similarities between the novel and eyewitness accounts of Istanbul during the era of Suleiman the Magnificent. In an afterword appended to the later Turkish edition of the novel and included in *Other Colors*, Pamuk implicitly responds to these accusations by discussing his sources and pointing to the narrator's postmodern method of rewriting archival documents (247–52).[2] Pamuk's first novel to be translated into English, *The White Castle* was welcomed with enthusiasm by his anglophone readers.

Released in 1990, Pamuk's fourth novel, *Kara Kitap* (1990 [*The Black Book*; 1994]) builds on material that Pamuk compiled in the mid-1980s at the Columbia University's Butler Library (*Other Colors* 257). Living away from Istanbul allowed Pamuk to revisit the Islamic and Sufi literature that he had previously dismissed. In particular, Mevlânâ Celâleddin Rûmî's *Masnavi-i Ma'navi* (1273 [Rûmî, *Masnavi*; 2004]), Şeyh Galip's *Hüsn'ü Aşk* (1783 [*Beauty and Love*; 2005]), and Farid ud-Din Attâr's *Mantiq ut-Tair* (1177 [*Conference of the Birds*; 1984]) inspired the allegorical aspects of *Kara Kitap*, to which Pamuk added a frame similar to that of *The Arabian Nights.* A series of newspaper columns written by one of the characters is interwoven with the plot, in alternating chapters, while the secular settings and everyday experiences of living in Istanbul are intertwined with the protagonist's physical and metaphysical search. The novel received unprecedented critical attention: within two years of its publication, the scholar Nüket Esen edited an anthology, *Kara Kitap Üzerine Yazılar* ("Writings on *Kara Kitap*"), and in 1999 Engin Kılıç edited *Orhan Pamuk'u Anlamak* ("Understanding Orhan Pamuk"). In Turkey some applauded Pamuk's reworking of Sufi tradition, defended his linguistic innovations, and welcomed the novel's postmodern turns. Others attacked his experiments with prose style: they accused him of marring the language with errors or found the narrative's preoccupation with endless stories and issues frustrating. In contrast to the mixed assessment at home, anglophone reviewers greeted the English translation with enthusiasm, praising its Eastern literary erudition, postmodern innovations, and noir style. Güneli Gün's English translation received harsh criticism from British reviewers, who found her idiomatic and colloquial style inappropriate. In 2006 a new translation by Maureen Freely appeared. Critics often point to James Joyce's *Ulysses* in reference to Pamuk's encyclopedic mapping of Istanbul. Yet the novel's density defies simple interpretations. In 2013 Pamuk collaborated with Darmin Hadzibegovic on *Kara Kitap'ın Sırları: Orhan Pamuk'un Yazı ve Resimleriyle* ("*The Black Book*'s Mysteries: With Orhan Pamuk's Handwritings and Drawings"), which includes Pamuk's reflections on conceiving and drafting his magnum opus, photographs from his private albums, his ballpoint-pen drawings, and snippets from his spiral-bound, graph-paper notebooks.

Chapter 15 of *The Black Book*, "Karlı Gecenin Aşk Hikayeleri" ("Love Stories on a Snowy Night") served as the basis for *Gizli Yüz* ("Hidden Face"; 1991), a screenplay Pamuk wrote in collaboration with the director Ömer Kavur. Mixing elements of the noir and the surreal, the film explores its female protagonist's mysterious search for a lost and unattainable object. The film received the Antalya Golden Orange Film Festival award for best original screenplay in 1991 as well as several awards in Europe and North America, including for best film at the Montreal World Film Festival in 1999.

Promoted by a vigorous publicity campaign, Pamuk's next novel, *Yeni Hayat* (1994 [*The New Life*; 1997]), became one of the most widely read books in Turkey. The cover appeared on billboards across Istanbul with the novel's provocative first sentence, "Bir gün bir kitap okudum ve bütün hayatım değişti" ("One day I read a book and my entire life was changed"; 7; 3). The novel weaves a dense intertextual web with Rainer Maria Rilke's *Duino Elegies* and Dante's *Vita Nuova*, borrowing stylistic elements of German romanticism while articulating a counterthesis to Ziya Gökalp's project of Turkish nationalism in his *Yeni Hayat* ("New Life"). Some critics were alienated by the novel's complexity and allusive nature, while others attributed the book's success to Pamuk's publicity campaign (Kılıç 226). In the wake of this criticism, in 1996 the literary scholar Yıldız Ecevit published *Orhan Pamuk'u Okumak: Kafası Karışmış Okur ve Modern Roman* ("Reading Orhan Pamuk: The Confused Reader and the Modern Novel"), a book-length analysis of the novel in relation to postmodern literary theories. Western critics, by contrast, appreciated the novel's style, referring to Jorge Luis Borges, Italo Calvino, Umberto Eco, and Thomas Pynchon in their reviews.

Pamuk's fifth novel, *Benim Adım Kırmızı* (1998 [*My Name Is Red*; 2001]) was an immediate success in Turkey and cemented Pamuk's reputation worldwide. His most lively and optimistic novel, *My Name Is Red* is a philosophical reflection on the relation between text and image; it depicts the struggle for cultural hegemony through the confrontation of Ottoman miniature painting with Renaissance portraiture. To gather material for his book, Pamuk studied illuminated manuscripts at Topkapı Palace in Istanbul and at the Metropolitan Museum of Art in New York City, mined the Ottoman archives, and read widely about the book's sixteenth-century setting in the historical and art historical scholarship. In Turkey, some criticized the book for employing orientalist stereotypes in the representation of the Ottoman Empire and for imitating Eco's style in his philosophical-historical murder mystery *The Name of the Rose*. Positive reviews called the novel an elegy to the forgotten Islamic aesthetics of miniature painting. The novel sold nearly half a million copies in China, where Pamuk was named "the most influential international author" ("Pamuk Receives Award"). In Italy, *My Name Is Red* was awarded the 2002 Grinzane Cavour Prize (Premio

Grinzane Cavour), and in France, the 2002 Best Foreign Book Prize (Prix du Meilleur Livre Étranger).

Published in the aftermath of the 9/11 attacks, Pamuk's most openly political novel, *Kar* (2002 [*Snow*; 2004]), generated controversy both at home and abroad. Some took it as a realist representation of the conflicts between "Westernization" and "Islamists" (Atwood) while others failed to register the complexities of the novel, accusing Pamuk of "marketing" his country unfavorably (İrdelmen) and of abusing the Turkish language (Kayra). More insightful reviewers noted the novel's provocative and defiant approach (Alpay, "Kar") and suggested Pamuk for the Nobel Prize (Updike, "Anatolian Arabesque"). Pointing to Fyodor Dostoevsky as a model and defending his authorial distance, Pamuk responded to partisan accusations thus: "Many of my characters hold ideas which run counter to my own. The challenge is to also make the voices representing opinions I find repugnant sound convincing" ("Turkish Trauma"). For him, the book's most important contribution was its self-reflexive concern with the ethics of representation (Shaw 260). After the publication of *Snow* in Germany in 2005, the book was awarded the prestigious Peace Prize of the German Book Trade (Der Friedenpreis des Deutschen Buchhandels), honoring Pamuk's commitment to a concept of culture based on knowledge and respect for others and to the idea that Europe and Muslim Turkey can coexist. Ultimately, this novel resulted in the awarding of the Nobel Prize to Pamuk in 2006.

Pamuk's seventh novel, *Masumiyet Müzesi* (2008 [*The Museum of Innocence*; 2009]), introduced a radically new mode of interaction between fiction and reality. Pamuk wrote it in tandem with his work on the physical Museum of Innocence—the book contains an admission ticket to the museum in Istanbul. The novel chronicles unrequited love; it also criticizes the Istanbul bourgeoisie for the contradiction of nostalgically longing for the Ottoman past while compulsively consuming everything Western. The Turkish newspaper *Hürriyet Daily* called it a "typical Turkish Yeşilçam or Hollywood-style love story" ("Museum of Innocence in the Formation Process") while anglophone readers compared the novel with Vladimir Nabokov's *Lolita* and Gustave Flaubert's *Madame Bovary*. The museum opened in Istanbul in 2012 and received eleven thousand visitors in its first three months. Its walls showcase eighty-three display cases, each corresponding to a chapter in the novel. By collecting and displaying these items, Pamuk materially evoked everyday bourgeois life in Istanbul in the 1960s and 1970s. One display box holds 4,123 cigarette butts discarded by the novel's heroine and collected by the novel's protagonist between 1976 and 1984; another is a cartographic allusion to other Pamuk novels with the "Literary Map of Nişantaşı" at its center. Selected among forty candidates, the museum was named the European Museum of the Year in 2014 by the European Museum Forum in Tallinn, Estonia ("Museum of Innocence: Turkish Museum").

Having given his novel physical form as a museum, Pamuk then recast the museum in a new textual form. Its catalog, *Şeylerin Masumiyeti* (2012 [*The Innocence of Objects*; 2012]), is an annotated visual tour of the museum's display boxes and pays homage to Pamuk's lifelong love of visual art. In addition to the museum's blueprints, the catalog includes a manifesto that advocates for small-scale museums that re-create individual stories instead of state-sponsored institutions based on fabricated national narratives. Behind the novel and the museum stands Pamuk's essential message about modern Turkey: dichotomies of East-West and Islamist-secularist are too simple to map the complexities of modern Turkish identity.

Pamuk's only experiment in short story writing is "Pencereden Bakmak" ("To Look out the Window"), which appears in *Other Colors.* The story narrates two days in little Orhan's life in 1958 Istanbul, crowded with family members, television and radio shows, 1952 Dodges, minibuses, and soccer matches that keep the narrator and his brother busy between quarrels. The story is also included in the third edition of the *Norton Anthology of World Literature.*

Pamuk's Nonfiction

Published in 2003, Pamuk's *İstanbul: Hatıaralar ve Şehir* (*Istanbul: Memories and the City*; 2004) is a self-portrait as much as a portrait of the city. Difficult to classify in a single genre, *Istanbul* is an amalgam of memories, reflections, and black-and-white photographs from family collections and from the photographer Ara Güler's archive. It features a chapter on Pamuk's description of *hüzün*, a melancholic mood that haunts postimperial Istanbul and is often cited in discussions of the book. In the autobiographical sections, Pamuk is less concerned with accuracy than with the ethical responsibility to question the means of representing himself as a historical subject. The memoir suggests that Pamuk could only have narrated his autobiography through the mediating role of the city's story, aligning these two accounts with accounts of Istanbul writers and those of European visitors such as the French writers Gerard de Nerval, Gustave Flaubert, and Théophile Gautier. The book is ideal for teaching empire, postimperial legacies, and nation building in the Turkish context.

A generous selection of Pamuk's interviews, literary criticism, and social and political commentary can be found in *Öteki Renkler* (1999 [*Other Colors*; 2007]). This self-reflective collection offers readers an intimate view of the writer and his world. In addition to entries on life, youth, paranoia, the art of the novel, and Pamuk's own novels, the Turkish version contains essays about Turkish literary figures such as Ahmet Hamdi Tanpınar, Kemal Tahir, Orhan Kemal,

Aziz Nesin, Oğuz Atay, Fethi Naci, Kemalettin Tuğcu, and Şavkar Altınel, as well as world writers who have been formative for Pamuk: Laurence Sterne, Dostoevsky, Borges, Thomas Bernhard, Philip Larkin, Patricia Highsmith, Mario Vargas Llosa, Guillermo Cabrera Infante, and Salman Rushdie. The English version includes only one-third of this content—it excludes, in particular, the essays devoted to Turkish writers—even as it adds several new pieces: a new preface, an essay that gives a poignant portrait of Pamuk's father, the essay "The Implied Author," a lecture to PEN, and a major 2005 interview in the *Paris Review*. The English version also includes Pamuk's Nobel lecture "My Father's Suitcase" (403–17), a deeply moving reflection on the meaning of literature and writing and on the personal and cultural legacy Pamuk has inherited.

Some significant essays that are available in English (outside *Other Colors*) are "Memories of a Public Square"; "My Turkish Library"; "My First Passport"; "Love, Death, and Storytelling"; "Freedom to Write"; "A Private Reading of André Gide's Public *Journal*"; "A Religious Conversation"; "The Anger of the Damned"; "Turkey's Divided Character"; "Salaam Bombay!"; and "A Taste of Death: Patricia Highsmith's Crime Time."

Delivered in the fall of 2009 at Harvard University, Pamuk's Charles Eliot Norton Lectures are collected in the volume *Saf ve Düşünceli Romancı* (2011 [*The Naive and the Sentimental Novelist*; 2010]). Building on Friedrich Schiller's distinction between naive and sentimental poets, these lectures reveal Pamuk's thoughts on the craft of the novel, its narrative elements, the ekphrastic relation of word and image, texts and museums, and what he calls "the center of the novel"—the deeply embedded enigma at the heart of the novel that constitutes its locus of meaning (153).

Interviews and Press

The following interviews with Pamuk appear in this volume's list of works cited under Pamuk's name. Online videos on Pamuk are legion by now. Among the most useful video interviews with Pamuk are "Interview with Orhan Pamuk," "Granta Conversation with Orhan Pamuk," "Big Think Interview with Orhan Pamuk," "Conversations with History—Orhan Pamuk," "An Evening with Orhan Pamuk," "University Lecture: A Discussion with Orhan Pamuk," "The Museum of Innocence: From the Novel to the Museum," and four interviews with *Charlie Rose*.

Among interviews published as texts that give insights into Pamuk's novels, ideas, and writing method are "Implementing Disform"; "Orhan Pamuk, The Art of Fiction No. 187" (also included in *Other Colors* [353–78] as "The *Paris*

Review Interview"); "Interview: Orhan Pamuk; 'I Was Not a Political Person'"; "Author in the Classroom: An Interview with Orhan Pamuk"; "Orhan Pamuk on Taksim Square, the Effects of *Breaking Bad*, and Why the Future of the Novel Is in the East"; "Conversation: Nobel Laureate Orhan Pamuk"; "Controversial Turkish Novelist Wins Nobel Prize in Literature"; and "Orhan Pamuk: Bridging Two Worlds."

Pamuk and His Translators

Very little is available in English from the rich and historically significant Turkish and Ottoman literary canons. Pamuk's novels gained interest in English only after he established himself as an important writer in Turkey. It was the awarding of the Nobel Prize to Pamuk that heightened international interest in Turkish letters and energized the translation activity from this important but much neglected language. Between 1949 and 2004 an average of only ten literary works written in Turkish were made available in English each year (Paker and Yılmaz). This limited translation activity produced a Turkish literary history in English ridden with gaps and inconsistencies that also characterize its limited reception. The uneven cultural flow between English and Turkish has impeded a fuller understanding of Turkish modernity, one that must go beyond the simplistic idea of Turkey as a bridge suspended between civilizational divides. Pamuk is often put forth as the embodiment of this idea, said to capture "the intricate spirit of a nation suspended perilously between east and west" (qtd. in Paker 11). The essays collected in this volume present more nuanced approaches to reading Pamuk in the context of Turkish literary history in dialogue with other literatures.

Translations have been critical to Pamuk's worldwide success. Well aware of their formative role, Pamuk has closely supervised translations into English, which in turn have served as the bases for many translations into other languages. His translators' increasingly timely work has reduced the lag between the publication of original editions and translations. The first interest for translation rights for one of Pamuk's works came in 1984, from the French publisher Gallimard, for his second novel, *Sessiz Ev*; Münevver Andaç's French translation (*La maison du silence*) was short-listed for the Prix Médicis Étranger and won the 1991 Prix de la Découverte Européene. These first foreign prizes awarded to the translation paved the way for Pamuk's recognition on the European literary stage. As of this writing, his first novel, *Cevdet Bey ve Oğulları*, is available only in German and in French, whereas his more recent works have been rapidly translated, sometimes appearing in the same year as the originals.

Erdağ Göknar's English translation of *My Name Is Red* (2001) received the prestigious International IMPEC Dublin Literary Award in 2003. The citation points to the novel's "intense beauty" and calls it a "timeless and timely" exploration of the Ottoman past ("Nominees"), aesthetic aspects that cannot be separated from the translation. Significantly, and for the first time, the translator was awarded a quarter of the prize money. Before the Nobel Prize, Pamuk was fortunate to enlist Victoria Holbrook to translate *The White Castle* (1990) and Güneli Gün to translate *The Black Book* (1994) and *The New Life* (1997). Pamuk's subsequent four books—*Snow* (2004), *Istanbul* (2004), *Other Colors* (2007), and *The Museum of Innocence* (2009)—were translated by Maureen Freely. A new translation of *The Black Book* by Freely appeared in 2006. Nazım Dikbaş translated *The Naive and the Sentimental Novelist* (2010); Ekin Oklap translated the museum catalog, *The Innocence of Objects* (2012) and *A Strangeness in My Mind* (2015). This list of translations, translators, and awards granted to translations attests to the crucial yet often invisible role translators have played in the creation of Pamuk's reputation as a *littérateur* on the world stage.

Resources for Teachers

Teachers will find the following book-length literary analyses useful in preparing to teach Pamuk's books: Erdağ Göknar's *Orhan Pamuk, Secularism, and Blasphemy: The Politics of the Turkish Novel*; Michael McGaha's *Autobiographies of Orhan Pamuk: The Writer and His Novels*; Azade Seyhan's *Tales of Crossed Destinies: The Modern Turkish Novel in a Comparative Context*; and Yıldız Ecevit's *Orhan Pamuk'u Okumak: Kafası Karışmış Okur ve Modern Roman*. Edited volumes available for further consultation on various aspects of Pamuk's works include *Orhan Pamuk'u Anlamak*, edited by Engin Kılıç; *Orhan Pamuk'un Edebi Dünyası*, edited by Nüket Esen and Engin Kılıç; *Global Perspectives on Orhan Pamuk: Existentialism and Politics*, edited by Mehnaz Afridi and David M. Buyze; *Essays Interpreting the Writings of Novelist Orhan Pamuk*, edited by Nilgün Anadolu-Okur, and *Orhan Pamuk: Critical Essays on a Novelist between Worlds*, edited by Taner Can and others. Yan Overfield Shaw's detailed literary biography of Pamuk has been included in *Turkish Novelists since 1960* (volume 373 of the *Dictionary of Literary Bibliography*).

Finally, we have found the following articles and book chapters insightful in their analyses of Pamuk's works: Barish Ali and Caroline Hagood's "Heteroglossic Sprees and Murderous Viewpoints in Orhan Pamuk's *My Name Is Red*"; Ian Almond's "Islam, Melancholy, and Sad, Concrete Minarets: The Futility of Narratives in Orhan Pamuk's *The Black Book*"; Walter G. Andrews's "*The*

Black Book and Black Boxes: Orhan Pamuk's *Kara Kitap*"; Aylin Bayrakçeken and Don Randall's "Meetings of East and West: Orhan Pamuk's Istanbulite Perspective"; Murat Belge's "Love Me or Leave Me? The Strange Case of Orhan Pamuk"; Marshall Berman's "Orhan Pamuk and Modernist Liberalism"; Colleen Ann Lutz Clemens's "'Suicide Girls': Orhan Pamuk's *Snow* and the Politics of Resistance in Contemporary Turkey"; Feride Çiçekçioğlu's "Difference, Visual Narration, and Point of View in *My Name Is Red*" and "A Pedagogy of Two Ways of Seeing: A Confrontation of 'Word and Image' in *My Name Is Red*"; Sibel Erol's "The Chronotope of Istanbul in Orhan Pamuk's Memoir *Istanbul*"; Nergis Ertürk's "Those outside the Scene: *Snow* in the World Republic of Letters"; Rachel E. Hile's "'The Spanish Tragedy' as Intertext for Orhan Pamuk's *Kar* (*Snow*)"; Djelal Kadir's "The Siege of Baghdad: Rashiduddin, Fazlullah, Orhan Pamuk, and the Commissions of History"; Mary Jo Kietzman's "Speaking 'to All Humanity': Renaissance Drama in Orhan Pamuk's *Snow*"; Sooyong Kim's "Master and Disciple: Sufi Mysticism as an Interpretive Framework for Orhan Pamuk's *Kara Kitap*"; B. Venkat Mani's "Turkish-German Reattachments: Orhan Pamuk's *The New Life*"; Karim Mattar's "Orhan Pamuk and the Limits of Translation: Foreignizing *The Black Book* for World Literature"; Jale Parla's "From Allegory to Parable: Inscriptions of Anatolia in the Turkish Novel" and "Dark Knowledge Befits Dark Colors: Turkish Novelists Interrogate the Ideology of Light"; Leonard Stone's "Minarets and Plastic Bags: The Social and Global Relations of Orhan Pamuk"; Kate Teltscher's "Reading Orientalism in Istanbul: Edward Said and Orhan Pamuk"; and Sevinç Türkkan's "Orhan Pamuk's *Kara Kitap*: (British) Reception vs. (American) Translation," "Orhan Pamuk's *Kara Kitap* (*The Black Book*): A Double Life in English," and "Pamuk, the Storyteller: Elements of *The Thousand and One Nights* in *The Black Book*."

NOTES

[1] This essay quotes from the 2006 Vintage Books edition of *Istanbul: Memories and the City*.

[2] This essay quotes from the 2007 Alfred A. Knopf edition of *Other Colors: Essays and a Story*.

Part Two

APPROACHES

Introduction

When Orhan Pamuk was awarded the Nobel Prize in Literature in 2006, the Nobel committee described him as a writer "who in the quest for the melancholic soul of his native city has discovered new symbols for the clash and interlacing of cultures" ("Nobel Prize"). Scholars have noted the resonance of these words with the political scientist Samuel Huntington's rhetoric of a clash of civilizations (Erol, "Reading" 403) even as the prize committee seeks to honor Pamuk's deep commitment to the history and complex legacy of the city of Istanbul. Yet neither image—of cultures clashing or interlacing—does justice to Pamuk's complex themes and stylistic innovations; such oversimplifications create artificial barriers to engagement with Pamuk's works.

Pamuk is not only a *littérateur* but a prominent figure in political and cultural debates, a critic, a cultural historian, and now the founder of an innovative museum. Instructors will find it enriching to introduce students to the various aspects of Pamuk's intellectual life in the context of Turkey's cultural and political debates and in the light of Pamuk's personal history as well as his dialogue with world literature. Before turning to questions of literary history and form, this introduction discusses Pamuk's prosecution for "insulting Turkishness," which placed him at the center of political debates in Turkey and reverberated globally. The trial and the attention he received forced Pamuk to negotiate politics at home and asymmetries on a global scale before he established himself firmly as a world writer.

The Author on Trial

The Pamuk trial threw a dark light on Turkey's problematic human rights record, a manifestation of long-term social inequality, authoritarianism, economic crises, and military interventions in the country. The trial's national and international publicity was also a troubling reminder of the problems of cultural translation and representation in and across languages, especially when statements concern contested personal, social, or political ramifications. In a 2005 interview with a Swiss journalist, Pamuk was reported as saying that a million Armenians and thirty thousand Kurds had been killed in Turkey. Immediately, various Turkish newspapers attacked Pamuk, accusing him of treachery and demanding his punishment and the public burning of his books. Pamuk was then legally charged with insulting Turkishness and denigrating Turkish identity. He responded by underscoring the taboo in Turkey against discussing such acts of violence. Following the initial charges, the Turkish press reported that in another interview, published in the German newspaper *Die Welt*, Pamuk stated that the threat to democratic development in Turkey was not the Islamic profile of the Justice and Development Party but the country's history of military interventions (Pamuk, "Meine Großmutter"). Pamuk was charged again, this time with insulting the Turkish army.

Both charges were based on Article 301 of the Turkish Penal Code, which states:[1]

> (1) A person who publicly denigrates Turkishness, the Republic or the Grand National Assembly of Turkey, shall be sentenced a penalty of imprisonment for a term of between six months and three years. (2) A person who publicly denigrates the Government of Republic of Turkey, the judicial bodies of the State, the military or security organizations, shall be sentenced to a penalty of imprisonment for a term of between six months and two years. (3) Where denigrating of Turkishness is committed by a Turkish citizen in another country, the penalty to be imposed shall be increased by one third. (4) Expressions of thought intended to criticize shall not constitute a crime. (Algan 2238)

Pamuk responded to the initial charges by pointing out that his words were taken out of context and that the quotation "Thirty thousand Kurds were killed here. And a million Armenians. Nobody but me dares to mention it" had undergone "double translation," from the English in which the interview was conducted, to the German in which it was published, and then to the Turkish in which it circulated (McGaha 4). The German "fast niemand" ("hardly anyone") was translated into Turkish as "hiç kimse" ("nobody") and made Pamuk appear aggressive and self-aggrandizing (4). His intention, in fact, had been to acknowledge the ongoing problems in the country, most notably the imprisonment of countless authors, scholars, journalists, and publishers for their political views ("Orhan Pamuk hakkında"). The ambiguous and problematic language of Article 301 allowed ultranationalist lawyers to charge Pamuk with threatening the stability of the country. During Pamuk's trial the antidemocratic and self-contradictory nature of Article 301 was further exposed; after considerable national and international debate, it was amended, though the parliament has never actually voted to repeal it.

For Pamuk, well aware of the prohibitions against freedom of expression in Turkey, the trial represented the ethical responsibility to speak openly about the Armenian Genocide and the violence committed against Turkey's Kurdish citizens:

> What am I to make of a country that insists that the Turks, unlike their Western neighbors, are a compassionate people, incapable of genocide, while nationalist political groups are pelting me with death threats? What is the logic behind a state that complains that its enemies spread false reports about the Ottoman legacy all over the globe, while it prosecutes and impris-

> ons one writer after another, thus propagating the image of the Terrible Turk worldwide? (Pamuk, "On Trial")

The paradox identified by Pamuk defies simple explanations. As a country considered for inclusion in the European Union, Turkey occupied a precarious position. With a glorious past and a volatile present, it was seen as a bridge suspended between Europe and Asia, caught between nostalgia for a lost empire and neoliberal global market structures. Economic stability and vitality were then the primary conditions for inclusion in the EU, but Turkey's religious differences—magnified from the European perspective—have refocused attention on the country's problematic human rights record. The Armenian question was particularly sensitive for many citizens when, as a provision to Turkey's admittance to the EU, European governments pressed Turkey to acknowledge having committed genocide (McGaha 2). Many Turks take pride in the fact that Turkey has never been colonized, yet the national struggle and the War of Independence (1919–22) was a response to the western partition of the Ottoman lands and Anatolia after the First World War. Similarly, the single-party regime and top-down mass mobilization of the authoritarian republican reforms disregarded minority rights and freedom of expression in the attempt to usher in westernization and to join the global economy. The incongruities between political and economic agendas and their social ramifications have resulted in destructive, intolerant forms of nationalism—and Pamuk became a victim of this nationalism. Even though Pamuk ardently advocated for Turkey's EU accession and openly identified with secularism, he became "a symbol of everything the nationalist-secularists despised" (Göknar, *Orhan Pamuk* 20).

Pamuk responded to this situation in an eloquent speech he delivered in Frankfurt when he accepted Germany's most prestigious literary award, the Peace Prize of the German Book Trade (Friedenpreis des Deutschen Buchhandels). Discussing the importance of the novel for understanding "the 'other,' the 'stranger,' the 'enemy' that resides inside each of our heads," Pamuk draws comparisons between two imagined writers: a German novelist who fails to imagine the difficulties faced by Germany's Turkish population and a Turkish novelist who fails to imagine the Kurds and other minorities in Turkey and who neglects to address the dark spots in his country's silenced history (Pamuk, "In Kars" 2). Both of these writers, Pamuk states, would produce works with holes at their center (3). He then compares them to a European Union that excludes Turkey. Addressing the question of European identity and the delicate situation it has generated for the Turks, Pamuk states:

> Here we are, knocking on your door, and asking to come in, full of high hopes and good intentions, but also feeling rather anxious and fearing rejection. I feel such things as keenly as other Turks. . . . As Turkey knocks on Europe's

> door, as we wait and wait and Europe makes us promises, and then forgets us, only to raise the bar. . . . The most cruel irony of all is that the fanning of nationalist anti-Turkish sentiment in Europe has provoked the coarsest of nationalist backlash inside Turkey. Those who believe in the European Union must see at once that the real choice we have to make is between peace and nationalism. Either we have peace, or we have nationalism. (6)

Pamuk is sensitive to the contradictions, ambiguities, and self-privileging attitudes underlining nationalist sentiments in Turkey and Europe. For him, a Europe that narrowly defines itself as Christian would not be dissimilar to a Turkey that identifies itself only with Islam. Both of these positions are divorced from reality and cancel any possibility of a peaceful coexistence between Europe and Turkey.

Pamuk's legal hearing was closely monitored by representatives of PEN; by Human Rights Watch; by the British, German, and European parliaments; by several European consuls; and by the Turkish media, lawyers, and writers. Pamuk called this a "drama (as Conrad might have said) 'under Western eyes,'" underscoring its ironies ("On Trial"). The court dismissed the charges, framing its decision in bureaucratic terms and citing insufficient evidence ("Orhan Pamuk davası düştü"). The Nobel Prize awarded to Pamuk the following year regrettably resulted in further polarization along political fault lines and culminated in death threats against Pamuk. Pamuk's trial revealed "the cultural logic Pamuk has had to negotiate to write novels that question the same logic" (Göknar, *Orhan Pamuk* 2). The trial shone a light on local and global contradictions, which became focused on Pamuk himself. Yet it would be wrong to interpret Pamuk's novels as straightforward statements about politics or culture. Fresh readings of his novels can reveal their potential to counter simplistic nationalist or orientalist interpretations of Turkish identity. The awarding of the Nobel Prize to Pamuk, the first of its kind in Turkey, is the most direct acknowledgment of Pamuk's and Turkey's cultural achievements. Since then, interest in the Ottoman and republican archival history has significantly increased and has begun to reveal many of the paradoxes that underlie the relation between Turkey and Europe, between Islam and Christianity, and between Ottoman history and modern Turkey.

Pamuk and the Novel in Turkish

It is important to read Pamuk's works in relation to the Turkish novel as well as in relation to world literature. North American readers aren't always aware of the literary tradition—and its historical and political contingencies—that Pamuk's novels adopt and rework. As a result, many foreign critics discuss Pamuk exclusively in relation to world novelists and in the light of European theoretical frames; in Turkey, however, his aesthetic innovations have been overshadowed by the polemics generated by the trial. On a global scale, his outspoken position has catapulted him to the domain of "world republic of letters" (Casanova, *World Republic*) while the Turkish cultural and literary context for his work has remained largely inaccessible because of limited translations, resulting in an incomplete assessment of his works. Ironically, the controversies surrounding Pamuk in Turkey and his criticisms of his home country made him agreeable as a Turkish writer in world literary circles, even though his novels have always interrogated a narrow understanding of Turkishness. Reading Pamuk as though he is a cultural and national informant neglects his formation as a Turkish writer and precludes more complex understandings of how he has negotiated the uneven terrains of world literature.

The Turkish and English editions of Pamuk's essay collection *Öteki Renkler* (*Other Colors*) show how differently Pamuk presents himself at home and internationally. The two editions also reveal how Pamuk viewed himself before and after winning the Nobel Prize, which cemented his position as a world writer. *Other Colors* (2007), the significantly abridged English version of *Öteki Renkler* (1999), showcases Pamuk's wide reading in literatures other than Turkish, with commentaries on such canonical figures as Laurence Sterne, Victor Hugo, Fyodor Dostoevsky, Vladimir Nabokov, Albert Camus, Mario Vargas Llosa, Salman Rushdie, and André Gide. Left out of the English edition are Pamuk's reflections on his first two novels, unavailable in English at that time, and some insightful commentaries that acknowledge his debt to the Turkish literary tradition, in particular to the writers Ahmet Hamdi Tanpınar, Kemal Tahir, Orhan Kemal, Aziz Nesin, Yaşar Kemal, Oğuz Atay, Fethi Naci, Kemalettin Tuğcu, and Şavkar Altınel.

The Turkish edition also includes a short entry, "Dünya Edebiyatı" ("World Literature"), which articulates Pamuk's acute awareness that global inequalities are obscured by world literature understood as a supranational phenomenon. As Erdağ Göknar and B. Venkat Mani suggest in their contributions to this volume, in this short essay Pamuk expresses skepticism about the division of labor required by local and global distributions of power. He also articulates the pain of being an outsider, residing at the edge of the map of world literature and not at its center. This aspect of the novelist's thought has remained largely inaccessible to his anglophone readers.

Pamuk has always been closely engaged with worldwide developments with respect to the contemporary novel as well as with the evolving, dynamic literary scene in Turkey. Fundamental to understanding Pamuk's place in Turkish literature is a familiarity with the literary culture in Turkey before and after the establishment of the modern state in 1923. Before the novel appeared in Ottoman Turkish in the second half of the nineteenth century, local literary forms—such as mystical verse romances, oral epics, shadow plays (*karagöz*), storytelling (*meddah*), improvised comedy (*orta oyunu*), minstrel tales, and Qur'anic as well as Sufi parables—were common (Evin 23–40; Göknar, "Novel" 473). These forms of cultural expression slowly began to wane following the establishment of the modern Turkish republic for social and political reasons.

Conceived by Mustafa Kemal Atatürk, the Turkish republic was a cultural project as well as a political and ideological one. Its hallmark, the language reform of the late 1920s replaced the Arabo-Persian alphabet with Latin script: Arabic and Persian grammatical features and vocabulary were eliminated or replaced with recovered Turkish words or neologisms. The proponents of these changes intended to modernize and simplify the language and to make it more accessible to the populace and more translatable into European languages. However, these changes significantly impeded writers, severed the younger generations from their Ottoman heritage, and created epistemological barriers between the Islamic Ottoman heritage and the newly established Turkish Republic (Brendemoen, "Turkish Language Reform"; Halman and Warner; G. Lewis). The wholesale transformation of the language partially explains what some anglophone critics came to see as the Turkish novel's belated entry into the modern era. But this is a reductive perspective that overlooks the complex forces that produced the Turkish novel; the reasons behind the novel's supposed belatedness remain yet to be analyzed and contextualized (Gürbilek 599).

Established as a vehicle of modernization, nation building, and self-reflection, the novel in Turkey has always been politically informed (Evin; Moran, *Türk Romanına*; Finn; Parla, *Babalar*; Göknar, "Novel"). It developed during the Tanzimat period (1839–76), when the Ottoman state reorganized its structure to accommodate the challenges posed by governing a heterogeneous population of a wide territory and by the external pressures of the British, French, and Russian empires. The first writers were members of the new intelligentsia who were involved in publishing as well as government service, acting as bureaucrats, authors, and disseminators of ideas (Evin 10). They admired the scientific, political, and social progress they witnessed in Europe and wrote novels to communicate government reforms and Western modernity to the people. However, pressing art into the service of education and reform was contrary to the traditional view of literature as primarily a medium of aesthetics, as E. Khayyat discusses in his contribution to this volume. The Tanzimat writers had to simplify Ottoman prose to bridge the gap between the language of the court and that of the masses. The novel thus emerged as a site of contradictory synthesis: it was informed by the established traditions of high Ottoman language and genres and served as a vehicle for practical ideas of progress and modernization.

The emergence of the novel also coincided with what later came to be identified as the East-West problem that is central to various interpretations of literary modernity in Turkey. The new intelligentsia saw no incongruity between Islamic values at home and the Western civilization they observed in Europe.

Still, their reformist ambitions were often interpreted as a total rejection of the past. The reformist ideal was certainly ambivalent, as it "faced, like the Roman god Janus, the East and the West at the same time" (Evin 17) and required a creative mind to accomplish the intended synthesis.

The development of the Turkish novel in the twentieth century reflects sociopolitical fluctuations in Turkey but cannot be understood independently from such fluctuations elsewhere. The First World War demolished the Tanzimat writers' aspirations for synthesis; instead, ethno-nationalist ideology emerged to counter the threat of European colonialism felt acutely in the transition from the Ottoman Empire to the Republic of Turkey. Made to serve the Kemalist reforms, the mainstream republican novel (*Cumhuriyet romanı*) of the early twentieth century abounded in nationalist propaganda. Another style of novel writing focused on social consciousness and narrated the difficulties of village life in Anatolia Minor, which evolved into the socialist village novels of the 1950s and 1960s. A strong opposition between nationalist and socialist factions of Turkish republican culture eventually led to the imprisonment of many novelists in the 1970s, which in turn created a tense social environment in Turkey. The so-called March 12 novels (in reference to the 1971 military coup) focused on the individual emerging out of a radical political discourse and environment. As Hülya Adak discusses in this volume, the 1970s was also a period of prison memoirs, coup novels, and committed feminist literature that opposed the ideologies of the patriarchal military state.

The effects of the military coups and the attendant atmosphere of fear and suspicion translated into novels that narrated personal experiences of imprisonment, torture, and interrogation. Novel writing changed after the 1980 military coup, which marked the most brutal interventions in the history of the Turkish republic—the military regime used intimidation, imprisonment, and even torture to suppress the leftist ideology that had spread since 1960. Disillusioned with the social realism of preceding decades, the authors of subsequent novels began to experiment with nonlinear narration, fantasy, and metafiction. Influenced by postmodern literary techniques, such narrative experiments were meant to question notions of westernization and progress.

This brief outline can't describe the full history of the Turkish novel, but it suggests generally what Pamuk inherited when he entered the Turkish writing scene. Though he began writing in the 1970s, a period marked by social realism, Pamuk's novels belong to post-1980s Turkey, influenced by the country's gradual integration into a global market economy and characterized by literary experimentation. Summarizing the atmosphere of that time, Pamuk states:

> When I decided to become a writer . . . the dominant view was that serious writers worked collectively, and their work was valued for the way in which it contributed to a social utopia and reflected a shared vision (like modernism,

> socialism, Islamism, nationalism, or secular republicanism). There was little interest in literary circles in the problem of the individual creative writer who drew from history and tradition, or who tried to find the literary form that best accommodated his voice. Instead literature was allied to the future: its job was to work hand in hand with the state to build a happy and harmonious society, or even nation. Utopian modernism—be it secularist, republican, or socialist egalitarian—has had its eyes so firmly planted on the future that it has, I sometimes think, been blind to the heart and the soul of just about everything that has gone on in the streets and houses of Istanbul over the past century. ("My Turkish Library")

Pamuk's keenness for alternative styles, forms, and themes led him to experiment with multiperspectival narration, the double motif, Sufi elements, allegory, and new ways to represent the city of Istanbul. Pamuk's first novel bears traces of the social realism prevalent in Turkish literature between 1960 and 1980, but beginning with his second novel, *Silent House*, and more acutely with his third, *The White Castle*, Pamuk directly raises questions related to national identity and the Ottoman archive, heritage, and cultural encounters. His linguistic innovations and the unusual style of his novels generated widespread controversy and alienated some of his readership. As Bernt Brendemoen discusses in this volume, critics found Pamuk's idiom bizarre and they disapproved of his subversive approach to the political ideologies of the republican tradition. Ironically, what generated negative criticism at home was admired and rewarded overseas, thus making Pamuk the most controversial novelist in Turkey.

Pamuk succeeded in situating his unique artistic perspective within the Turkish narrative tradition by building on the writing of predecessors who, like himself, experienced a dual East-West identity. Pamuk's admiration for Ahmet Hamdi Tanpınar (1901–62) is not surprising. In an essay in *Öteki Renkler* (not included in *Other Colors*), Pamuk designates Tanpınar as "the most significant local writer of the twentieth century":

> Tanpınar appreciated Western culture, French poetry and novels, the poetry of Valéry and Gide, for instance; and at the same time established a deep connection to local poetry and music. The deep feeling of pain that nourishes this writer's works is grounded in the loss of traditional arts and life. However, his reaction is not that of a superficial conservative's accusation of others, but of personal pain and a feeling of guilt. This is because he came to understand and appreciate Western culture both as an uninhibited child would do and with feelings of guilt. By placing his own feeling of guilt and silent melancholy between East and West, he endowed his work with an exceptional authenticity. It is because his books are nourished by and embrace both worlds that they are so profound and his characters so complex. (190; my trans.)

Pamuk feels kinship with Tanpınar's attempt to synthesize (*terkip*) his experience of the painful divide between tradition and modernity, East and West. However, Pamuk departs from Tanpınar in capitalizing on this divide: his novels interrogate these dichotomies and reject simplistic either-or classifications.

Pamuk's essays, his Nobel speech, and his Norton lectures attest to this writer's ongoing preoccupation with literary legacies. In 1874, during the Tanzimat era, Namık Kemal articulated the reformist perspective regarding the prevailing literary scene at home: "In our country . . . the novel is the most deficient among the genres of literature produced. Perhaps not even three stories can be found and read with pleasure" (qtd. in Evin 16). The comparison between Turkish and European novels is implicit here, and the European novel is unequivocally accepted as a yardstick against which to measure Turkish novelistic success. Even though the Turkish novel is now an established genre, it has always been evaluated within such frameworks of implicit comparisons, and its generative form continues to challenge its practitioners. More than a century after Namık Kemal, one of Pamuk's narrators articulates similar sentiments:

> [T]his newfangled plaything called the novel, which is the greatest invention of Western culture, is none of our culture's business. That the reader hears the clumsiness of my voice within these pages is not because I am speaking raucously from a place which has been polluted by books and vulgarized by gross thoughts; it results rather from the fact that I still have not quite figured out how to inhabit this foreign toy. (*New Life* [1997] 243)

The Nobel prize has certainly alleviated Pamuk's acutely self-conscious assessment of his craftsmanship. His continuous preoccupation with literary legacy and expression at home and beyond has made Pamuk the master of defining himself in contrast to and at times in rigorous dialogue with other writers, other legacies, and other modernities. Once a writer who admitted the challenges of "inhabiting" the novelistic genre, "this foreign toy," today Pamuk is an established Istanbul chronicler and historical novelist who has turned cultural ambivalences into creativity.

The Structure of This Volume

Pamuk's works reveal the complex, shifting, and ideological nature of literary and cultural cartographies, which makes them highly valuable in courses that have a literary and cultural component. The task of approaching Pamuk's variegated, multifaceted oeuvre may appear intimidating at first, given the wealth of material, genres, narrative techniques, and themes that have concerned him over the past fifty-five years. His books can fill the syllabus of an entire seminar;

more often, teachers include a single novel in world literature surveys or in courses with a comparative angle, his memoir in courses on life writing, or his Norton lectures in courses with theoretical components. The essays in this volume support all these ways of including Pamuk in course curricula: they provide a solid historical and cultural context for his works, address recent concerns emerging from teaching Pamuk in English translation, and offer ways to teach his works in interdisciplinary courses on aesthetic and visual representation. Most of the essays focus on a single work or pair of works, yet collectively the essays survey Pamuk's oeuvre as a whole. Instructors who are teaching just one work by Pamuk will likely find relevant discussions in several other essays beyond the one or two devoted directly to the work they are teaching.

The volume begins with essays on historical and cultural contexts by Bernt Brendemoen, Hülya Adak, and E. Khayyat. Brendemoen analyzes Pamuk's use of the Turkish language in comparison with other contemporary Turkish authors and in the light of the "catastrophic success" of the Turkish language reform (G. Lewis). Adak explores the tense relation between aesthetics and politics in Pamuk's novels against the backdrop of coup d'état novels and denial narratives regarding the Armenian Genocide. E. Khayyat, tracing the link between Pamuk and Tanpınar, discusses how Pamuk builds on, but also modifies, Tanpınar's prescriptions regarding the impasse between tradition and modernity in the Turkish context.

In the second section, Sevinç Türkkan, Gloria Fisk, and Jennifer Malia address problems and nuances in teaching Pamuk in translation and in transnational contexts. Türkkan argues that teaching *The White Castle* with sensitivity to the novel's paratextual elements and to the translated nature of the text can illuminate Pamuk's relation to the Ottoman literary and historical legacy while complicating world literature approaches to the novel. Fisk treats the illegibility of the original Turkish text in the English translation of Pamuk's *Snow* as a pedagogical challenge that enables students' entry into contemporary debates on world literature. Malia explores comparative approaches to such notions as belonging, government censorship, and freedom of expression by comparing her experience teaching Pamuk's essays in North America and in the Middle East.

Djelal Kadir opens the section "Teaching Pamuk beyond the East-West Divide" by reading Pamuk's work through the lenses of *The Naive and the Sentimental Novelist*, *Other Colors*, and *Istanbul*. Göknar offers a syllabus that situates Pamuk in a comparative context of world literature and discusses how such an approach teaches students to read Pamuk's novels as artifacts of negotiation beyond simplistic dichotomies. Barish Ali explores *My Name Is Red*'s central question of representation and how this question is presented through debates about Eastern and Western styles of painting. Carolyn McCue Goffman places *Istanbul* in dialogue with two late Ottoman and early Turkish writers to demonstrate how Pamuk's treatment of Turkey's complicated relation with its past is part of a longer literary tradition. Esra Mirze Santesso concludes this section by proposing that the intricacies of *Snow* can empower students to maintain a critical distance from Pamuk's highly complex discussions of identity politics.

Section 4, "Teaching Pamuk in Dialogue with World Literature," opens with John Limon's argument that in *Silent House*, Pamuk transcends his reliance on Faulkner's modernism by way of postmodern fictionality. B. Venkat Mani presents an approach to teaching Pamuk's works through print culture, using library and print cultural histories in tandem with the enterprise of translation and world literature. Didem Havlioğlu discusses how she overcomes the spatial, cultural, and linguistic distances presented by the dense narrative of *The Black Book* in a course on Islamic literatures. Delia Ungureanu explores *The New Life*'s intertextual encounters with the visionary dreamworld of Dante's *La Vita Nuova* and with the modern metafictions of Jorge Luis Borges and Italo Calvino to argue that Pamuk's home is the world of fiction as much as it is Istanbul. David Gramling argues that *Snow* reverses the orientation of the world literature curricular design, casting light not on representations of the normative foreign but on the selection and translation protocols that induce such representations. Building on Georg Lukács's *The Historical Novel*, Bruce Robbins discusses ways to teach *Snow*'s politics from the perspective of the love triangle formed by the politically disengaged Ka, the Muslim activist Blue, and their mutual love interest, İpek.

The final section of the volume, "Aesthetic Representations and Visual Studies," begins with Darcy Irvin's argument that in *My Name Is Red* identity formation is a result of the interaction of supposedly clashing visual ideologies of sight and image production. Drawing on the work of Michel Foucault, Walter Benjamin, and John Berger, Nhora Lucía Serrano employs the term *textual visuality* to engage with divergent questions of representation in Pamuk's works. Yin Xing concludes the volume by tracing the link between Pamuk's novel *The Museum of Innocence* and its physical counterpart in Istanbul, which students can experience through the museum catalog *The Innocence of Objects*; this approach enhances students' understanding of world literature as a unique preservation of human experiences that embraces popular and elite culture alike.

We hope that the information and pedagogical strategies provided in the following essays will support instructors in helping students explore Pamuk's worlds, deepen their understanding, and even increase their pleasure in reading Pamuk's often challenging but always seductive works.

NOTE

[1] Article 301 of the Turkish Penal Code was revised in 2008. The version quoted here is from before the revision, when Pamuk was charged.

Pamuk's Use of the Turkish Language

Bernt Brendemoen

Because of the profound effects of the language reform on the Turkish vocabulary, the contemporary literary language is rich in synonyms. In the first part of this essay, I give a brief account of the reform and compare Orhan Pamuk's vocabulary with that of other contemporary Turkish authors. Special features of the syntax in *The Black Book* are the subject of subsequent sections, which also include a brief introduction to Turkish sentence structure. I conclude by looking at Pamuk's word order in sentences that introduce direct speech and in more complicated structures and by discussing the possible influence of English sentence structure on Pamuk.

The Language Reform

One of the most important reforms initiated by Mustafa Kemal Atatürk as part of his efforts to westernize Turkey was the language reform, which took place with varying intensity mostly between 1928 and 1980. The aim of this reform was to replace words and grammatical constructions of Arabic and Persian origins—which had entered the language since the Turks accepted Islam in the Middle Ages—with words of pure Turkish origin. The first step, replacing the Arabo-Persian alphabet with Latin script, was initiated in 1928. However, because Atatürk did not fully understand the depth of the lexical influence from Arabic and Persian, he underestimated both the scope of the reform and the difficulties in finding pure Turkish substitutes for the foreign elements. Consequently, the work of the Turkish Language Association (Türk Dil Kurumu), which was founded in 1932 to lead the reform, was partly suspended in 1935; it resumed with full intensity after Atatürk's death in 1938. From that point until

1980, when the Turkish Language Association was transformed into a more scientific language academy, the language underwent a complete transformation. The aim to eliminate all words of Arabic and Persian origin proved impossible, partly because many basic words such as *kalem* (pen), *kağıt* (paper) and *kitap* (book) were strongly established and not perceived to be foreign, and partly because of the difficulties in finding adequate Turkish replacements. Nevertheless, the reformed language that gradually developed was so different that texts written before the 1920s were unintelligible to the later generations. The older generations, unable to easily adapt, found such a comprehensive reform unnecessary. A formidable gap was thus created between the old generation, who continued to talk and write as they were used to, and the newer generations, who were exposed to the reformed language at school and through media. In *The Turkish Language Reform: A Catastrophic Success*, Geoffrey Lewis surveys the reform process from its beginning and heavily criticizes the cultural loss created by the Turkish Language Association's methods.

The language reform also became a political issue. The left wing Republican People's Party (CHP) strongly welcomed Atatürk's westernization policy. Its immensely popular leader, Bülent Ecevit, who was elected prime minister five times between 1974 and 2002, adopted the new vocabulary in his addresses to the nation for clear political purposes: to liberate the language from Ottoman elements that he regarded as outdated or reactionary and to continue Atatürk's political line. His use of the new language undoubtedly contributed to the success of the reform. More conservative and religious parties and individuals, on the other hand, continued to use a more old-fashioned language. The divergent language of newspapers representing various political views is evident up to the turn of the twenty-first century. Today there is less opposition to the reformed language. Representatives of the Justice and Development Party (AKP) show a preference for the older vocabulary. On the whole the official written and oral language of the media today is more homogeneous than it was in the 1980s. However, because of globalization English has had a strong impact on the language. In the thirty-five years since the reform work began tapering off, the Turkish Language Association has identified a new target: finding Turkish replacements for English terminology. The reformed language has become generally accepted, since the generation that fervently opposed the reform has passed away. If someone today were to use in a political context the old-fashioned vocabulary used by conservatives in the 1970s, the message would be ineffective.

Educated people today have a passive knowledge of the older language. Certain authors from the first half of the twentieth century are still popular, but they are often read in modernized editions. Today the Turkish literary language is rich: the old vocabulary is still familiar to some readers, and the language includes a vast number of synonyms and quasi-synonyms. For example, the words *yavaş* and *aheste* both mean "slow." Of Persian origin, *aheste* is known by educated people because they study Ottoman poetry in school. The word has a strong poetic connotation and can be used to describe, for instance, the "slow movement of snowflakes falling down from heaven." Despite the criticism of the language reform—mostly by foreign Turkologists such as Lewis—today's literary language provides writers with endless possibilities for stylistic variation. In what follows, I address the lexical aspects of Pamuk's writing and discuss his place in modern Turkish literature with respect to his use of the Turkish language.

Pamuk's Vocabulary

Some contemporary Turkish authors, among them Pamuk, know how to benefit from the treasure of synonyms that has emerged from the language reform. Unlike the works of Turkish novelists up to 1990, most of Pamuk's novels have urban settings inhabited by characters who—considering their educational background—are to some extent in command of the old-fashioned vocabulary. Prominent Turkish authors such as Yaşar Kemal (1923–2015) and Adalet Ağaoğlu (b. 1929) use fewer words of Arabic and Persian origin than Pamuk does—Kemal because his settings are villages that he describes in simple (but nevertheless extremely poetic) sentences where old-fashioned vocabulary would be out of place stylistically; Ağaoğlu because her literary language was shaped during the peak period of the language reform, when it was natural for politically progressive young writers to adopt the reform.

Historical novels are naturally written in a more old-fashioned language than novels in contemporary settings. Thus, in his novel *Yedinci Gün* ("Seventh Day"; 2012), set in upper-class Istanbul at the very end of the nineteenth century, the author İhsan Oktay Anar (b. 1960) uses old-fashioned words more extensively than Pamuk does. Actually, Anar risks alienating some readers by using rare words not found in modern dictionaries. In Pamuk's historical novel *My Name Is Red*, the frequency of old words is higher than in his other novels. But Pamuk does allow its characters to speak modern Turkish, a problem he addresses in a passage in which the *meddah*, or the storyteller, impersonates a dog and tells the readers: "I'm a dog, and because you humans are less rational beasts than I, you're telling yourselves: 'Dogs don't talk.' Nevertheless, you seem to believe a story in which corpses speak and characters use words they wouldn't possibly know" (11).[1] Pamuk is aware that he has introduced anachronism by letting his characters speak modern Turkish and by using words that were created during the language reform.

The large number of synonyms and other linguistic possibilities of the Turkish literary vocabulary provides Pamuk with variation, which lends elegance and sophistication to his writing. Ottoman Turkish observed the pattern of gender in Arabic grammar to a great extent. Certain nouns or adjectives denoting male persons could be made feminine by adding the suffix *-e*. This feature has survived in very few words in modern Turkish. While *memur* originally meant a "male official" and *memure* a "female official," the feminine form is infrequently used today, while *memur* has become gender-neutral. But Pamuk will introduce the gender distinction, for instance, in *Masumiyet Müzesi* (*The Museum of Innocence*), to give the sentence elegance and to give his style an intellectual touch:

> İpek İsmet, Şaziye, Solak Şermin ve Madam Mualla gibi bir zamanlar Füsun'un annesinin arkadaşı ve rakibesi olan ünlü sosyete terzileri . . . (93)
>
> As for Silky İsmet, Şaziye, Left-handed Şermin, Madame Mualla, and all the other seamstresses who catered to society ladies and had once been friends and competitors of Füsun's mother . . . (80)[2]

Here, the Arabic word *rakip* (competitor, rival) has acquired a feminine suffix (*rakibe*), which is grammatically correct in the old language, but quite unnecessary because a Turkish reader will automatically understand from their names that these individuals are females.

Other aspects of Pamuk's language have been heavily criticized by Turkish writers such as Tahsin Yücel (b. 1933), a well-known writer and professor of French literature at Istanbul University. *Kara Kitap* (*The Black Book*) in particular has been the object of his criticism. In an article starting with the sentence "Can a bad writer be a good novelist?," Yücel claims that Pamuk's language is almost unreadable, grammatically speaking. Yücel attacks the novel's literary aspects and points to the writer's "erroneous choice of words." But Yücel neither states what exactly is wrong nor explains how Pamuk should have expressed himself. I will address Yücel's views on Pamuk's syntax below.

Syntactic Characteristics of Pamuk's Language

Even though his criticism is exaggerated and subjective, Yücel is right to point out that Pamuk's language in *The Black Book* is different from that of his contemporaries. In addition to its effect on vocabulary, the language reform in Turkey aimed to westernize the language and to bring written language closer to spoken language from a syntactical point of view. In Ottoman administrative and factual prose, sentences tended to be extremely long and seemed to have neither heads nor tails. Literary prose in the initial years of the republic became less complicated, and the effort of the language reform movement resulted in a trend toward shorter sentences, culminating with the so-called village novels, which gained popularity in the 1950s. Schools encouraged the new generations of language learners to write short sentences. Accordingly, in Pamuk's first novel, *Cevdet Bey ve Oğulları*, long sentences of the kind found in his later novels are relatively rare. (One could argue that *Cevdet Bey ve Oğulları* would not have received the Orhan Kemal Novel Prize in 1983 had its language not abided with the norms of the time.) There are several reasons why Pamuk's sentences became longer and more complicated in his later novels; for one, he probably wished to create a style of his own, different from the structurally simpler style of his contemporaries. Although his dialogue style resembles everyday speech, he also projects himself as an intellectual and erudite writer. He signals his erudition with a relatively heavy writing style in which long chains of argumentation are constructed by the subordination of several secondary clauses within one another like Chinese boxes, in the same way as in Latin. The styles of older writers, such as Marcel Proust (1871–1922) and especially Ahmet Hamdi Tanpınar (1901–62), have decisively shaped Pamuk's style. The complex, long sentences in *Istanbul: Memories and the City* enable Pamuk to pursue his arguments and to analyze more easily how the city has influenced writers of the last couple of centuries.

The Black Book is structured around alternating chapters. In half of the chapters the young lawyer Galip frantically searches for his wife, Rüya, in the streets of various Istanbul neighborhoods. The alternating chapters, which interrupt this search, are articles from a daily newspaper column written by Galip's cousin, the celebrated journalist Celâl. There are important stylistic differences between the Galip chapters and the Celâl chapters. The slow, careful style of the Celâl chapters is syntactically traditional: the sentences are long, but their structure complies with the commonly accepted rules of Turkish syntax. In the first part of the novel before Galip reaches Celâl's apartment, however, the sentence structure of the Galip chapters is more chaotic, possibly reflecting Galip's turbulent state of mind. In what follows, I explain how Pamuk's unique language in these chapters differs from traditional sentence structure.

Turkish Sentence Structure

In Turkish sentence structure, the subject comes before the object, and the verb comes at the end (SOV). Adverbial constituents denoting time or place may come at the beginning of the sentence or between the subject and the object. Modifiers such as adjectives precede the constituents they describe. Dependent clauses (as in English) are nominal, adjectival, or adverbial, and they are placed within the main clause in the same position as nouns, adjectives, or adverbs. As Lars Johanson points out, special emphasis accrues to the word in the position immediately before the verb (1191). Thus, "Mehmet washed the car yesterday" is expressed with no particular emphasis by "Mehmet dün arabayı yıkadı," where *dün* means "yesterday," *arabayı* "the car," and *yıkadı* "washed." If the subject is placed immediately before the verb, as in "Dün arabayı Mehmet yıkadı," Mehmet is emphasized, and the meaning is: "It was Mehmet who washed the car yesterday." To emphasize that he washed it yesterday and not some other day, one would write, "Mehmet arabayı dün yıkadı."

Especially in oral language, sentence constituents may also be put after the verb in order to de-emphasize them. Words that can be understood from the context, and are uttered as an afterthought, are frequently in this position (Erguvanlı 50–56). In Turkish literary prose, writers use this structure as a dramatic device to draw the reader's attention; a sentence in which the verb is followed by one or more constituents is called *devrik cümle* ("twisted sentence"). As Eser Erguvanlı points out, a reader would least expect to find this structure in the initial paragraph of a novel, where everything is new, but, by the same logic, *devrik cümle* may arouse the reader's curiosity when it appears in such an unexpected place (68). Pamuk uses this device frequently. The following excerpt introduces Celâl's chapter "Cellât ve Ağlayan Yüz" ("The Executioner and the Weeping Face") in *The Black Book*:

> Gözyaşları içindeki bir erkek niye telaşlandırır bizi? Ağlayan bir kadını, günlük hayatımızın sıradışı, ama duygulu ve acıklı bir parçası olarak görebilir, içtenlik ve sevgiyle benimseriz onu. Ağlayan bir erkek ise bir çaresizlik duygusuyla doldurur içimizi. (*Kara Kitap* 265)

> Why does the sight of a man in tears make us nervous? We perceive a weeping woman as an exceptional but sad and touching part of our lives, accepting her with affection and sincerity. But a weeping man makes us feel helpless. (*Black Book* 248)[3]

In the three Turkish sentences, the objects—"bizi" ("us"), "onu" ("her"), and "içimizi" ("our interiors"; or "our minds")—are placed after the main verb. In the second sentence, the de-emphasis of "onu" is justifiable because the woman has been mentioned earlier in the sentence. But this is not the case for the de-emphasized words in the other two sentences.

Unfortunately, it is impossible to illustrate the effects of the different word order in the translation because changing the order of the elements in English does not produce the same variation. I suggest that the word order of the three Turkish sentences above places an increased emphasis on the verb. Such sentences are common in the Galip chapters in *The Black Book*, but they also appear in the Celâl chapters. For instance, in the chapter "Uzun Süren bir Satranç Oyunu" ("A Lengthy Chess Game"), which consists of a letter given to Celâl by one of his readers and which Celâl characterizes as written in "pasha" ("general") style, this structure is frequent:

> Kaptan kulesinde toplanmış kalabalığın üzerinden İstanbul'a, insanlara ve sanki tarihe çevirmişti gözlerinin projektörlerini. (289)
>
> Raised above the heads of the crowd on the bridge, he seemed to have fixed his eyes like two searchlights on Istanbul, the populace, and history. (271; my emendation: "to have turned the projectors of his eyes")

And:

> O zaman anlamış her şeyin şimdi olduğu gibi gelişeceğini, tam şimdi olduğu gibi olmasa da. (291)
>
> That was when he had an inkling that things would turn out as they had, although not exactly as it was now. (273; my emendation: "That was when he understood")

In these two sentences, too, the objects—"gözlerinin projektörlerini" ("the projectors of his eyes") and "her şeyin şimdi olduğu gibi gelişeceğini, tam şimdi olduğu gibi olmasa da" ("that things would turn out as they had, although not exactly as it was now")—are placed after the main verbs ("çevirmişti" and "anlamış"). Even though the objects are semantically heavy, the verb is emphasized.

Pamuk's prolific use of *devrik cümle*, a highly individual aspect of his style, in *The Black Book* is specific to this novel. He employs it differently in *My Name Is Red* and *The Museum of Innocence*, where it appears frequently in dialogue but rarely in narration. The use in dialogue is more expected, since *devrik cümle* is mainly a feature of oral communication. Moreover, in these two novels the elements placed after the verb are typically short adverbial phrases, or, in some cases, definite objects, a usage that lends the language of these two novels a more fluent and transparent quality compared with *The Black Book*.

Rendering Direct Speech

In all his books Pamuk makes use of *devrik cümle* to introduce direct speech. According to Turkish grammatical structure, in the sentence, "Mehmet said 'I'm not at home,'" "Mehmet" is the subject, the utterance "I'm not at home" is the object, and "said" is the verb. Accordingly, the normal word order should be "Mehmet 'Evde değilim' dedi" ("Mehmet 'I'm not at home' said"). However, Pamuk puts the direct speech first, then introduces the verb, and finally the subject: "'Evde değilim' dedi Mehmet" ("'I'm not at home' said Mehmet"). In the *Black Book*, again, the length of the phrase placed in the final position is unusual, as in: "'Müstesna bir kişilik!' dedi fötr şapkalı adam durumu özetleyerek" ("'An extraordinary personality!' the man with the fedora hat said, summarizing the situation"; *Kara Kitap* 172; *Black Book* 162). The traditional way to express this sentence would be: "Fötr şapkalı adam, durumu özetleyerek 'Müstesna bir kişilik!' dedi" ("The man with the fedora hat, summarizing the situation, said: 'An extraordinary personality!'"). In the same way, in *The Museum of Innocence*, expressions such as "diye devam etti Feridun" and "dedi Füsun" ("Feridun went on" and "said Füsun") are more common than constructions with the subject of the verb placed in front of the utterance.

This construction for direct speech follows the rules of *devrik cümle*, since the de-emphasized subject (the speaker) has usually already been introduced. Accordingly, in the following sentence, the subject "Babaanne" ("Grandma") comes in the expected position because it has not been mentioned earlier in the same paragraph, and thus is more important for the context: "Babaanne, Rüya'nın hikâyesini sabırla dinledikten sonra, 'Berber birazdan gelir,' derdi, ama Dede berberden söz edilirken sevinmezdi" ("After listening to the dream patiently, Grandma would say, 'The barber is due to arrive soon,' but Grandpa wasn't cheered by the talk of the barber"; *Kara Kitap* 13; *Black Book* 7). Pamuk may prefer using *devrik cümle* to render direct speech because the identification of the speaker is slightly de-emphasized. The most economical, least disruptive way to render dialogue is to omit references to the speakers' identities. However, it is often necessary to tell the reader who said what, especially if more than two people are engaged in a dialogue. In English and other European languages, the personal pronouns *he* and *she* can identify two persons of opposite gender in dialogue. Because the Turkish personal and demonstrative pronouns are gender-neutral, indicating a speaker of dialogue requires words such as *adam* (man), *kadın* (woman), or the names of the conversation partners; however, these options are semantically heavier than using pronouns. One way to lighten the semantic weight of the nouns *adam*, *kadın*, and proper names is to place them after the verb that describes the utterance, as Pamuk does. The result is lighter and more fluent dialogue. English dialogue structure may have inspired Pamuk to use this model, but there is nothing un-Turkish about it either. In *The Black Book* the Celâl chapters do not contain direct speech, and their style thus comes across as more traditional. Similarly, in *The White Castle* there are few instances of *devrik cümle* since there is almost no dialogue.

Pamuk exploits the potentials of Turkish grammar, but does not break its rules. However, at times he produces linguistic constructions that give the impression that he has stretched the rules to or beyond their limits.

Unusual Sentence Structures

In *The Black Book* Pamuk revived the Ottoman Turkish style of long, complex sentences, which was unusual in modern Turkish; this became the hallmark of his style. However, Turkish word order presents a challenge if the sentences become very long. When the distance between the main subject and its verb grows, there is a risk that the subject may be forgotten by the time the reader has reached the verb at the end of the sentence. Pamuk often tries to mitigate this risk in sentences where an adverbial clause precedes a main clause and they have a common subject by placing the subject between the two clauses. Yücel characterizes this as clumsy and claims that it gives Pamuk's prose the "impression of bad translation." In English one can write either "Seeing his friend's new car, Mehmet got quite envious" or "Mehmet, seeing his friend's new car, got quite envious." In traditional Turkish sentences, the latter construction is more common. But Pamuk uses the former construction frequently, especially in the Galip chapters. For example: "Sirkeci'den Galatasaray'a gelirken takside yanına oturduğu siyah beyaz filmlerden çıkmış adamı yeniden gördüğünde, Galip, Türkân Şoray benzerinin odasından yeni ayrılmıştı" ("The next time he saw the man with whom he'd shared the cab, the one who looked like a character from a black-and-white film, Galip had just left Türkân Şoray's look-alike's room"; *Kara Kitap* 148; *Black Book* 139). In normal Turkish prose "Galip" would have been at the beginning of the sentence rather than the middle.

Pamuk uses this construction most commonly when the first clause is adverbial, but there are also more complicated examples, such as the following: "Bundan sonraki hikâyeye başlayan uzun boylu adamın, adını şurada burada daha önceleri işittiği bir yazar olduğunu Galip İskender'in sözünden anladı" ("Galip caught İskender's drift that the tall man who started yet another story was a writer whose name he'd previously heard bandied about"; *Kara Kitap* 150; *Black Book* 141). Here, the subject "Galip" is not the subject of the initial nominal clause ("who started yet another story") but of the relative clause within it that starts with "whose name." Traditionally, the subject is placed in the initial position, but here, for no obvious contextual reason, it has been placed after the nominal clause, which is the definite object in the main clause. This is Pamuk's way of pointing out the subject to his readers. According to Yücel there are at least one thousand examples of this construction in *The Black Book*.[4] Though less common, this construction is not idiosyncratic to Pamuk alone; it is also used by other modern Turkish authors. Its frequent use by Pamuk might suggest that it is a syntactic borrowing from English. In the example from the previous paragraph, in the English translation the temporal clause has only "he" as a subject, while "Galip" is named as the subject only after the temporal clause. The opposite construction is equally valid in English: "The next time Galip saw . . . he had just left . . ." The flexibility of this type of construction in English may have encouraged Pamuk to use the less typical Turkish construction more freely.

Pamuk sometimes places the subject immediately before the verb—in the position of greatest emphasis in the sentence—even when there is no contextual reason to do so. In participle and gerundial constructions, the most common way of expressing subordinate clauses in Turkish, word order is stricter. The following example is quite remarkable: "Ortalığı iyice altüst ettikten sonra, biraz da umutsuzlukla baktığı kutulardan birinde, altmışlı yılların başında Celâl'in kesip sakladığı çeşitli gazete kesikleri . . . arasında kitabı bulduğunda . . ." ("After turning the place completely upside down, when he finally came across the book among the news clips from the early sixties that Jelal had saved . . ."; *Kara Kitap* 282; *Black Book* 264; my emendation: "among the news clips that Jelal had saved in the early sixties"). Here the expected position of the unemphasized but definite subject "Celâl'in" would be as the first word of the subordinate clause, that is, in front of "altmışlı." Without the context to clarify its meaning, the sentence would read in English thus: "After turning the place completely upside down, when he finally, in the early sixties, came across the book among the news clips that Jelâl had saved. . . ." Another example is: "Masanın ucundaki dosya kâğıtlarının duruş şekli, Celâl'in anlattığı hikâyeleri Rüya'nın yazmaya başladığını . . . gösteriyordu" ("The way the papers were placed on the table revealed that Rüya had begun to write down the stories Jelâl had been dictating . . ."; *Kara Kitap* 414; *Black Book* 389). To a reader used to traditional word order, the last phrase would mean "revealed that it was Rüya who had begun to write down." However, there is no contextual reason that this should be the intended meaning. According to word order conventions, "Rüya'nın" should have been placed before "Celâl'in." As I have shown elsewhere, sentences of this kind are also sporadically found in older Turkish ("Orhan Pamuk" 155–56). Perhaps this is why none of Pamuk's harshest critics have commented on them.

Even if English language structure influenced Pamuk's syntax in *The Black Book*, all the constructions he uses have precedents in recent or older Turkish prose. One could speculate that Pamuk chose complex sentences in the Galip chapters as a conceit: the reader's search for the heads and tails of Pamuk's sentences parallels Galip's search for his wife in the streets of Istanbul. Regardless of the reasons behind the author's choice, Pamuk's predilection for complex sentences has made significant innovations to the syntax of modern Turkish.

NOTES

[1] This essay quotes from Erdağ M. Göknar's translation of *My Name Is Red* published by Faber and Faber in 2001.

[2] This essay quotes from Maureen Freely's translation of *The Museum of Innocence* published by Faber and Faber.

[3] This essay quotes from Güneli Gün's 1994 translation of *The Black Book.*

[4] For similar examples in *Snow*, see Alpay, *Dilimiz* 140.

Coups, Violence, and Political Turmoil: Aesthetics and Politics in Pamuk's Novels

Hülya Adak

The works of Orhan Pamuk are replete with intertextual references, ranging from Islamic mysticism to the entire history of Turkish and European literature, including writers as varied as Jalal ad-Din Rûmî, Farid ud-Din Attâr, Dante, Fyodor Dostoevsky, and Georges Perec. Significant as such literary allusions are, their historical and political meanings are equally important to understanding Pamuk's works. *Cevdet Bey ve Oğulları*, *Silent House*, *The White Castle*, and *My Name Is Red* are only a few of the works that focus on the East-West divide while analyzing Ottoman culture, the arts, and modernization in Turkey in the twentieth century. Pamuk's other novels problematize the Kemalist reforms and the rapid secularization process in Turkey in the 1920s and 1930s.[1] In this essay I focus on the background of the three military coups in Turkey (1960, 1971, and 1980). While *Silent House*, *The Black Book*, *The New Life*, and *Snow* all relate to the coups, I analyze *The Black Book* in particular, referring also to *Snow*.

Successive Coups

In *Angry Nation*, Kerem Öktem argues that the Turkish military coups cannot be interpreted without understanding the "behind-the-scenes politics" of the "guardian state" in Turkey that started with the 1950 elections. Backed by the United States, which wanted to secure Turkey's partnership in NATO, the guardian state destabilized successive governments, starting with the government of Adnan Menderes (1950–60) through the use of mass violence. From the 1950s, a conservative democracy, challenged by "a radicalized socialist left and extreme right," emerged in Turkey (40).

A staged arson attack on Mustafa Kemal's house in Thessaloniki prepared the ground for the 1960 military intervention. The event generated enmity toward Greeks and other non-Muslim minorities. Public outrage was expressed by general looting and destruction in İstanbul, İzmir, and İskenderun, which came to be referred to as the 6–7 September Pogroms in 1955 (Öktem 44). Organized by members of a group called Cyprus Is Turkish, the pogroms targeted roughly five thousand businesses and several Greek Orthodox churches. Amid the looting, some fifteen Greeks and Armenians were murdered and several hundred women were raped. The two days of violence was prepared by the Special War Office (Özel Harp Dairesi). Öktem describes this office as "one of the secret organizations which NATO countries created to wage psychological warfare against communism and to prepare the ground defense in the case of a communist attack . . ." (45).

The pogroms had many consequences. In the immediate aftermath of the 1960 coup, the guardian state used the Democratic Party (Demokrat Partisi) of Adnan Menderes, the first prime minister in Turkey to be elected democratically, as a scapegoat for the events of 1955, even though the Menderes government was only partially responsible for the pogroms. Further, many non-Muslims, their hopes for equal citizenship diminished, emigrated after witnessing the 1955 pogroms (45). Lastly, and most important for Pamuk's works, in 1953 İstanbul had marked the five-hundredth anniversary of Fatih Sultan Mehmet's conquest of Constantinople with a jubilee that celebrated the Ottoman heritage—yet only two years later the city mourned the loss of its Ottoman cosmopolitanism.

During the ten-day jubilee festivities in 1953, Fatih Sultan Mehmet was portrayed as a "secular leader," "a good Kemalist sultan," and "a man of the Renaissance" who, ignoring Islamic prohibitions, had hired Italian masters to paint his portrait (Danforth). The hailing of secularism, Renaissance humanism, peace, and brotherhood through the national hero of the Kemalist Mehmed the Conqueror came to an abrupt end with the pogroms and the vandalism targeting the Ottoman capital's cosmopolitan culture and heritage. In Pamuk's first novel, *Cevdet Bey ve Oğulları*, in *The Black Book*, and most significantly in his memoir, *Istanbul: Memories and the City*, the remnants of an empire and the loss of Ottoman cosmopolitanism are recurrent themes in the exploration of the urban culture of Istanbul and its inhabitants, a loss crystallized in the concept of *hüzün*—melancholy, tristesse, sadness, lament—described in the memoir.

The 1960 coup was the first manifestation of military intervention in Turkish politics. In 1961, Prime Minister Menderes, the finance minister, and the foreign minister were executed, and courts were set up to try opponents of the guardian state. Concomitant with the 1968 European student movements and protest movements against the Vietnam War, university students in Turkey also became politicized. By the late 1960s the polarization between different university student groups turned into violence. The state-sponsored nationalist and Islamist groups were fighting against Marxist and Kurdish political associations, and the violence gradually escalated.

In 1971 Prime Minister Nihat Erim declared martial law in eleven provinces, as "Turkish radio stations broadcast an armed forces memorandum that accused the parliament and the government of having led the homeland into anarchy, fratricide and social and economic discord" (Öktem 49). In response the Marxist youth movement arranged for the abduction of the Israeli ambassador, Efraim Elrom, in Ankara and had him assassinated the same year. The state used the political murder of Elrom as an excuse to imprison and torture roughly ten thousand leftist activists and some members of right-wing organizations. Some activists were sentenced to death (49). Pamuk's *Silent House* is set against this background of political polarization and turmoil.

Leading up to the third military coup, the situation in Turkey was characterized by violence, random killings, and daily assassinations. The 1980 coup, under General Kenan Evren, was designed to take over government affairs and restructure the spheres of politics, economics, and culture. Finally, in 1989 General Kenan Evren "handed over power to the democratically elected president, Turgut Özal, the first civilian ever in this position since the foundation of the republic." This act "marked the symbolic end of almost a decade of brutal military oppression" (Öktem 56).

The space most emblematic of the military violence and human rights abuses of the 1980s was the Diyarbakır prison in the Kurdish region, where thousands of left-wing and Kurdish nationalists were incarcerated and tortured. In this atmosphere of brutal violence and oppression, many Kurdish political activists joined the Kurdistan Workers' Party (Partiya Karkeren Kurdistan [PKK]) under the leadership of Abdullah Öcalan (known as Apo) to press for Kurdish independence and for more political and cultural rights for Kurds within the Republic of Turkey. In 1984, with the goal of Kurdish autonomy, the PKK launched a war against the Turkish military that lasted until the PKK announced a unilateral cease-fire in 1999 and resulted in around 35,000 recorded casualties (Göçek 411).

Coup Literature

Three decades of coups and curfews produced a unique set of literary genres and aesthetic preoccupations. The literary landscape in the 1970s, as Pamuk started his writing career, was dominated by political novels. According to Murat Belge, 12 March (in reference to the 1971 coup) was not only an academic area for research but a space for aesthetic experimentation (*Edebiyat* 114). Belge argues that the "12 March novels" differed greatly from political novels of earlier decades. The "12 March novels" take up the problem of torture, attempting to narrate the inhumane practices suffered by the (leftist) revolutionaries incarcerated in Turkey. While the novelists were not themselves imprisoned, they shared the ideology of those imprisoned (115). Because the novelists wanted to ennoble the incarcerated revolutionaries, they sought to represent them as innocent victims oppressed by the state. Further, the novels do not mention the revolutionaries' actions before their prison terms (118, 120). Citing many examples from the novels of Tarık Dursun, Füruzan, and Erdal Öz, Belge ably demonstrates that most of the protagonists of these novels were robbed of their political histories (123, 125, 127). The revolutionaries are represented as possessing childlike naiveté—they are simple victims of state torture. In exonerating the revolutionaries from any complicity in violence, the novels remain abstract and narrate general existential anxieties, including struggling to survive as a victim of torture, rather than specific political issues within the context of the coup period. For instance, in Öz's *Yaralısın* ("You Are Wounded") the torture the protagonist undergoes is discussed in existential terms (128). Because freedom of expression was restricted during the coup periods, the political details of the texts could have been censored by the authors themselves or by editors or publishers.

The Decade of Terror and Denial Narratives of the Armenian Genocide

The period between 1975 and 1985 is referred to as the decade of terror as well as the period of radical Armenian violence. During this decade, the Armenian Secret Army for the Liberation of Armenia (ASALA) and the Justice Commandos of the Armenian Genocide (JCOAG) killed some four dozen people, mostly Turkish diplomats, and injured several hundred more. The aim of both groups was to bring the Armenian Genocide—the systematic extermination of at least one million Armenian citizens in the Ottoman Empire in the early decades of the twentieth century—to the attention of Turkish and international communities. ASALA also had territorial demands for an Armenia to be established in Eastern Anatolia and part of Soviet Russia (Göçek 424).

Even though the attacks perpetrated by ASALA and JCOAG brought international attention to the Armenian Genocide, they did not endorse the recognition of genocide within Turkey itself. Denial narratives and defensive nationalist propaganda regarding the Armenian Genocide proliferated as Turkish intellectuals, diplomats, and retired generals used the attacks to prove Turkish innocence and Armenian culpability, not only during 1915–16 but throughout the twentieth century (Göçek 391). Women also contributed to this genre of denialist writing, for instance, the famous Islamic Sufi mystic Sâmiha Ayverdi (1905–93) wrote *Türkiye'nin Ermeni Meselesi* (1976), which was translated into English as *The Armenian Question in Turkey* (1980) during the period (Adak, "Gendering").[2]

Pamuk and the Armenian Genocide

Pamuk's novels do not explicitly deal with the First World War or the Armenian Genocide. But in February 2005, Pamuk gave an interview to the Swiss newspaper *Tages-Anzeiger*, in which he remarked that roughly thirty thousand people had died in the conflict in the Kurdish region between 1984 and 1999 and that one million Armenians had been massacred during the First World War. He was also inaccurately quoted as saying that "nobody but me dares to talk about it."[3] A groundbreaking conference at Istanbul's Bilgi University in September 2005 opened up a public conversation about the Armenian Genocide. When Pamuk made his remarks, however, acknowledgment of the massacres was still taboo in Turkey. Pamuk was charged with denigrating Turkishness, under Article 301 of the Turkish Penal Code, which states that it is illegal to insult the republic, parliament, or any organs of the state. His trial followed in December 2005, but it was abandoned in 2006. Had Pamuk been found guilty, he could have faced up to three years in prison ("Avoiding").

Pamuk's fiction includes subtle allusions to the Armenian Genocide. In *Snow*, the characters İpek and Ka meet for the first time in a patisserie in Kars and talk about an Orthodox church that had formerly stood there. They mention that the church had been torn down in 1967 and that its door was exhibited in the Kars Museum, which housed a special section on the Armenian massacres (31).[4] The narrator remarks in a stark, satiric tone that some tourists who visited the Kars Museum thought this section was about the Turks who had massacred the Armenians but later found out that it was the other way around (31). This comment refers implicitly to the denial narratives—particularly those written in the decade of terror—that reverse the roles of Armenians and Turks, describing Armenians as perpetrators and Turks as victims.

Another narrative in *Snow* hints at the violent history against Armenians. Navigating a thin line between fact and fiction, Pamuk relates a story of Kemalist soldiers on stage firing real bullets at the audience. Many years after the violent scene, the only remaining bullet hole left unrepaired was on the wall of the box reserved for the Armenian leather merchant Kirkor Çizmeciyan. Pamuk writes that Çizmeciyan and his family, all of them dressed in fur, regularly visited the theater during the first decade of the twentieth century (161). Pamuk touches on the significance of memory and history: he reveals that formerly the audience of the National Theater was wealthy Armenians in Kars. The passage is an excellent one to discuss in class, prompting many questions: Where are the Armenians? Why did they leave? Why was the shot directed at the box of Kirkor Çizmeciyan the only trace of the violence that was allowed to remain in the theater? The reader also learns that the mayor, Muhtar Bey, who is giving Ka a tour, would like him to write positively about Kars and its people. Muhtar Bey tells Ka that denying the massacres and representing Kars positively are the only way to make the poor people of Kars a little happier (161). The passage experiments with the idea that placing the burden of denial on a writer frees the contemporary inhabitants of Kars, a poor class oppressed by neoliberal policies, from the horrible burden of a tragic history.

The Burden of Politics

Fredric Jameson describes "national allegory" as a mode of expression of Third World literature (69). In their engagement with national allegory, Pamuk's novels wrestle with the tense relation between aesthetics and politics. In *The Black Book* chapters revolving around the protagonist Galip's wanderings in Istanbul alternate with chapters that consist of the journalist Celâl's essays. The novel is about reading, writing, and the process of becoming a writer: Galip, through reading Celâl's essays, gradually becomes a writer himself. The particular themes explored under the acts of reading and writing include the function of the columnist, the journalist, the writer, and the production and reception of the essay genre (and of literature more generally) in the Turkish context.

Both *The Black Book* and *Snow* include discussions of the *mission civilisatrice* of art and literature. As Sibel Irzık argues, "*Snow* is a satire on the imagined, experienced, displaced, and manipulated boundaries between the East and the West" (191). In *Snow*, one of the functions of art is a "civilizing mission, the means of educating a backward people, an instrument of modernization. Related to this is also the conception of the East as a peculiarly malleable entity, raw material to be hammered into a new form according to the Western model" (189). Similarly, the style of Celâl's essays in *The Black Book* is didactic, with "the tone of a patient teacher trying to educate an ignorant audience" (Adak, *Pamuk's Encyclopedia* 27). Celâl's style resembles that of the prominent Turkish sociologist, writer, poet, and political activist Ziya Gökalp (1876–1924) in *Türkçülüğün Tarihi* (*The Principles of Turkism*). Gökalp also carried on this *mission civilisatrice* in his essays, and his thought could be characterized as a "cult of nationalism and modernization" (Erickson 97).

The double functions of the essayist—occupying roles both public and personal—involve social and political engineering (Adak, *Pamuk's Encyclopedia* 25). Hilary Clark observes, for instance, that both Ezra Pound and Michel de Montaigne work with "a public/personal tension at the heart of the essay form . . . which is directly related to the essay's interplay between fiction and non-fiction" (6). From the nineteenth century onward, the essay in Turkey carried the social and political function to engineer Ottoman society; the genre was used to educate and guide the Ottoman and later Turkish public. At the same time, the essayist has often had an autobiographical function as the exemplary national hero.[5]

The essay as a genre is highly significant in *The Black Book*. In his daily column, Celâl makes extensive use of the loose structure and the variegated themes typical of the essay form. His topics range from descriptions of personal experiences and other literary works to social problems meant to guide his reader (Adak, *Pamuk's Encyclopedia* 26). Further, *The Black Book* acknowledges the trouble with the columnist's prophetic role—a role bestowed by the columnist's readers. While the columnist is supposedly endowed with the qualities of a messiah, always coming to the rescue of the people (Adak, *Pamuk's Encyclopedia* 27), Celâl is alienated and unable to carry the heavy burden placed on him by people seeking answers to social problems and enigmas. A good passage to look at in class to explore this theme is the scene in which Celâl gets his hair cut:

> . . . I immediately knew that this person sitting in the chair looking at his reflection in the mirror was someone else. When the barber asked, "How much should we take off the front?" the head he touched, like the neck that carried it, and those shoulders, and that chest—they did not belong to me, but to the columnist, Celâl Bey.
>
> I had nothing to do with this man. This was so clear to me that I was sure the barber would see it too, but he paid no attention. It was almost as if he was going out of his way to make me forget myself and really feel like a columnist—questions like "If war breaks out, can we defeat the Greeks?" "Is it true that the prime minister's wife is a prostitute?" "Is it the vegetable sellers who are driving up prices?" I am at a loss to describe the oppressive genie that kept me from sharing my own thoughts on these matters, insisting instead that this gruesome columnist staring back at me from the mirror mumble the usual smart-alecky nonsense: "Peace is a good thing." "It's important to realize that you can't bring the prices down just by hanging a few men!" And so on. (*Black Book* 183)[6]

The scene illustrates the multiplicity of roles ascribed to columnists in Turkey: they are supposed to function like professors, autobiographers, gossip writers, and prophets who can foretell the future of the Turkish nation.

Despite the speedy modernization brought by the Kemalist reforms, people's connection to texts, to the book, and to the alphabet has remained stable. A secular form of *hurufism*—the mystical, kabbalistic Sufi doctrine prominent in the fourteenth and fifteenth centuries in Western Persia, Anatolia, and Azerbaijan—is practiced in *The Black Book* by a retired colonel. In the column entitled "The Discovery of Mystery," the use of the Latin script alphabet is shown not to have changed the sacrosanct quality that people endow to letters and texts:

> According to F.M. Üçüncü [Fatih Mehmet the Third], it was on Turkish soil that the Messiah who would become the savior of all the East would make His appearance, and it therefore followed that, in preparation for that day, if they were to recover the lost mystery, His future followers should begin by establishing the correspondences between faces and the new Latin alphabet that Turkey adapted in 1928. To this end—and drawing from forgotten Hurufi pamphlets, Bektaşi poems, Anatolian folk art, the ghostly ruins of pristine Hurufi villages, the figures etched on the walls of dervish lodges and pashas' mansions, and thousands of calligraphic inscriptions—he demonstrated the "values" accorded to various sounds when they were translated from Arabic and Persian into Turkish, after which he went on to show, with a terrifying precision, where each individual letter could be found on human faces. (317)

The way the retired colonel, as propagandist and as spokesperson for the guardian state, engages with letters and with hidden meanings has resonances with Islamic *hurufism*.

Moreover, the articles by Celâl are interpreted by certain readers in the novel as secret codes of conspirators plotting to bring a new political regime to Turkey. Hence, the columnist's life is put in jeopardy because of his messianic role. Fatih Mehmet the Third, one of Celâl's most loyal readers, asks the columnist to describe utopias that give hope to the people:

> O brother mine, I know you are possessed of a mighty pen, a pen that can realize all these dreams—and tales far more implausible than these—and miracles others might deem impossible. With your beautiful words, and with the astonishing memories you will soon be pulling from the bottomless well that is your mind, you can bring these dreams to life. . . . In this wretched land of ours, what other path is open to us except to write? (363)

Frustrated that Celâl has his own agendas, and that he has perhaps given up supporting an "imminent coup" that could bring order and save the nation, Fatih Mehmet the Third announces his desire to kill Celâl: "I am going to kill you because you deceived us all, deceived the entire nation with your bold lies, scandalous dreams, paranoid obsessions, insinuating refinements, elegant turns of phrase, and endearing antics—for years and years, you fooled even me" (381–82). When Celâl is murdered, Fatih Mehmet the Third remains one of the most probable suspects.

The function of literature as a sacred text with a prophetic political message is Janus-faced. On the one hand, texts may possess a certain power: a particular literary text is related to its readers in a similar way that a sacred text is related to a community of believers. On the other hand, a weakness: if the prophetic functions of an author fail, or if the author chooses not to fulfill the role of the prophet, the result may be apocalyptic. The author-prophet fails to rescue the nation and his readers lose faith in his prophetic abilities. In trying to free himself from the chains of national allegory or political prophecy, the author risks becoming a traitor.

"The Only Consolation"

As Galip takes over Celâl's column and becomes a writer in the last section of *The Black Book*, entitled "But I Who Write," readers too are invited to write. In the interplay between texts of different histories and geographies, we are encouraged to move beyond the role of passive readers and to instead create new meanings. In addition, the pronoun for the narrator shifts from *I* to *we*:

> Together we think of Rüya and look out onto the dark streets of Istanbul; together we go to bed to drift between sleep and wakefulness, and whenever I see some sign of Rüya on the blue-checked quilt, we are both plunged into misery and surprised back to life: because nothing is as surprising as life. Except for writing. Except for writing. Yes, of course, except for writing, the only consolation. (461)

Much Turkish literature operates in line with Jameson's notion of national allegory, as "the story of the private individual destiny" that is "always an allegory of the embattled situation of the public third-world culture and society" (69). Writing in the Turkish context might carry a civilizing mission, as writers take on the role of educators and of social and political missionaries to an uneducated reading public waiting for instruction. Without political prophecy, Turkish writers know that their texts might not contribute to the act of rescuing the nation, causing them to be alienated from national goals, resulting in feelings of shame, embarrassment, and perhaps of being irrelevant to their community. They might be pushed into being propagandists of the guardian state, and perhaps even punished for not complying with its demands. Writers might want to write coup d'état novels that idolize their narrators, denying them any sense of history, political belonging, and individuality, in order to exonerate the activist who may have been militant during the period of political polarization in the 1970s and to prove the warrantless violence of the guardian state. Against this background and knowledge, the last lines of *The Black Book* nonetheless invite readers to be the writers of their lives as well as the writers of new texts. Such a task will not take place by dismissing the burden of politics in writing but by embracing it. Through the confrontation with the political, and through the limitless freedoms offered in writing, we might "see some sign of Rüya on the blue-checked quilt," "as we go to bed to drift between sleep and wakefulness." In the zone between consciousness and unconsciousness, between the burden of the political and the dream of emancipation from the burden, some sign of Rüya (the dream) might be found. Lurking in some dark corner of life and of writing lies hope: *jouissance* (Barthes, *Pleasure*).

NOTES

[1]Mustafa Kemal Atatürk's reforms of the 1920s and 1930s included a series of economic policy, cultural, social, religious, legal, and political changes aimed at the modernization of Turkish society through political and cultural westernization. The reforms included but were not limited to changes in the constitution, the adaptation of European laws, jurisprudence, dress, and linguistic engineering.

[2]*Türkiye'nin Ermeni Meselesi* and its translation, *The Armenian Question in Turkey*, were written by Sâmiha Ayverdi but published under the name of Neşide K. Demir.

[3] For more, see "The Author on Trial," in the introduction to this volume.

[4] This essay quotes from Maureen Freely's translation of *Snow* published by Vintage Books in 2005.

[5] For example, in his work on Irish nationalism, David Lloyd in *Nationalism and Minor Literature* acknowledges the correspondence between autobiography and nationalism: "Biography or autobiography is intimately linked to the aesthetic politics of Romantic nationalism. The biography of the national hero is the repetition of the history of the nation. . . . Autobiography, including fictional autobiography, tends to represent the ethical self-realization of the writer from a perspective of self-consciousness through which the repetition of a life endows it with the appearance of a providential or a predestined pattern" (160).

[6] This essay quotes from Maureen Freely's translation of *The Black Book* published by Vintage Books in 2006.

Pamuk and New Turkish Literature

E. Khayyat

In 1939 the Turkish novelist, poet, and critic Ahmet Hamdi Tanpınar was appointed the chair of the newly established Department of New Turkish Literature at Istanbul University. The creation of the chair was part of two related developments: the establishment of European humanities in Turkey and the reorganization of the traditional educational institution (*İstanbul Darülfünûnu*) into Istanbul University. The university—where, incidentally, Pamuk would study journalism decades later—was among the first national, European-style universities in the Muslim world. Many prominent figures who influenced Turkish and world literature were involved in the creation of the university, including Erich Auerbach, who, having fled Nazi aggression, chaired the Department of Western Languages and Literatures and penned *Mimesis* and "Figura" there.

Tanpınar's appointment marks a crucial moment in the history of Turkish literary and cultural criticism and modern Turkish fiction. Tanpınar planned to write the first comprehensive history of modern Turkish letters as a two-volume work but only completed the first volume, *XIX. Asır Türk Edebiyatı* ("Nineteenth-Century Turkish Literature"; 1949). Tanpınar briefly explains why the verbal arts in what he calls the Muslim Orient before the nineteenth century did not develop into a full-blown literary enterprise and then offers a lengthy account of the many attempts to cultivate modern Turkish fiction in the nineteenth century. He describes many of these modern attempts as failures but regards them all as having paved the way to his own era. According to Tanpınar's somewhat subjective periodization, there are three phases to this history: the failure of the Muslim Orient to produce literature in the modern sense, because of its own peculiar, and at times charming, way of making things with words; the modern Ottoman and Turkish failure, bound to the ways of the Muslim Orient, to engage in literary activity proper; and Tanpınar's own extraordinary struggle and his reluctant, melancholy achievement as an accomplished man of letters.

Tanpınar is the writer with whom Pamuk feels "the closest bond" (*Istanbul* 110).[1] According to Pamuk, Tanpınar offers "the deepest understanding of what it means to live in a rapidly westernizing country among the ruins of Ottoman culture" (209). In this essay I imagine understanding Tanpınar's work as a barricade between the Ottoman past and Pamuk's era allows us to locate the coordinates of Pamuk's writing in the history of Turkish literature. Tanpınar is the ultimate figure that divides the past—a past difficult for Pamuk's generation to access—from the present. Tanpınar himself, the barricade "standing tall" (225), presents a historical image of a world that no longer exists and a melancholy account of his own moment in modernity.

Tanpınar narrates a progression toward modern Turkish letters. Driving this progression is a conflict between two different ways of relating to reality, which is linked to relating to words and things, and, by extension, of relating words to things. Tanpınar places himself between these two ways, one belonging to the preliterary Muslim Orient and the other to his rapidly westernizing present. For Pamuk, melancholy is the legacy of Tanpınar and his contemporaries. Tanpınar professes a literature that is melancholic and derives from his nostalgic dedication to "our old poetry" (*XIX. Asır Türk Edebiyatı* 20–24), but also revolutionary, pointing to the future. Pamuk's works bear marks of the conflictual history Tanpınar narrates, but Pamuk follows Tanpınar's prescription to step out of melancholy and impasse.

This essay charts Pamuk's place in the long history of Turkish letters to help teachers understand Pamuk's concerns about the Ottoman past and his fixation on the relation of real objects to fiction (his own peculiar realism). Pamuk shares Tanpınar's preoccupation with questions about the political and historical relevance of writing; in fact, writing is a major motif in Pamuk's fiction. This essay outlines Tanpınar's perception of Muslim oriental art as a dead end on the way to literary modernity, describes Tanpınar's quest to discover a way out of this impasse, and then explains how Pamuk sidesteps Tanpınar's paradox and ultimately surpasses Tanpınar and his predecessors.

Failure

"Şiir ve İnşa" ("Poetry and Prose"; 1868) is one of the first literary critical works written in Ottoman Turkish. Its author, Ziya Pasha (1825–80), is thought to have used "Poetry and Prose" for his title because he lacked an Ottoman Turkish word that corresponded to the French *littérature*. As Tanpınar would later explain, prose was an almost nonexistent genre in the Muslim Orient; Muslim poetry surpassed prose in quality and quantity, and because of its prominence poetry also overburdened prose with its peculiar intransitivity. Comparing the couplet ("beyit") to European poetry, Tanpınar describes the poetry of the Muslim Orient as a radically different way of making things with words. The couplet—a fragment, as opposed to the solid stanza of European poetry—is the essence of Muslim oriental art, he argues. The binding of stanzas with "themes" is irrelevant to the Muslim oriental couplet, as are "narratives" that bind statements into stories or novels and "frames," visible or invisible, that in Western plastic arts enable a particular vision and its representation. While such elements may exist in Muslim oriental art, they remain secondary; the *beyit* shapes the art and dictates its movements. Tanpınar argues that the second line of a couplet in

Muslim oriental poetry is usually either redundant or superficial semantically, while the two lines together resemble a jewel. The first line gives the saying, while the second says almost nothing, expressing submission to form in following the first line formulaically. The second line appears empty of content, an embellishment of the motif introduced in the first line. One half of the couplet annuls the content promised in the other and pushes the motif—the singular object, sentiment, or thought expressed in the first line—to the fore. Couplets cannot be unified into a single meaningful work, regardless of the length of the poem (*XIX. Asır Türk Edebiyatı* 28–46). Tanpınar sees parallels of this phenomenon in nonartistic realms as well. Quoting Louis Massignon, he argues that "there is no time in the Muslim Orient, but only moments" (32). In Tanpınar's view, there were no stories in the Muslim Orient, not even storytelling pressed into the service of history. Poems only provided impressions and images—not "realistic" images, but images typical of miniatures, lacking perspective and proportion. The trouble with "our old poetry" was that it treated words as things, as precious stones.

This oriental poetic way of making things with words paralyzed Turkish prose, according to Tanpınar. Turkish prose could not become literary in the modern sense, could not enable the writing of novels, for instance, because it was stuck in the peculiar intransitivity of the oriental "verbal arts":

> No doubt one of the important reasons for the obsession with the verbal arts overwhelming the old prose was that it was deprived of the *terbiye* [manners, habit of mind, discipline] that plastic arts and painting had enabled in other languages, paving the way to the possibility of a clear vision. . . . In a literature [or regime of writing], and particularly a prose tradition that had never confronted the line, the image or the sculpture, or simply the volume and the color; in a writing that had never before tested in these the *nizam* [order] of attesting to the real and the accompanying notion of *nisbet* [proportion], hence deprived of their *terbiye* of *tecrit* [isolation, abstraction], the contact with the thing and the external world would obviously remain superficial.
>
> (46; my trans.)

Here, Tanpınar relates ways of saying to ways of seeing. Making things with words, as with lines and colors, conditions vision and relation to the world. Properly literary, "realistic" writing, like realistic depiction, enables realistic vision. Such vision and relation are possible as a habit of mind, cultivated through exercises in realistic representation, verbal or visual. Tanpınar developed the habit of mind to forge the kind of "contact" with "the external world" that is not "superficial," but here "historical," elsewhere "realistic" and literary. His "melancholy" derives from his inability to reconcile this historical, literary-realistic contact with the habits of mind of the Muslim Orient. As a humanist, he feels that the only option is to describe the old Turkish, Muslim oriental ways of saying and being as problematic and inaccessible, as an impasse on the way to westernization and progress. Yet he still recognizes these traditions as his own, referring to "our" old poetry and prose.

How would these matters look from the perspective of a Turkish novelist of Pamuk's caliber? Pamuk's work often addresses the question of "contact with the thing and the external world," comparing, and at times equating, literary writing with visual representation. A miniature of a tree Pamuk draws in *My Name Is Red*, for instance, tells us that it was not depicted realistically "not because I fear that if I'd been thus depicted all the dogs in Istanbul would assume I was a real tree and piss on me: I don't want to be a tree, I want to be its meaning" (51).[2] The "unrealistic" depiction of a tree—as a miniature, as a figure in an abstract painting, or here as a character in a novel—is governed by a particular choice between ways of relating to things in the world. In *My Name Is Red* different ways of "contact with the thing and the external world" are presented as different options for relating to the world, yet there is no sense of a hierarchy to these options.

Pamuk offers the option of simply not choosing from among these different means of expression. The fragmented narrative of *My Name Is Red* privileges moments more than time. Its chapters resemble miniatures or Tanpınar's miniature-like couplets. Yet despite the fragmented narrative, the simple plot of this detective fiction effortlessly frames and unifies these miniatures. Could one argue that where Tanpınar fails, Pamuk prevails? If so, in what ways? Does *My Name Is Red* reconcile the novel with what Tanpınar calls the verbal arts of the Muslim Orient? To answer these questions, let us consider the implications of the role Tanpınar and Pamuk each assigns to verbal and visual representations in life.

Tanpınar's perspective considers the weight of an entire civilizational history and the overbearing tension that arises when this history confronts another. The main character of Tanpınar's *The Time Regulation Institute*, Hayri İrdal, an author, carries this burden. Cut off from the past, he can hardly understand Ottoman Turkish. He is far from appreciating "our old poetry." His employment at the institute initiates him into another way of writing and reading, saying and being. The mission of the institute is to enable citizens to develop a more precise sense of temporality, of one's place in time. İrdal is involved in an intellectual project—the writing of history—that challenges the traditional ways of experiencing time and place. His crowning achievement is his best-selling biography, whose completely fictional, yet historically probable, story ends up driving its inventor mad. The tensions of the civilizational conflict exhaust İrdal. The type of writing he practices at the institute is in conflict with the Muslim oriental way, a conflict experienced daily by the Turkish people. In this account, literature is the site of a social and political conflict. Moreover, Tanpınar involves himself politically in this conflict by writing both fiction and history about it (Pamuk, *Istanbul* 225).

İrdal's madness can be compared to Galip's perplexity in *The Black Book*. When Galip sets out to find his wife in Istanbul, the entire city, real and concrete, transforms itself into a labyrinth of signs, every object and event overburdened with meaning. The way Pamuk weaves signs together and folds the narrative onto itself numerous times shows how a different way of relating to words and things can transform the entire world beyond one's intentions or understanding. The famous scene from *Snow* in which the soldiers on stage fire live rounds at the audience can help elucidate the broader implications of Pamuk's position on the truth of fiction:

> As someone from the back rows stood up and made straight for the stage with blood streaming from his head, there came the smell of gunpowder. . . . Even so, the literature teacher Nuriye Hanım, who attended the National Theater every time she visited Ankara and was full of admiration for the beauty of the theatrical effects, rose to her feet for the first time to applaud the actors. (156–57)[3]

The eruption of fiction into reality in these lines must be understood against the background of Tanpınar's commentary on different habits of mind and their relations to reality. What is at stake here is the truth of fiction. The stage fires live rounds. Fiction does real things in the real world. Nuriye Hanım, the literature teacher, does not seem to understand what is happening, and appears a little mad, like İrdal, perhaps a little like Tanpınar as well. But *Snow*, which Pamuk described as his first political novel, is not the story of Nuriye Hanım, who is but a minor, comic figure in the narrative. Galip, unlike İrdal or Tanpınar, navigates the city, heavy with signs and meaning, with ease. We will see how Pamuk's politics is fairly different from the civilizational impasse Tanpınar describes in *The Time Regulation Institute*. Tanpınar himself prescribed a different, specific politics of literature as a way out of this impasse.

Manufacture

Not surprisingly, Tanpınar describes Muslim oriental art as above all craftsmanship: "our old poetry" was making things with words, rather like producing textiles rather than texts, and was related to reality only superficially. Making literature requires perspective, context, and proportion, that is, a more intimate relation to reality. In his 1960 essay "The Fundamental Differences between the Orient and the Occident" (*Edebiyat* 132–35), Tanpınar explains how the difference between Muslim oriental art and modern Western literature is related to different styles of making, quite literally:

> It is always possible to reduce the most apparent differences between the Occident and the Orient into a few notions, which then would allow critical engagement. As I understand it, first come the behaviors of these two distinct mentalities vis-à-vis the good and the thing. Needless to say here . . . we consider the good and the thing, but also the stuff of thinking and imagining, all the material of mental and social life, which is to say we consider the "object" in the face of the thinking mind and the processing hand. The Orient accepts the thing as is or as it appears in the first differentiation it is assigned at the first encounter. . . . In the first encounter [the Orient] even arrives at certain perfections, so much so that sometimes after the first encounter, perfection of the same caliber becomes forever unattainable. . . . The Occident grabs the thing to turn it around, holds it before the mind, looks for additional traits to assign and other possibilities of perfection to pursue, wrestles to know the thing as thoroughly as possible and as a result of all this endeavor makes the thing into almost something other than itself. . . . Sometimes it is as if the Orient simply borrows the good from nature. The Occident owns the good completely by understanding its bodily constitution and testing all of its possibilities. (132; my trans.)

For Tanpınar, diamond cutting is the perfect example. "At least until the conquest of South African mines," Tanpınar writes, "the Orient was the home of precious metals" (132). While the most precious and the most beautiful jewels were originally oriental, the processing of precious metals had become an occidental business. It was originally an oriental business, argues Tanpınar, but "a special care and a way of knowledge that expands all the way to speculation has transformed" this sort of making: "This care is speculative, because it is based on observation and knowledge concerning the capacity of light to be refracted. In the Occident, in poetry, in music and language, in all the fields of fine arts and in all issues concerning thought and society, we always encounter this care and this economy of knowledge." In the Orient, however, "imagination resembles those figures of old fables that stumble upon precious stones. It gathers whatever it can gather on the isolated mountain tops where it flies on the back of a Phoenix" (133). In these few lines, Tanpınar reduces all literary history, an entire history of art in the East and the West alike, into a history of manufacture, of literally making. To answer the question of what art is, one must simply consider "the 'object' in the face of the thinking mind and the processing hand."

One can interpret Pamuk's carefully crafted, labyrinthine plots, which display a craftsmanlike care and precision, in the light of these insights. The Hoja in *The White Castle*, for instance, spends years to discover the origin of his

Venetian slave's colorful stories in order to learn how to tell stories himself. But he masters storytelling (so much so that he can become the Venetian himself) only after understanding that the slave's stories owe their effectiveness not to the slave's ability to mine secrets but to a particular way of crafting narratives. But if there is one single work that puts to mind Tanpınar's premise it is Pamuk's *The Museum of Innocence.* Kemal introduces the reader to multiple everyday objects related to his beloved, Füsun, each representing a discrete moment of bliss. In every chapter, together with the narrator, readers grab one object after another, "turn it around, hold it before the mind, . . . make the thing into almost something other than itself." In the meantime, by making the novel itself into a thing—one of its pages is a printed ticket to the physical Museum of Innocence in Istanbul—Pamuk underlines the dumb reality of the book as an object. Moreover, the actual museum displays a collection of objects typical of everyday life in Istanbul during the period in which the novel is set. In the museum, objects are exhibited as if they were "precious stones," remnants of a mythic past, of a world that never was or is no more. *The Museum of Innocence* reveals how conflicting ways of being and different ways of relating to words and things, real and concrete, exist together in this part of the world. Pamuk's approach to realism releases the tensions inherent in Tanpınar's civilizational conflicts. In the next section I will consider how Pamuk achieves this.

Faith

Ziya Pasha's landmark essay "Poetry and Prose" identified a problem relating to the distance between written and vernacular languages, a distance that had stunted the development of literature in the absence of properly equipped readers. The pasha proposed educational and curricular shifts and a standardized orthography that would enable everyone to take part in a community of letters. Ahmet Midhat Efendi (1844–1913), one of the first modern Turkish novelists, thought that the problem lay elsewhere: the failure could be attributed to the rootlessness of Turkish literature (5). The problem was that Turkish literature had no classics: Midhat wanted to create modern Turkish classics rather than imitate Western classics or adopt them as part of Turkish culture and believed that Ottoman youth should read what is appropriate and useful to Muslims. Later Ömer Seyfeddin (1884–1920) explained that some of Midhat's readers traveled to the printing facilities where Midhat had his works published in order to find out if a certain fictional character of Midhat's was a real person: "People did not know anything about this genre of writing that is the novel, they took fictional persons to be real persons! And yet, *elhamdülillah* [praise be to God], we do not live in that age that takes the novel to be the real event" (Seyfeddin 292; my trans.). The emerging awareness of fiction writing was only the beginning of the path toward Turkish literary production.

For Ziya Pasha the creation of a common, simple language and standardized orthography would support the development of literature because it would create an informed community of readers and writers. But Midhat believed that Ziya Pasha's ideas could be destructive if one did not ensure that the emerging literary public was not in conflict with Muslim society, which had its own traditions of writing and communication. For Seyfeddin the modernization of literature followed the modernization of life. Turkish life could not yet be represented by novels, just as Turkish people were not yet ready for "[the] streetcar or the boat" (292). In the minds of all three writers, the question of literature is inextricably linked to certain cultural, societal, and educational changes that must take place before this literary impasse could be overcome. The literary failure was a failure to communicate and to be a people in the modern, Western sense. Literary criticism was thus social critique and its call to action was political.

Tanpınar explains that literary writing is neither a tool to be employed for Ziya Pasha's revolutionary purposes or Midhat's reactionary purposes nor is it dependent on a culture that shares a modern lifestyle. In the early nineteenth century, people's relation to things and words began to change in this part of the world, slowly and painfully because change requires the loss of tradition. Tanpınar juxtaposes what he deems an "idealist" account of "our failure in literature" with a "determinist" one. Idealists argue that the Turkish men of letters remain ignorant about their society while wishing to transform it; they are elites who lack contact with the common culture of the simple folk. Tanpınar accepts that art forms are transmitted and imitated across cultures, and therefore finds that the issue of Turkish writers copying Western examples has been exaggerated. The determinists argue that Turkish letters fail because "our communal life" is not fit to be represented by a modern genre such as the novel. Tanpınar agrees with this judgment as well, but proves it to be faulty with the following argument: "Our life is narrow, it is intricate. This said, in the final analysis it is and we are living it, we love and hate, suffer and die. Is this not enough for the novelist?" (*Edebiyat* 37; my trans.).

Coming from an author as political as Tanpınar, the statement is shockingly indifferent. *The Time Regulation Institute* comes close to putting on paper the narrow and intricate life Tanpınar refers to, although the deep melancholy of the tragicomedy proves that "we are living, we love, . . . and die" does not suffice for Tanpınar the novelist. Yet this is exactly what he seems to prescribe for future writers: in place of revolutionary or reactionary politics, he suggests political indifference, or better still, a politics of indifference. For Pamuk this ideal will take the form of naiveté, as he expresses in *The Naive and the Sentimental Novelist*. It would be a mistake to associate this indifference or intentional naiveté with an apolitical position. Tanpınar's fascinating, if still somewhat melancholy, passage below displays the political foundations of indifference:

> The novelist must believe in the people. It is this faith that produces art. Wherever there is life, there is also the joy that is nothing other than lights and colors overflowing this faith. . . . I believe that when we recognize these issues in their actuality, we will find ourselves elsewhere, in a place where we don't anymore take life to be something we bear, something like fate. A place where we take hold of life, looking around us with the self-confidence of the great makers. Yet to find this spirit of making we need first to find the pleasure of life. We need to taste the happiness of life in the exact same way the great nature appears to be happy simply to be. This is only possible by believing in the people of this society. It is futile to look at this society through alien lenses, or to recreate it as if it were the product of some intellect, as if it did not have a reality of its own. (*Edebiyat* 44–45; my trans.)

Faith in the people, in the life in common, requires coming to terms with the realities of the life in common, even when this life is narrow and intricate. Neither nostalgia for bygone glory nor ideals about origins nor fixation on the greener grass will do. The spirit of great makers, which Pamuk certainly possesses, is "the joy that is nothing other than lights and colors overflowing this faith." What makes Pamuk a Turkish novelist is not what makes Ziya Pasha, Midhat, Seyfeddin, or Tanpınar Turkish men of letters. Pamuk stands out, perhaps in the direction Tanpınar points to, as a great, naive, and sentimental novelist of world literature, with Istanbul at the center of his world. He stands out as a great maker, an artisan who gives a glimpse of the "lights and colors" of the city, crafting stories out of memories, hopes and despairs, angers and joys, of its past and present inhabitants.

NOTES

[1] This essay quotes from Maureen Freely's translation of *Istanbul: Memories of the City* published by Alfred A. Knopf in 2006.

[2] This essay quotes from Erdağ M. Göknar's translation of *My Name Is Red* published by Alfred A. Knopf in 2001.

[3] This essay quotes from Maureen Freely's translation of *Snow* published by Faber and Faber in 2004.

The White Castle: Reception, Paratexts, and the Politics of Translation

Sevinç Türkkan

In my graduate seminar Major Authors in World Literature, I use translation as a lens through which we read Pamuk's works to explore the ethics and politics of translation, circulation, and international reception. This essay focuses on *The White Castle* and reflects on my teaching the text both as a translation and as a narrative that performs translation. I highlight the role of writers and translators as interpreters and help students develop skills in reading the text as a translation. Ultimately, together with my students I aim to formulate a new definition of world literature, one that recognizes the politics of translation in canon formation and is cognizant of the role of translators in literary influence and cross-cultural dialogue.

When designing world literature syllabi, one is compelled to place Pamuk not in the context of Turkish literary history but in the comparative zone created by the interaction of various texts, temporalities, and cartographies. It is rewarding to read Pamuk as a world author, as his works open themselves up in a variety of ways to comparative analysis. For example, one could read *The White Castle* with sections from Hegel's *Phenomenology of Spirit* and Plato's *Symposium* to discuss the master-slave dialectic; or one could combine *The White Castle* with Edgar Allan Poe's "William Wilson," Fyodor Dostoevsky's *The Double*, Oscar Wilde's *Portrait of Dorian Gray*, and Robert Louis Stevenson's *Dr. Jekyll and Mr. Hyde* in a study of the motif of the double. *The White Castle* could be taught in a course on metafiction side by side with Italo Calvino's *If on a Winter's Night a Traveler* or *The Castle of Crossed Destinies* in order to compare metafictional techniques in different historical and cultural contexts, or with Jorge Luis Borges's "Story of the Warrior and the Captive" as another role-reversal tale. One could teach the novel in a course on travel writing and the Ottoman Empire's interaction with early modern Europe by combining sections from Evliya Çelebi's *The Book of Travels* and Miguel de Cervantes's "The Captive's Tale." Studying *The White Castle* side by side with Abdelfattah Kilito's *Thou Shalt Not Speak My Language* opens up avenues for exploring the role of the other in the formation of one's self-image in and through language. Such juxtapositions span time, place, and languages and allow students to gain cross-cultural understanding in ways that reach beyond national categorizations. Reading texts comparatively, students see how each text reflects others as though in a series of mirrors, recalling the physical mirror at the center of *The White Castle* that serves as a node of cathexis to generate a sense of mutual identity between the narrator and Hoja, the two main characters.

However, Turkish literature occupies a precarious place in North American comparative literary studies. Texts written in Turkish and circulating in translation have to negotiate various power differentials and barriers as they enter this uneven field. Identifying translation as a lens circumvents some of the difficulties teachers encounter with Pamuk's novels. Taken as an analytical category, translation teaches students to recognize the mediated nature of the translated text and to develop ways to read translations that differ from the ways they read other texts. Students understand that their interpretations and critical exercises are contingent, situated in a particular language and cultural moment, circumscribed by institutional constraints that could change as new translations appear. For instance, I tell my students that I assign *The White Castle* not just because of its intrinsic value but because there is only one translation available in English. This makes students aware of the double focus of the discussion: we address the text not only in its cultural and historical context but also in our own moment and context. Such sensitivity limits free-floating interpretations of the English text and draws attention to the material and mediated conditions of its existence. Would Pamuk have reached the attention of the Nobel Prize committee had his novels not been available in English, French, and German? Is this even an issue for writers of English or other major European languages? What is the implication for texts that never reach an afterlife in another language? What does it mean to be translated, to gain, and to travel in translation? I have observed how students' recognition of these constraints open up different ways of grasping the text and their own position as readers in relation to the translation.

Contemporary Approaches to Translation

Approaches to translation span a wide spectrum—some see translation as an insurmountable difficulty while others deem it necessary. Robert Frost stated that poetry is what gets lost in translation (159); Walter Benjamin, on the other hand, postulated that without translation the original is barren ("Task" 74). As an afterlife and an interpretation of the original for a new audience, translation gives a work a future in the transnational field. Similarly, approaches to methods of translating are divided into two camps. According to Friedrich Schleiermacher, "either the translator leaves the writer in peace as much as possible and moves the reader toward him; or he leaves the reader in peace as much as possible and moves the writer toward him" (49). Building on Schleiermacher's proposition, Lawrence Venuti identifies "foreignizing" and "domesticating" as the predominant approaches to translation in the Anglo-American domain (*Translator's Invisibility* 20). Domesticating translations erase differences between languages and cultures to make the translation transparent and fluent, almost as if it were an original work. Foreignizing translations, on the other hand, validate difference and retain the foreign. Adopting an ethical and political agenda, Venuti calls for foreignizing methods that counter the "ethnocentric violence" of translation; he urges us to "write and read translated texts in ways that seek to recognize the linguistic and cultural difference of foreign texts" (41). Needless to say, ideal translations strike a balance between the two approaches. Highly foreignizing translations create barriers for readers, while heavily domesticating translations defy the logic of their existence. These theoretical approaches provide students with a critical framework for reading *The White Castle* as a locus of difference and also for rethinking what cultural assumptions they bring to reading a foreign text in English. In teaching *The White Castle* in translation, issues of language, style, and form can be approached through the novel's themes as well: set in seventeenth-century Istanbul, *The White Castle* is a tale of conversion and translation of selves, the Venetian and the Ottoman.

Teaching Reception

Translated into English as *The White Castle* by Victoria Holbrook, *Beyaz Kale* (1985) is Pamuk's third novel and the first he published in English (in 1990 in the United Kingdom and 1991 in the United States). A class session could begin by discussing the timing and choice of the translation and its significance for readers of world literature. Pamuk's second novel, *Sessiz Ev* (1983), appeared in English as *Silent House* only in 2012, and as of 2017 his first novel *Cevdet Bey and His Sons* still awaits English publication. Gaps and inconsistencies in the translation history of Pamuk's novels limit our ability to grasp the intertextual references across them, and, as Erdağ Göknar has pointed out, these gaps resulted in misinterpretations of this writer's "literary modernity" ("Occulted Texts" 178). Pamuk made a strategic choice to defer English translations of his first novels; he might have seen them as products of his apprenticeship period or suspected that they were closely tied to a certain chapter in modern Turkish history and therefore untranslatable. Willing to experiment with narrative form and technique, Pamuk crafted *The White Castle* in ways that radically departed from his first two novels while maintaining intertextual continuity with them. Pamuk's experimentation is most visible through the main characters, Hoja and the Venetian scholar, whose dialogic relationship questions essentialist understandings of self and identity, revealing them as interchangeable and translatable. The intertextual continuity is established with the return of *Silent House*'s disillusioned historian, Faruk, as the writer of the preface to *The White Castle* (12).[1] Similarly, *Silent House* establishes the connection to *Cevdet Bey* through Fatma, who remembers her visits to Nigân, Cevdet Bey's wife (150, 329).

The White Castle allowed English-speaking readers their first glimpses into Pamuk's literary world. Holbrook's translation renders Pamuk's novel in a clear, eloquent, and fairly elevated style: "Thus, to find an appropriate end to my story and my life, I think of Him to my heart's content" (147). These aspects of the text are balanced with occasional contractions and colloquialisms. Syntactically, Holbrook opted for pithy sentences free of embellishments and ornate or complex language. These stylistic choices generated a text that doesn't attract attention to itself. Instead, it carries the plot forward and allows for immersion in the story. Questions of style were rarely noted in the reviews of the translation, which introduced its author as an "emerging writer" from "the East" writing in a predominantly "postmodernist" and "experimental" mode (P. Berman; Updike, "Vagueness"; McGrath; Marien). The reviewers often find similarities between this novel and those of Kafka (Parini; Lehman-Haupt), Borges (Parini; Updike, "Vagueness"), Calvino (Updike, "Vagueness"; Lehman-Haupt), Nabokov (Lehman-Haupt), and Proust (Updike, "Vagueness"), and even the figure of Scheherazade (Parini). Many anglophone reviewers and critics read the novel as a commentary on a "clash of civilizations,"[2] taking Hoja and the Venetian as analogues to "Islam" and "the West" (P. Berman; Hitchins; Lehman-Haupt). Almost uniformly, reviews focus on thematic concerns and ignore the fact that the text is a translation. Some fail to list the translator in the headnotes or don't mention that the book is a translation, quoting and commenting as if the text were written in English (Carver; P. Berman; Kellman). They refer to the narrative's "shimmering tone" and its "effortless gymnastics" (Updike, "Vagueness" 102), its "coolly recited" narrative and Pamuk's "easy Cartesian cerebralness" (P. Berman 38), the novel's "echoing word patterns" and its "exotic" style (Lehman-Haupt), the "elegant postmodernist twist" and "skillfully constructed paradoxes" (Steinberg), the "slow, unmoving" pace (Nielson 222), the novel's "accessible" nature (McGrath), and how it is an "elegant and important meditation on East and West" (Carver).

As these quotations demonstrate, reviewers notice the narrative's stylistic aspects and hear its allusions to other texts, translations, and writers. However, reviewers treat *The White Castle* as if it were a transparent copy of the original and fail to acknowledge the translator who crafted the text. Teachers could assign students to research the book's reception in reviews and criticism and to discuss the language and style of the translation in relation to how these aspects of the novel have been addressed in book reviews. For instance, what aspects of the text are highlighted and what aspects are evaded? What references, if any, are made to the translation? How are quotations from the translation addressed and interpreted? Does it matter if a review does or does not engage with the text's second frame (the translation being the first)—the paratextual elements that are the dedication, epigraph, and fictional preface? This assignment is even more effective when reviews by anglophone critics are juxtaposed with critical essays by scholars of Turkish literature (Göknar, "Ottoman Legacy"; Bayrakçeken and Randall). Turkish scholars excavate the text's Ottoman elements, complicating the dominant narratives about Turkish modernity, references that in anglophone reviews are conspicuously absent or substituted with orientalist readings. This discussion could further lead to an investigation of the packaging and presentation of the translation, the cover and copyright pages, and the introduction and references to the translator (or lack thereof).

Teaching Paratextual Elements

Not only did anglophone reviewers typically dismiss the text's status as a translation and decline to engage with its paratextual elements, they also failed to understand the role of "Faruk Darvınoğlu," the writer of the (fictional) preface and the translator of the archival manuscript that constitutes the novel's chapters. As Gérard Genette points out, texts rarely exist without paratextual devices. Framing the text from inside and outside, paratexts contribute to the text's presence, reception, and consumption, and they constitute a translation and transaction zone between the book and its readers (1–2). I would also add that paratexts serve to illuminate the roles of the translator and publisher, important brokers of world literature today. Thus, as a signifying threshold, paratexts act as a key to a more complete reading and better understanding of the materiality of texts.

The White Castle is structurally framed by a dedication, an epigraph, and a preface. It consists of eleven chapters, the last of which could be read as an epilogue, and an afterword that Pamuk penned a year after the publication of the Turkish edition. The afterword appears in no English editions of the novel, but teachers can find it in Maureen Freely's (somewhat incomplete) translation included in the essay collection *Other Colors*. The novel begins with a dedication to "Nilgün Darvınoğlu, a loving sister (1961–1980)." Who is Nilgün? A muse, the ideal inspirer, the one responsible for the work dedicated to her? Who is the dedicator of this unsigned dedication? What is the symbolic resonance of the time frame "1961–1980"? From Pamuk's second novel, *Silent House*, we know that Nilgün is Faruk Darvınoğlu's leftist-socialist sister. The dedication in

The White House posits a personal and symbolic relationship that must be "at the service of the work" (Genette 134). Faruk's ability to produce the subtle tale of translational identities that follows is conditioned by the death of his sister, whose life coincides with the flourishing of leftist-socialist ideology in Turkey. Thus, the dedication is an intertextual link to Pamuk's previous novel, and the sister's death marks a symbolic break from the ideologies of that era, moving toward a new kind of writing represented by *The White Castle*.

The dedication is followed by an epigraph:

> To imagine that a person who intrigues us has access to a way of life unknown and all the more attractive for its mystery, to believe that we will begin to live only through the love of that person—what else is this but the birth of great passion?
>
> —Marcel Proust, from the mistranslation of Y. K. Karaosmanoğlu

More than simply a quotation from Proust's *À la recherche du temps perdu*, the epigraph reveals the presence of another text in this one, a proof of an (in)direct textual support, the presence of another in the self and of the self in the other. It is also a concrete manifestation of cross-cultural interaction through translation. Ironically, or perhaps necessarily, the identification with the other is through "mistranslation." The Turkish text renders the author of the quotation as "çeviren," that is, "the translator of," while the English translation renders it as "mistranslation." How do we understand this glaring discrepancy?

Pamuk has confided in me that he read Proust first in Karaosmanoğlu's Turkish translation, came across the sentence, thought it relevant to his novel, and decided to use it as an epigraph (Pamuk, "Karaosmanoğlu (mis)translation?"). When Pamuk and Holbrook reviewed the final proofs of the English translation, they searched for Karaosmanoğlu's sentence in both the French and English versions (performing a back translation) but couldn't find one that precisely corresponded to it. They deemed Karaosmanoğlu's a mistranslation and took the opportunity to correct it in the English version. Is this a correction or a further authorial displacement and a genuine way to retain the act of mistranslation? This anecdote allows me to generate discussions regarding the impact of translations on originals, on intertextuality in translation, and the idea of a translation as a metaphor for the original, a rewriting and mediation across texts. Translators necessarily fix a singular meaning for the proliferation of meanings and intertextual significations in the source text, provide explanations to compensate for the loss (thereby creating an excess of meaning), or supply corrections. Such textual meddling can result in further proliferation of signification, belying any pretense for linguistic equivalence or ideal translation. Authors and translators perpetually mistranslate as they carry meaning, say, from French to Turkish to

English and back, only to recognize that there will always be something that resists complete assimilation into one language.

To highlight these questions of mistranslation and equivalence in translation, one could juxtapose Holbrook's translation in *The White Castle* with C. K. Scott Moncrieff's acclaimed English translation of *Swann's Way*, in which the sentence reads: "The belief that a person has a share in an unknown life to which his or her love may win us admission is, of all the prerequisites of love, the one which it values most highly and which makes it set little store by all the rest" (139). Holbrook's translation emphasizes the place of the unknown and mystery in the complexity of love and passion for another, while Moncrieff's translation prioritizes the lyricism and timelessness of Proust's swirling poetic ecstasy. Holbrook's translation is conditioned by its context: it is an epigraph to an allegory of interchangeable identities. Moncrieff's translation makes sense only in the context of the larger text from which it is taken, and in relation to Proust's long, complex sentences that rise and fall dramatically to express sentiments and longing for an ideal. Could we deem one translation better or more accurate than the other? Does checking a translation's accuracy against an original benefit our understanding of how texts signify and circulate? This exercise can help students deepen their understanding of the assumed singularity of source texts and to rethink the translational zone of world literature, where texts are constantly written, rewritten, (mis)interpreted, and (mis)translated.

The epigraph condenses multiple authorial identifications and displacements (Holbrook, Pamuk, Karaosmanoğlu, Proust, Darvınoğlu) and blurs distinctions between writers, translators, and narrator. But Pamuk's choice of the epigraph's author-translator reveals another layer of signification, often overlooked. The writer, poet, translator, journalist, and diplomat Karaosmanoğlu (1889–1974) lived during the transitional period between the Ottoman Empire and the Turkish Republic; his novels comment on the cultural crises of the republican era and explore the challenges citizens faced under the perverse logic of westernization and nationalism. The republican ideology that promoted purging the Turkish language of its words derived from Arabic and Persian entailed borrowing French words to replace them. The Translation Bureau established by the Ministry of Education during the reform period launched an active program of translating Western classics into Turkish. Its World Literature series prioritized French literature—Karaosmanoğlu's Turkish translation of Proust was part of this program. Thus the epigraph also comments on the role of writers and translators in the project of nation building.

Formally, the epigraph is also a textual link between the fictional dedication and the preface. It is an ironic comment on how Turkish modernity, a project of intralingual and interlingual (mis)translation, replaced the disavowed Ottoman past. The epigraph links not only languages but also different temporalities and divergent cultural and ideological constructions. This much is condensed in the epigraph, but it still leaves my students in a state of uncertainty: How does it connect with the dedication? Does it signify incestuous love between brother and sister, or submission to taboo by sublimating the love object? Genette writes that an epigraph is "always a mute gesture whose interpretation is left up to the reader" (156). I suggest that the epigraph comments on and justifies the book's title, whose meaning it indirectly specifies. In the preface Darvınoğlu comments, "It was not I who chose the title of the book, but the publishing house" (12). In a gesture of further authorial displacement, the narrative highlights other guardians of meaning, the editors and publishers, who exercise control on how texts signify and circulate. The epigraph complements the title and comments on the text that follows by way of a preliminary warning that this is not a historical novel or a naive representation but an evocation of the predicaments of identity. That is, the title is to be taken figuratively, as a sublimation of an ideal and a comment on the impossibility of univocal meaning or identity.

Especially rewarding was a class discussion on the title of the novel and character names. The Turkish title, *Beyaz Kale*, translates as "the white castle" or "the white fortress." Students reflected on various connotations and denotations of *castle* and *fortress* as I posed questions regarding their different significations and how these two options might be supported (or not) by the narrative. How is the title related to the castle named Doppio (meaning *double*), whose resistance to the Ottoman siege prompts the Venetian and Hoja to exchange identities? Should a translation render the title literally or aim for an aesthetic re-creation or metaphoric allusion to other texts? We also discussed the main characters' names, their meanings, and their allusions to Eastern and Western traditions. *Faruk* means "one who discerns truth from falsehood," and *Darvınoğlu*, the ironic last name Salahattin of *Silent House* takes when the new government requires citizens to register surnames, stands for "son of Darwin." How does Faruk's name relate to his role as the disillusioned Ottoman historian and professor, dweller in the archive, smuggler and translator of the manuscript? What are the analogies between Darvinoğlu and Karaosmanoğlu, the Proust translator? How do we read the superimposition on one character of Eastern and Western names? What do these uneasy superimpositions, or juxtapositions, tell us about contemporary Turkish identity?

The title "Hoja" raises similar complex questions suitable for class discussion. Holbrook retained the title, adding only a brief explanation instead of a footnote: "'Hoja,' meaning 'master'" (23). In Turkish, the term *Hoja* carries both secular and religious meanings. In contemporary usage it refers to a professor employed at a secular university. In an Ottoman Islamic context it refers to a seminary (*medrese*) graduate with specialized knowledge of Islamic theology. Thus, the term allows Pamuk to highlight the secular and fundamental contradictions of contemporary Turkish identity that are embodied in this word. My students debated whether names should be rendered in translation as they are in the original, transliterated into the target language's alphabet, or supplemented by annotations and explanations. This discussion led one student to ask about the word *Allah.* Class discussion focused on whether translators should transliterate the word and emphasize difference, or translate it as "God" and underscore commonalities across monotheistic religions. How did Holbrook handle this key word? How does her choice of vocabulary affect the translation and the reading experience overall? Thus the class discussion drew attention to the translator's crucial role in negotiating religious differences.

Signed by the fictional narrator Darvınoğlu, the preface is a commentary on the tale that follows. Darvınoğlu introduces himself as the translator-writer of the manuscript he has found in a "forgotten 'archive' . . . at the bottom of a dusty chest" (9). I ask my students to imagine the moment of discovery and think about the work historians perform. How does a seventeenth-century Ottoman archival manuscript transform in the hands of a historian in 1982? To generate discussion on the role of the historian as a writer and on the status of the historical narrative as one version of events, I assign chapters 14 and 18 from *Silent House* and the chapter "The Historical Text as Literary Artifact" in Hayden White's *Tropics of Discourse.* In the *Silent House* chapters, Faruk reflects on the "strangeness" of his profession (124) while White argues that historical narratives are verbal fictions "as much invented as found" and thereby have more in common with literature than with science (82). The archive supplies incomplete records that the historian must rewrite and reassemble into a continuous narrative—how does our knowledge of this assemblage affect our understanding of historical narratives? What skills do we need to read narratives collected from the archives? Could the pamphlets on (pseudo)science, zoology, and the plague, as well as the autobiographical confessions the narrator and Hoja produce, be the "records" Darvınoğlu finds in the archive and weaves into the story "The Quilter's Stepson"? My goal is to challenge students to think about historians as writers and translators who, in the process of creating a historical text, emphasize some elements while censoring and demoting others, similar to the plotting of narrative in fiction.

Negligence in the archive allows Darvınoğlu to steal the manuscript and revise "the book into contemporary Turkish: after reading a couple of sentences from the manuscript I kept on one table, I'd go to another table in the other room where I kept my papers and try to narrate in today's idiom the sense of what remained in my mind" (12). In the archive, records are in the Ottoman language and require both transliteration (from Ottoman to Latin script) and translation (from Arabic- and Persian-inflected Turkish to "today's idiom," modern Turkish). Translation in this context entails carrying across temporal, historical, and linguistic divides for readers of Turkish who are only familiar with the Latin alphabet (not to mention the further translation required to render the text in

English). In a gesture that is characteristic of historiographical metafiction, Darvınoğlu comments that "some events described in the story bore little resemblance to fact" yet "our 'knowledge' of history generally verified the events in the book" (10). The ambivalence is parodic and renders any claims to historical veracity problematic. Further, the novel's final chapter is an extreme form of unreliable narration and troubled certitude. Here, the source text as an archival document is transformed into a fictional story that offers a sense of the past that can only be known from the traces it left in literature through translation. Therefore, Darvınoğlu's acts of revision and transliteration are also acts of resisting what should have remained untranslated.

Darvınoğlu's translation is also a metaphor for the historical transition from the Ottoman state to the modern Turkish republic, as articulated in the republic's modernization reforms. These reforms include not only changing from Ottoman to Latin script (1928) but also abolishing the Ottoman sultanate (1922), shifting the capital from Istanbul to rural Ankara (1923), abolishing the Islamic caliphate and religious courts (1924), adopting European-style dress (1925), adopting the European calendar and various civil codes (1926), removing Islam as the state religion from the constitution (1929), granting women voting rights (1934), and declaring secularism and nationalism as constitutional principles (1937). Darvınoğlu's act of translating is described as shuttling from one table to another, from one room to another, and from the Ottoman script to the Latin alphabet. This shuttling is the fate of the modern historian, scholar, and writer, and is symptomatic of the dislocations left by the project of nation building. The idea of translation that emerges from the preface, therefore, is a metaphor for the method of rewriting the fragmented archival record and rendering it into a legible whole for a new audience. Such translation also gives an afterlife to the historical archive in world literature.

The White Castle *as a Theory of Translation*

Darvınoğlu's act of translating between two temporalities, settings, scripts, and cultural constituencies could also be read as a commentary on contemporary translation theories. It is both domesticating (making a legible, fluent, and readable story) and resistant (Faruk produces a text that speaks in multiple tongues and presents an alternative historiography). Contrary to Venuti's argument that acts of domestication are hegemonic, in the Turkish context the act of making the archive legible is an act of resisting the dominant republican ideology. By returning to the archive and translating the past for the benefit of the present, Darvınoğlu challenges the fabricated history of the modern Turkish state. Instructors and students may wish to contemplate how the end of the Ottoman Empire and the beginning of the Turkish republic are historically delineated.

What are the violences of Eurocentric chronologies that equate modernization with westernization?

My purpose has been to show that a mode of literary analysis that takes translation as a lens complicates students' understanding of Pamuk's novels and of their own place in the world. Students perceive the politics of world literature against the backdrop of available, selective, or absent translations. Students can then evaluate the text's reception and recognize the reviewers' silences regarding translators and translations in order to develop political readings that bring these elements back to the text. Instead of equating the English text with the original, students analyze paratextual elements; ask questions regarding voice, discourse, and ideology (rather than verbal accuracy); question their own status as consumers of translations; and work from within the text to formulate their own definitions of translation, world literature, and readership.

NOTES

[1] This essay quotes from the Carcanet edition of *The White Castle*.

[2] On the notion of a clash of civilizations, see Huntington.

Teaching *Snow* as a Translation

Gloria Fisk

If contemporary comparatists advance any single thesis by consensus, it might be this: the translation of literary texts requires processes that are much more complex—culturally, politically, economically, and linguistically—than they first appear. That consensus is naturalized by decades, if not centuries, of scholarly debate among critics from Pascale Casanova to Edward Said, who catalogue the difficulty with which literature travels across all manner of borders. Those difficulties seem obscure to even the ablest undergraduates, however, and not only because they have yet to learn the intricate theories to which these critics' names refer. In their eagerness to glean knowledge about the nonfictional world, the newest arrivals to scholarly conversation become not just susceptible, but indeed committed, to what Lawrence Venuti calls "the illusion of transparency." That is to say, they read with implicit trust that a good translator conveys texts across languages and cultures without leaving a trace. Assuming "the translator's invisibility," as Venuti describes it, they interpret Orhan Pamuk's *Snow* (2004) as if it "is not in fact a translation" of the Turkish *Kar* (2002), "but the 'original'" in every way that matters (*Translator's Invisibility* 1). And, in its transparency, *Snow* gives English-speaking readers access to a faraway world as real as we are.

This prevailing blindness to the translator's mediating presence on the page limits my students' entry to recent critical debates in translation theory, postcolonial studies, area studies, and world literature. It also girds their more general tendency to read fiction as ethnography, which is anathema to literary study altogether. When my students read *Snow* as an artifact of the Turkish writer's hand, they trust it as a source of reliable information about nonfictional Turks and Turkey, but they become less able to read it as a work of literature. Its value becomes contingent to its transparency; its literary features become irrelevant if not obstructive.

I coax my students onto more literary terrain by asking them to read *Snow* as a translation. This assignment seems to me fundamental without being at all easy, and the particular ways in which it is difficult have varied in proportion to the kinds of courses and students I've taught: first to freshmen in a writing seminar at Princeton University, then to Turkish undergraduates reading in English at Koç University in Istanbul, and now to undergraduate and graduate students at Queens College of the City University of New York.

Despite the differences among these groups of students, they share a striking similarity: their tendency to read *Snow* as if its status as a translation is a mere technicality, largely irrelevant to its interpretation. And they protect this assumption of the translator's invisibility energetically when I work to dispel it, which suggests to me that it is embedded in beliefs about world literature that are as pervasive as they are deeply held. That leads me to suspect that a nascent critic gains benefits beyond the obvious when he or she learns to read a translation as such, and I see that suspicion confirmed every time I teach *Snow*.

Few of my students—in Princeton, New York, and Istanbul—have come to our discussions about *Snow* with much factual knowledge about life in eastern Turkey, where *Snow* is set. Most of my students in North America have entered my classes with an acute awareness of their relative ignorance of Turkish politics and culture. Most have found that gap in their education highlighted for them by their initial foray into *Snow*, which makes them wonder how well they can read the novel without knowing more. As they read the narrator's descriptions of Ka's travel to the remote eastern city of Kars, they perceive themselves to be out of their depth—not knowing, for example, what is implied by Muhtar Bey's assertion to Ka that the religious men in town are "unlike Westernized Turks," because "they don't instinctively despise the common folk" (62).[1] They wonder what it means that the denizens of Kars suspect a conspiracy around the Kurdish sherbet shop, or, more centrally to the plot, precisely why some Turkish girls refuse to remove their headscarves in school and on stage.

My Turkish students knew volumes about "the headscarf issue," as it's colloquially known, but that knowledge did not make them certain that they were part of *Snow*'s implied audience. Studying at a private university in a suburb of the nation's cultural capital, they had participated actively in the debates about secularism and national identity that suffuse *Snow*, but they had no acquaintances like the fictional fundamentalist boy, Fazıl, or the provincial Muhtar Bey. *Snow*'s characters live on the opposite side of the country from Istanbul, at the end of long, treacherous mountain roads that my students would have no reason to travel. In fact, few of them had traveled east of the coastal swath of the country that has historically been home to the most educated Turks. Sons and daughters of the secular elite, they belonged to a demographic that is acculturated to be a likely audience for Pamuk, and they demonstrated to me the mutual exclusivity between his potential readership and the characters he depicts in *Snow*. The Europeanized protagonist, Ka, provides the only cultural coordinate that is proximal to Turkish literary circles, which are about as far away from Kars as my students in Queens are from Fargo, North Dakota.

And as my Turkish students came to *Snow* with imprecise knowledge of its landscape, they also felt their foreignness to the realist literary tradition that it extends. My students in the United States have also noted how granular details bury *Snow*'s plot as steadily as snowflakes blanket the city of Kars in drifts, slowing the pace, but they relate this technique to literary traditions that they recognize generally. They are not surprised to learn that Pamuk cites Fyodor Dostoevsky, Gustave Flaubert, and Thomas Mann among his influences, all of whom write novels that an undergraduate might initially deem boring, slow, and unrelatable. With those adjectives, my students at Princeton and Queens locate *Snow* in the realist tradition that they know in the broadest sense—if not through Pamuk's influences, then through their literary relatives who appear more regularly on North American reading lists: Jane Austen, Herman Melville, or John Steinbeck. Those references were lost on my Turkish students, who were schooled in other traditions entirely.

On both sides of the Bosphorus, then, Pamuk asks his readers to negotiate a path between the foreign and the familiar, and to extend their imaginations to regions where they do not travel with ease. He writes in cultural grammars that are mostly exclusive from each other, with references ranging from the Kurdistan Workers' Party (PKK) to Emma Bovary; at one point or another virtually all his readers are excluded from his implied audience. Whenever I teach *Snow*, I make the case that Pamuk extends that exclusion to all his readers by turns, and I use that argument to raise broader questions about the best way to read world literature by any definition. *Snow* makes its readers' relative ignorance a constitutive feature of the text and renders its implied reader a thought experiment in the conditions for literary circulation; it guarantees that all its readers will read beyond the limits of our expertise. Translation in the literal and metaphorical senses of the word seems essential to that project.

I gesture toward these deeper logics by asking my students to imagine the reader who could grasp all *Snow*'s cultural references. They consider the possibility of a Turkish person who is educated in Western traditions, and they identify Ka as a counterexample, noting how he travels as a foreigner in Germany and also in Kars. At home nowhere, he is a bad reader of cultural cues everywhere. Agreeing, I suggest that the novel implies a reader who is a unicorn, existing only in a fictive sense. Pamuk drowns the plot in a wealth of detail to make the actual readers' ignorance perceptible as a feature of the reading experience. If that is true, then the challenge of reading beyond the limits of what we know becomes central to the experience of reading *Snow*. I posit this hypothesis, and I ask my students to notice the moments when *Snow* makes them feel as if they possess insufficient knowledge to read it well.

The Assignment

As my students read the first ten chapters of *Snow*, I ask them to identify a passage or a scene that strikes them as foreign in some way, and to write an informal response that analyzes the source of that semblance of foreignness. From the following prompt, students are to respond in about two pages:

> Identify a passage that you find hard to read. Analyze as precisely as you can *what* seemed notably unfamiliar to you in the passage, and *how* you responded

> to that sensation of strangeness. What specific gap in your knowledge halted your progress through the novel? How and to what degree did the novel enable you to proceed past this impediment? Reflect on the ways that you used context clues to gather some of the knowledge you lacked, and consider how you made sense of this scene without knowing more than you do. As you look toward the rest of the novel, ask yourself what this momentary exclusion from the text suggests to you about the novel as a whole, or about the reader it assumes.

These questions are too many and too varied for students to answer them all, so I emphasize the exploratory purpose of this assignment, which paves the way to the formal essay they write later. I encourage students to pick and choose among the questions, noting that I've formulated them to be more generative than confining, leading to writing that is more speculative than certain. I ask students to retrace their steps as readers and, putting aside the imperative to follow a logical structure or to advance a convincing thesis, to narrate their reading experience, noting how the novel engages them as well as where and why their attention flags. I always provide my grading criteria for these assignments to indicate that these informal responses may include narration or reflection that would otherwise be too subjective, inconclusive, or self-contradictory for the conventions of academic writing. At the same time, I say explicitly that a good response paper requires at least one direct reference to the text, and that it analyzes that passage with care and close attention.

Those written responses prepare the ground for our first class discussion about *Snow*, which I open by asking who learned something—about the text or about themselves as its readers—from the informal response that they wrote. I take volunteers, and we practice close reading together. We focus on the passages that students identified, noting how and when the novel called their attention to their distance from the text or its referents. One of my primary goals in this conversation is to delineate the difference between two objects—the literary text and the nonfictional phenomena it represents—and to trace, through specific passages that my students select, how the difference is constructed.

One passage that recurs in these discussions is the bulk of chapter 5, whose English title is "Excuse Me, Sir: The First and Last Conversation between the Murderer and His Victim." This short chapter consists largely of the fictional transcript of a conversation between the director of the Education Institute and the religious extremist who shoots him at the end of the scene. The assassin has targeted the director as an enemy of Islam for enforcing the law of the secular state, which has historically required Turkish girls to remove their headscarves when they enter public buildings such as schools: "What good can come to this country if women uncover their heads?" the man asks, pointing a gun at the director, who wears the microphone that enables the transcript of the conversation we read. The man says, “Give me one good outcome. Say something you believe with all your heart. Say, for example, that by uncovering themselves they’ll get Europeans to start treating them like human beings. At least then I’ll understand what your motives are and then I won’t shoot you. I’ll let you go” (44).

When my students identify this passage as one that seems to require knowledge that they lack, I ask them what questions it raises that they are unable to answer. We distinguish those that are answerable with research—for example, are girls really required to remove their headscarves in Turkish schools, and, if so, why?—from those that are not, for example, what are Pamuk’s positions on the limits of secularism in an Islamic culture and the limits of Islamic practice in a secular state? In these conversations my students disentangle Turkey from Pamuk’s representation of it; they also note the partiality of any comparison they draw between the two. They categorize a list of the questions that *Snow* raises for them: “Answerable with Reference to Fact,” “Answerable with Reference to Fiction,” and “Probably Not Answerable at All.” We tabulate their progress with those questions, mapping precisely how Pamuk engages his readers with people, places, and literary devices that they might otherwise find excessively remote. And we subject that reading experience to analysis through the secondary texts that I assign—including short excerpts from Venuti (“How”), Emily Apter (*Against* 265–97), Said (3–4)—which posit every translation as an interpretation that becomes legible only in terms of its culture, language, politics, and history. These readings and class discussions prepare students for the essay prompt that I give:

> What methods of interpretation enable you to read *Snow* as a text that was written in a language that you don’t speak? Devise a thesis that answers this question, identify the methods you use, and demonstrate how they work with a close reading of the text. Define your key terms with reference to any of the theorists we’ve read and show precisely how your reading of the English text benefits from your acknowledgment of the Turkish text that Pamuk wrote.

Why This Assignment Is Difficult

My students incline to protect the translator’s invisibility from any critical practice that works against it, and I think I understand why. As Venuti observes, Anglo-American literary publics cling persistently to their assumption that “the more fluent the translation, the more invisible the translator, and, presumably, the more visible the writer or meaning of the foreign text” (*Translator’s Invisibility* 2). The assumption that a text can reveal the real world as it actually is—and, moreover, that a translation can perform that act of revelation from a great distance—weighs heavily on the ways my students read Pamuk in North America. Like the vast majority of Pamuk’s Western critics, my students at Queens hope to find in Pamuk’s novels a humanistic supplement to the daily news, and they take comfort in the possibility that a novel can render Turkish life more imaginable and more proximal. That feat of imagination becomes much easier when students can interpret the English words they read in *Snow* as if Pamuk wrote them.

The fiction of the unadulterated Turkishness of the English text rests on another related, more profound fiction. My students' desire to believe that *Snow* offers them an unobstructed view of real Turks and Turkey hinges on their belief that every great novelist conveys realities that are culturally specific and perfectly whole. Supporting this fantasy, the translator's invisibility extends the cultural logic that instrumentalizes literature as a source of "windows into foreign worlds"—which is, as David Damrosch observes, the logic by which world literature is read in the contemporary period (*What* 15). I understand why my students scowl when I ask them to notice the distance that separates them from the Turkish text of *Kar*. They bring to *Snow* laudable desires for greater understanding of the nonfictional world, and for greater proximity to other people who live in it—and who am I to interfere with that?

I wriggle out of this affective swamp by reframing the problem in methodological terms, aiming to render it an interpretive problem as solvable as any other. I note that translation proves unwieldy as an object of literary study, even for experienced critics who have at hand multiple linguistic traditions plus volumes of theory and practice, because it implies a comparative gesture precisely when comparison is impossible: how can *Snow*'s English-speaking readers factor *Kar* into their interpretation of the text when their inability to read it is precisely the problem? I invite my students to answer that question provisionally by putting scare quotes around what it means "to read" a text in this context, so they can interpret the English text in the light of the Turkish one that is unavailable to them—by acknowledging its existence and using that acknowledgement as the ground from which to work. For many of my students at Queens, that invitation is not entirely abstract: more than half of the student body was born outside of North America, so many are multilingual, and all of them live in New York City, so they frequently communicate with nonnative speakers of English. But, still, they ask me quite reasonably, what does it mean to "read" a text that they are categorically unable to read?

How This Assignment Becomes a Little Easier

The question of how to "read" a text in a language one doesn't know becomes more answerable when I preface it with other conversations about reading in translation—and, ideally, when I support those conversations with some comparative textual work. That preface comes readily to me when I teach *Snow* in a senior seminar that investigates the question that gives Damrosch a book title: What is world literature? Students enter a critical conversation with Pascale Casanova, David Damrosch, Gayatri Spivak (Damrosch and Spivak, "Comparative Literature"), scholars at the Warwick Research Collective (Deckard et al.), and others about current uses of the term *world literature*; they also read seminal texts that have exemplified it: *The Arabian Nights*, Sophocles's *Antigone*, and Flaubert's *Madame Bovary*. We read all those texts in translation, which generally goes overlooked until I note it.

To show why it matters and prepare for our discussion of *Snow*, I teach the translations of *Madame Bovary*, which has a textual history that is longer and richer and whose significance is easier to grasp. Some discussion about Flaubert's innovation of free indirect discourse precedes our conversation about Lydia Davis's translation; I say that we are lucky to read it, because it renders nineteenth-century French so lucid and contemporary in English. To make that point by contrast, I ask my students to contemplate the history of Flaubert's text, which was translated by Eleanor Marx Aveling, the daughter of Karl Marx, and revised decades later by Paul de Man. With that historical oddity in mind, we trace the differences between the Aveling and de Man translation and the Davis translation.

For example, I ask the students to read part 3, chapter 1, from Aveling and de Man's translation:

> Monsieur Léon, while studying law, had been a fairly assiduous customer at the Chaumière, a dance-hall where he was particularly successful with the grisettes who thought him distinguished looking. He was the best-mannered of the students; he wore his hair neither too long nor too short, didn't spend all his quarter's money on the first day of the month, and kept on good terms with his professors. As for excesses, he had always abstained from them, as much from cowardice as from refinement. (183)

I then ask them to compare Davis's translation:

> Monsieur Léon, while pursuing his legal studies, had quite often frequented La Chaumière, where indeed he achieved some nice successes with the grisettes, who found him *distinguished*. He was the most seemly of the students: he wore his hair neither too long nor too short, did not squander all his quarter's allowance on the first of the month, and stayed on good terms with his professors. As for excesses, he had always refrained from committing them, as much from timidity as from fastidiousness. (205)

One of the first differences students notice is the italic font in Davis's translation, which lends an ironic cast to the "distinguished" impression that Monsieur Léon makes on the "grisettes." Whose idea, they ask, was that—Davis's or Flaubert's? When I say the italics were Flaubert's, indignation ensues, as my students are aghast that Aveling and de Man altered the text in this way. They are also intrigued to see that neither translator rendered "grisettes" in English, and they smile when they realize how easily they can guess the rough meaning of the word. We debate possible translations in the various slangs they speak, and consider what each would imply.

I agree with their preference for Davis's restoration of Flaubert's italics that Aveling and de Man had deleted, but I also suggest that no translator could possibly preserve the source text in its entirety. To make this point, I ask where the translator's hand is evident in the text, and my students are quick to respond: in the difference between "cowardice" and "timidity" in the last sentence, for example, as well as the difference between "refinement" and "fastidiousness." We debate what these varying translations imply about Léon's character as we try to think of English words for which both "cowardice" and "refinement" might seem synonymous. If I have two students who speak the same language other than English, I ask them whether they can agree on a word that could produce both of those translations in that other language, too. Then I ask what this discussion implies about the work of close reading, and about the power of translators to determine how the text is read. I rarely need to belabor the point that every translator alters the meaning of the text by degrees, because my students see that inevitability clearly.

The next challenge is to carry these insights from *Madame Bovary* to *Snow*, which I approach by adapting an annotation assignment created by the digital humanist Mark Sample (Sample). In my adaptation, this assignment gives students credit for reading the translation closely:

> *Annotation Assignment*
>
> Your assignment is to represent your close reading of *Snow*, attending particularly to passages that make you wonder about the Turkish text that is unavailable to you. What questions does this passage raise about the decisions the English translator makes? As you read, develop a system of noting important passages, key terms, and your questions and observations. Your notes should represent all your reactions as a reader—the analyses and connections you make, the questions you raise, the resistances you have, etc.
>
> Begin by copying a two-page spread from *Snow* that seems to warrant further analysis. Represent your analysis by annotating the text heavily. Your annotations should not advance a coherent argument. Rather, they should represent the variety of analytical responses that you have as a critical reader. Then, type up your annotations, including any commentary and analysis that doesn't fit on the page. Your typed annotation will be chronological, beginning at the top of the left page and ending at the bottom of the right.

> Finally, write a reflection of 2–3 pages on your annotations. What themes emerged from your analysis, and what did you learn about the text in the English translation—or about yourself as a reader of it—by looking so closely at it? How might your analysis of these two pages contribute to your analysis of the novel as a whole?
>
> You will submit these three things: the copied page with your notes, the typed annotations that are more extended, and the reflection.

The assignment fosters a recursive practice that slows the practice of reading to make time for close textual analysis. Making literal the integral relationship between reading a text and writing a paper about it, it also forces students to acknowledge the existence of the Turkish *Kar* that is latent in the English *Snow.*

This assignment also grows out of my experience of teaching *Snow* to Turkish students. It seemed bizarre to me initially to assign Maureen Freely's translation to my students who were native speakers of Turkish, but they assured me that they found it easier to read Pamuk in the English translation. Perhaps, they speculated, this was because Freely had abbreviated Pamuk's sentences to make them more accessible, or because they were simply more practiced readers of difficult texts in English, the language in which they were taught at school. Certainly, both facts are relevant to the larger context in which Pamuk is read and taught.

Why This Assignment Is Important

Like many universities outside the English-speaking world, Koç University states its mission to prepare its students for success in fields where global English is the lingua franca. The university prepares its graduates to "become leaders in their professions and, true to Mustafa Kemal Atatürk's principles, contribute to the betterment of society," which is imagined on a national and global scale. The assumed compatibility between those two registers of citizenship—national and global—is implicit also in the assertion that "Koç University consistently strives to advance knowledge through its efforts and to serve Turkey and humanity as a model of institutional excellence" ("Koç University Mission Statement"). The imperatives of a cosmopolitanism that coexists easily with Western humanism are entwined here with a nationalist narrative that renders every Turkish citizen a guardian of the secular legacy of Atatürk. Those seeming opposites are conjoined in the discourse of the global economy, which obligates the most successful Turks to do much of their business in English. That obligation dictates the university's English-only policy for all class work and discussions, even those about Pamuk. I defied that policy mildly when I asked my students to read his Turkish text next to Freely's English, to write an annotation assignment for each, and to write an essay that describes the patterns that they observed.

Few of Pamuk's readers are able to see those patterns in his translations, since most read him only in languages other than Turkish. He reflects on this fact of his transnational audience in a short essay titled, "Who Do You Write For?," which I usually assign in conjunction with *Snow* (*Other Colors* [Vintage, 2007] 241–46). Locating himself among "literary novelists" writing "in the age of global media," Pamuk says that he writes for the public that wants to read him, and it is spread thinly over the world. He joins a new cohort of "literary writers" who "are gradually writing less for their own national majorities (who do not read them), than for the small minority of literary readers in the world who do" (242). He earns his reputation for bringing "the bestseller to Turkey" despite the smallness of his Turkish audience, because he has sold "hundreds of thousands of copies of his books in a nation with a notably small reading public" (Vaisman). And that small minority has analogs in literary subcultures all over the world, where Pamuk's novels sell well and to great acclaim.

The global scale of his audience makes his translators crucial to his success and his legacy, and translation a significant matter to interpretation of his work. *Snow* suggests as much to its readers by ensuring that they lack the context on which the novel seems to rely. As I make this point to my students, I urge them to abandon their dual efforts to approximate a reader who is steeped in the knowledge they lack and to see the real world in the fiction they read. Instead, they should ask, how can I read literature most responsibly given the ignorance—linguistic and cultural—that will remain with me no matter how much I learn?

NOTE

[1] This essay quotes from the 2004 Faber and Faber edition of *Snow*.

Pamuk's Essays in Multicultural Classrooms in North America and the Middle East

Jennifer Malia

Multicultural Education in North America and the Middle East

An increasing number of students studying in North America come from foreign countries, and many North American students study abroad in countries around the world. In addition, many universities abroad, including those in the Middle East, offer students an American-style education. To make curricula more relevant to the increasingly multicultural student body in today's classrooms, instructors can incorporate the works of diverse authors from around the world. Teaching Orhan Pamuk's essays "My First Passport: What Does It Mean to Belong to a Country?," "On Trial," and "My Father's Suitcase" can help promote multiculturalism, encourage students to appreciate world literatures and cultures, and inspire them to explore the world by taking advantage of study abroad and other international opportunities. Pamuk's essays also help students think about what it means to belong to a country and understand how government censorship can result in social media bans and limit freedom of expression.

I teach Pamuk's nonfictional works as literature in my world literature courses and as examples of rhetorical modes, such as narration and persuasion, in my literature-based composition courses. Since most of my students have not even heard of Pamuk, I introduce him as a Turkish author of fiction and nonfiction who received the Nobel Prize in Literature in 2006. Pamuk's "My First Passport" helps me share with students some of the linguistic and cultural challenges Pamuk faced as a child when his family relocated from Istanbul to Geneva. I have also taught Pamuk's "On Trial" as a persuasive essay that addresses freedom of speech and the international controversies that have surrounded Pamuk and his works. Pamuk's "My Father's Suitcase" helps me teach the rhetorical strategies of comparing and contrasting while discussing Pamuk's views about the place of Turkish literature among other national literatures and how his concept of world literature has changed over the course of his life.

I have taught Pamuk's essays to vastly different student populations at universities in North America and the United Arab Emirates. At Norfolk State University (NSU), a historically black, state-funded university, the majority of students are African American and come from the Hampton Roads area of southeastern Virginia. Many students are first-generation college attendees, have economically disadvantaged backgrounds, and rely heavily on financial aid. Most NSU students have had little or no experience traveling outside southeastern Virginia, let alone to other countries. In the past two years, only eighty-five of the university's roughly 6,300 students have studied abroad. Some students have had international experiences other than study abroad, but the total number of students who have traveled outside the United States is still quite small, which encourages me to raise awareness about international education in my courses.

At NSU I have taught Pamuk's essays in two lower-level, literature-based composition courses, which are required for all degree-seeking students, and in an upper-level world literature course, which is required for English majors and fulfills a general education requirement in the humanities. Before I arrived at NSU, my colleagues had self-published a common textbook for our world literature course. Intended as an overview of world literature to the present, the collection mainly includes Western literature published before 1923. I therefore supplement our textbook with non-Western works such as Pamuk's essays, "The Porter and the Three Ladies of Baghdad" from *The Arabian Nights*, and Azar Nafisi's *Reading Lolita in Tehran*. In my two literature-based composition courses, I also teach Pamuk's essays to supplement our common textbook, which includes works by authors such as George Orwell, Jamaica Kincaid, Jhumpa Lahiri, and Amy Tan. My goal is to include authors representing diverse geographic regions on the syllabi for both courses.

I have also taught Pamuk's nonfictional works at the American University of Sharjah (AUS), a private, independent, co-ed university in the United Arab Emirates. Most students were from the Middle East and North Africa and came from a variety of cultural, social, and economic backgrounds. The local Emirati students were typically from privileged families, while many of the students who came from other countries in the Persian Gulf were sponsored by their governments or by the companies their parents worked for in Dubai. Unlike most NSU students, AUS students frequently traveled outside their countries. In fact, most were pursuing their bachelor's degrees by studying abroad at AUS for four years. Though AUS is not an American university, it is reputed to be one of the best universities in the Middle East and offers an American-style education. AUS recognizes the importance of promoting multiculturalism by hiring diverse faculty and administrators, by admitting a diverse student population, and by encouraging multiculturalism in the curriculum. At AUS I taught Pamuk's essays in a lower-level, literature-based composition course, a course required for all degree-seeking students. My department self-published the common textbook for this course, *Majlis of the Others: A Reader for Writers in the Gulf*, which includes authors from around the world and has a strong focus on Middle Eastern authors, such as Pamuk, Abdul Rahman Munif, and Alaa Al Aswany.

Travel Abroad with "My First Passport"

Whether the course is face-to-face, online, or blended, I make use of an online course management system (Blackboard) and often assign students discussion questions that they answer on an online discussion board. My main goal is to get students to think critically about the class readings and to develop a habit of writing frequently. In my online courses, the discussion board is the center of the course, allowing students to virtually discuss the course readings with one another and with me. I have also found discussion boards to be an essential part of my face-to-face courses, since students tend to have more developed responses to the readings if they put them in writing before we meet for in-class discussions. I tell my students that these discussion board responses should be treated as informal writing assignments, as the written equivalent of what they might say during class discussion, and I give them credit for completing them. While an electronic journal response can serve the same purpose as a discussion board in helping students reflect on what they read, I prefer assigning discussion board responses because students can easily share their comments about the readings with the entire class and can reply to one another in writing. I maintain a strong presence during the online session by participating in the discussions and by posting a concluding note that summarizes the main points discussed. In my experience, most students stay on topic and address the prompts; if they have tangential responses, I encourage them to find textual evidence to support their claims.

Here is a sample prompt for my discussion board on "My First Passport":

> Please respond to the following in 150–200 words: To what extent do you relate to the experiences Pamuk describes in his essay "My First Passport"? If relevant, relate specific examples from Pamuk's essay to your own experience of traveling, studying, or living abroad. If you have not been abroad, please relate his essay to an international experience you hope to have someday. Please quote or paraphrase from Pamuk's essay in your response and use specific examples to support your claims. In addition, please respond to another classmate's commentary in 50–100 words. In your response, you should ask follow-up questions, build on the discussion by taking the analysis a step further, or suggest additional examples to support your classmate's points.

Pamuk's "My First Passport" promotes cross-cultural understanding not only by raising student awareness about the possibilities of international travel but also by stimulating them to think critically about the advantages and disadvantages of living in a culture that is different from their own. I inform students about international opportunities that they may wish to consider and share my own experiences of living, traveling, and studying abroad. Through the discussion board it became apparent that some NSU students overlooked that the author of “My First Passport” is Turkish; they assumed the essay was written by an American who had traveled abroad to Europe. While a careful reader would recognize that the author is from Turkey, this oversight could indicate that some students do not have sufficient experience with literatures and cultures other than their own. Reading texts in English translation also reinforces the assumption that the author is from an English-speaking country. When students mistake Pamuk’s nationality, I emphasize the importance of closely reading the contextual clues in the work and point to the moments in the text when Pamuk reveals his nationality. Many NSU students who have never been to a foreign country expressed their interest in study abroad after reading Pamuk’s essay and hearing what other classmates had to say about their travels abroad. Students studying foreign languages at NSU, for instance, talked about their desire to study abroad in order to improve their fluency in another language. They identified with Pamuk’s point that he was silent at the French school because he did not understand the language, and his observation that “my tendency to turn inward protected me from life’s difficulties, but it also deprived me of life’s riches.” One student noted that Pamuk’s essay made him think about the advantages of living in a foreign country at a young age because it is easier to learn another language and to adjust to a different culture.

Some of the responses pointed out the differences students have experienced when visiting other cultures. Most students who had traveled abroad went to the Caribbean, which suggests that they are more comfortable in places that are not particularly foreign to southeastern Virginia. Their choices are probably also influenced by the costs of traveling since most of them come from low-income families. One student discussed the difference between shopping at retail stores in the Hampton Roads area of southeastern Virginia and buying homemade goods from the locals wandering the streets of the Bahamas. Another student talked about her regular visits to Jamaica to stay in her mother’s childhood home. The student who could perhaps relate the most to Pamuk’s experience lived in İzmir, a city in western Anatolia, for three years. He identified with Pamuk’s uncomfortable living arrangements, difficulty adjusting to school, and problems communicating. Describing his time abroad as life-changing, his response focused on challenges communicating with locals and learning new customs when living in Turkey. On the discussion board I respond to students by asking them to elaborate on the linguistic and cultural challenges they faced as well as the positive experiences they had in other countries. For those who have yet to travel abroad, I ask them to name specific places and cultures that they are interested in exploring and to reflect on how the experience might be useful for their intended majors and careers.

Unlike some of the NSU students, the AUS students never mistook Pamuk's nationality. Because of their extensive international experience, AUS students had a broad multicultural awareness; moreover, they were accustomed to course assignments that expected them to read authors from a variety of different countries. My goal in teaching world literature texts at AUS, then, was to reinforce the appreciation of national literatures and cultures, especially those with which students were not familiar. Many of these students readily identified with Pamuk because they had traveled to foreign countries at a young age. For instance, in "My First Passport" Pamuk compares the living conditions in Istanbul to those in Geneva. My students coming to the Emirates from other Gulf countries noted that the observations Pamuk makes—"the streets were cleaner and emptier," there was more "variety in the shopwindows," and there were more cars—also applied to their own experiences.

Many AUS students indicated that when they traveled abroad, they did not feel as though they really belonged in the countries they visited, especially the Emirates. Pointing to economic and social differences between the United Arab Emirates and their home countries, AUS students who came from other poorer countries in the Middle East and North Africa suggested that they were treated as visitors who should feel privileged to be afforded the opportunity to live and go to school in the Emirates. They could identify with Pamuk's claim that "another country was a country that belonged to other people. We had to accept the fact that the things we were using would never belong to us, and that this country, this other land, would never belong to us, either." Many undesirable jobs in the Emirates are filled by foreign workers from countries such as India, Pakistan, and the Philippines. Students who were citizens of these countries confided that they were careful not to offend Emirati citizens because they feared being deported from the Emirates.

Other students focused their responses on the ending of Pamuk's essay, which considers "how much we belong to the country of our first passport and how much we belong to the 'other countries' that it allows us to enter." Having grown accustomed to the local culture and living conditions, some AUS students were comfortable living in the Emirates, especially those who had spent most of their lives there as foreigners. One of my female Saudi Arabian students, for example, compared the restrictions on girls and women in Saudi Arabia—where she was afraid to speak about women's rights and had to wear an *abaya* (a robe-like dress) and *niqāb* (a face veil covering everything except the eyes)—to the comfortable lifestyle she led in the Emirates, where a woman could speak more freely and choose to cover herself or not.

I drew students' attention to Pamuk's comment that "a passport is not a document that tells us who we are but a document that shows what other people think of us" to get them to consider what it means to be a citizen of a country and to discuss how others perceive you when you travel abroad. Many students identified with Pamuk's decision to remain silent in school as a way of handling living in another country. When I asked a follow-up question to inquire why they thought Pamuk reacted in this way, some ventured that silence was a defensive mechanism he used to protect himself from ridicule or from "life's difficulties," as Pamuk puts it. Others suggested that his reaction helped to avoid drawing unwanted attention to himself, a technique they also used in the United Arab Emirates to blend in. AUS students' reflections on Pamuk's essay helped them to think critically about their own experiences studying and living in the Emirates and the challenges of being immersed in a culture that was different from their own.

Freedom of Speech and "On Trial"

In my literature-based composition courses, I have taught rhetorical persuasion with Pamuk's essay "On Trial" by using a discussion board with instructions similar to those I provide for "My First Passport." The main questions I ask students to address for "On Trial" include: What is Pamuk's argument? What evidence does he give to support his argument? To what extent were you surprised by the Turkish government's reaction to Pamuk's criticism? How do you expect the US government to react when American authors criticize it? With this activity, students often recognize that some topics, such as the Armenian Genocide, are taboo in Turkey, and that defying the taboo may result in government censorship or even in punishment by law. Students usually cite Pamuk's 2005 trial under Turkish law for having "publicly denigrated Turkish identity" by criticizing the position of the Turkish government ("On Trial"). They often point out that Pamuk had alluded to Turkey's role in the Armenian Genocide in an interview published in the Swiss newspaper *Tages-Anzeiger*, saying "a million Armenians and thirty thousand Kurds had been killed in Turkey" ("On Trial"). In addition, students often acknowledge that the reaction to Pamuk's statement resulted in "newspapers launching hate campaigns against [him]," "groups of nationalist extremists organiz[ing] meetings and demonstrations to protest [his] treachery," and "public burnings of [his] books."

I inform students that after Pamuk's trial death threats were made against him and that he had to flee Turkey until the charges were dropped. To supplement "On Trial," I recommend some optional readings, including an article in *The Guardian* that emphasizes Pamuk's advocacy for freedom of speech. This article discusses Pamuk's opening address at the Frankfurt Book Fair in 2008, in which he spoke about the "oppression" of Turkish writers by pointing to "a century of banning and burning books, of throwing writers into prison or killing them or branding them as traitors and sending them into exile, and continuously denigrating them in the press" (Flood, "Frankfurt Book Fair"). To emphasize the widespread censorship of authors' works around the world, I also recommend that students read an article titled "Twelve Nobel Laureates in Literature Who Have Been Banned, Censored, or Exiled in the Past Twenty Years" (Burkett). I want my students to recognize that Pamuk is not the only Nobel laureate to be punished for speaking freely and to understand that many world authors have taken risks by openly expressing their political views in the face of dire consequences. Another article in *The Guardian* I suggest as optional reading is "Turkey and Twitter: Major Authors Join PEN International Appeal to End Ban," which articulates concerns with social media bans in Turkey (Flood, "Turkey"). Pamuk continued to advocate for freedom of expression when he joined other well-known authors to write a joint letter from PEN International to oppose the *Twitter* and *YouTube* bans in Turkey in March 2014, which have since been lifted. In their letter these authors stated that the social media bans in Turkey are an "unacceptable violation of the right to freedom of speech." One of the advantages of teaching a contemporary author like Pamuk is that students can see how the discussion about freedom of speech in "On Trial" applies to more recent events, such as social media bans.

The responses of NSU students to "On Trial" suggested that they were shocked Pamuk was put on trial for criticizing the Turkish government, revealing their assumptions about social justice and freedom of speech in parts of the world less familiar to them. For the most part, they were unfamiliar with censorship laws in Turkey and were surprised to hear that Pamuk was tried and sentenced for contradicting the Turkish government's decrees regarding freedom of speech. However, a few students with military experience in the Middle East were familiar with this sort of censorship; some had interacted with Iraqi and Afghani citizens who were afraid to criticize their governments. NSU students unanimously agreed that Pamuk was treated unfairly and should have been free to express his opinions even if his views were critical of his government. On the discussion board, students recognized the high consequences of Pamuk's criticism of the Turkish government, even though the author had valid reasons for doing so, and the low consequences of American journalists' satirical treatment of the United States government, even if the journalists' reporting could at times be ill-informed, irresponsible, and partial. As a follow-up activity to students' discussion board responses, I asked them to provide links in their posts to examples of how American news media criticizes the US government. They found newspaper articles with satiric political cartoons poking fun at President Obama's healthcare plan and news broadcasts with political analysts criticizing the government's decision to send military troops abroad. This activity helped students make cross-cultural comparisons by reflecting on how the American and Turkish governments respond to criticism.

Unlike most NSU students, most AUS students were not surprised about the Turkish government's response to Pamuk's statements because they came from countries where they feared the consequences of speaking about politics. They were all too familiar with government censorship and did not expect to have the right to freedom of speech. Some AUS students felt that Pamuk was wrong to say anything negative about the Turkish government, and some even felt he was a traitor to his country for speaking out in this way. I asked follow-up questions in an attempt to get students to discuss freedom of speech in their own countries, but many of them were careful not to speak negatively about their own governments. They often expressed their views as a collective opinion rather than an individual one, saying, for example, that "we in Lebanon believe . . ." In some cases, students responded by saying that they were not willing to express their own views on freedom of speech, claiming that they could be punished—even though they knew the discussion board was a closed forum to which no one outside our class had access. On the other hand, some students were comfortable openly sharing their views, and reading "On Trial" seemed to have given them the courage to criticize their own governments for prohibiting freedom of expression. An Iranian student, for example, disagreed with his government's insistence on how Islamic law or historical events, such as the Iranian Revolution in 1979, had to be interpreted. Regardless of whether or not they were comfortable openly expressing their opinions, discussing "On Trial" helped students think critically about a topical social issue such as freedom of speech.

World Literature and "My Father's Suitcase"

In my literature-based composition and world literature courses, I have also used a discussion board to teach Pamuk's essay "My Father's Suitcase." I ask students to address several questions about this essay: How did Pamuk's experiences as a child and young adult influence what he thought about Turkish literature? How has his opinion of Turkish and other national literatures changed over time? How does your own view of what constitutes the center of world literature compare and contrast with Pamuk's view? In their discussion board responses, many NSU and AUS students suggested that although Pamuk grew up thinking that Western literature was at the center of world literature, he canonized Istanbul by writing about the city for more than thirty years. In "My Father's Suitcase," Pamuk writes: "In the centre of the world, there was a life richer and more exciting than our own, and with all of Istanbul, all of Turkey, I was outside it. . . . In the same way, there was a world literature, and its centre, too, was very far away from me. Actually what I had in mind was Western, not world, literature, and we Turks were outside it." Pamuk admits that reading Western literature allowed him to vicariously experience a life more appealing than his own in Istanbul. The NSU students had the same experience, just in the opposite path: as Westerners they found non-Western works of literature appealing in their foreignness to their own lives. Works such as *The Thousand*

and One Nights allowed them to temporarily escape to a place and time that was more exciting than their lives in southeastern Virginia. NSU students generally concluded that there was no center to world literature, because they were able to appreciate a variety of national literatures and cultures.

AUS student responses, on the other hand, indicated that they identified with the way Pamuk felt in his childhood and early adulthood, mainly believing that Western literature is at the center of world literature. They appreciated reading the literature of their home countries but preferred reading Western literature, not because it was more exciting for them but because they thought it would be more useful to know. From their point of view, learning more about American and British literatures and cultures would help them become successful in their careers. Many of them studied in an American-style educational system because they believed it would lead to better employment opportunities. They felt they would be more economically successful living in North America, for instance, than in the poverty-stricken Middle Eastern countries where they were born. Just as Pamuk "read novels to escape his life and flee to the West," they believed Western literature provided an outlet to break free from their own cultures ("My Father's Suitcase"). Students identified with Pamuk's description in "My Father's Suitcase" of his father's library, which contained a vast collection of books of world literature, with Turkish literature on one end and Western literature on the other. Even though I pointed out that the division of world literatures and cultures into Western and Eastern is a useful, albeit problematic, construct for organizing the world around a specific center, many AUS students assumed that most of the world sees the West as the center. I encouraged students to appreciate world literatures and cultures on their own merits rather than as part of a classification such as Western or Eastern. Pamuk's "My Father's Suitcase" helped students better understand the construct of East-West dichotomies in discussions about world literatures and cultures.

In both North America and the Middle East, Pamuk's essays taught students the importance of grappling with cross-cultural perspectives when reading world literature. They benefited from working with texts written by an author who comes from a culture different from their own. In their responses to Pamuk's essays, students reflected on their experiences of traveling abroad (or their desire to do so), discussed what it means to be a citizen of a country, considered issues concerning social justice and freedom of speech, and shared their appreciation for world literatures and cultures. My main goal was to help students gain the education and skills to become better critical readers, thinkers, and writers—informed global citizens who are comfortable functioning in an increasingly diverse, plural, and interconnected world.

How to Read Pamuk? Naively and Sentimentally, Of Course

Djelal Kadir

Few novelists are as articulate on their vocation and practice as Orhan Pamuk has been in the course of his career. A well-read, historically knowledgeable, politically astute, and theoretically informed author, Pamuk is often coy and ambiguous in his statements, which offer a set of diagnostic tools for the reading and teaching of his novels. Pamuk claims, "I am a novelist. However much I have learned from theory, having at times even been beguiled by it, I have quite often felt the need to steer clear of it. I now hope to entertain you with a few stories and, through them, suggest a few ideas of my own" (*Other Colors* 283).[1] And, indeed, he does. A diagnosis is by definition discernment through pulling things apart and, literally, knowledge about two things at once: ("Diagnosis"). In the case of Pamuk, a novelist haunted by duality—of cultures, of individual identities, of languages, of temporalities, of geographies, of histories, of representations—pursuit of this twofold understanding amounts to a negotiation of ambiguity and ambivalence, including that equivocal terrain between what a novelist does and what he says about what he does. As critically discerning readers, we are obliged to focus on what the novelist Pamuk tells us and, at the same time, to remain mindful that his declarations function as telltale symptoms beyond what we are told.

Negotiating this terrain is a rewarding challenge, one that is necessary to all critical reading, but especially so in the case of an author explicitly engaged in what is simultaneously a conversation with himself for the benefit of his readers and, inevitably, a revealing dialogue with the literary traditions in which he is historically embedded. Pamuk's work is a laboratory in which he operates on various literary traditions and where the author's acts of reading are as illustrative as his acts of writing. I have found Pamuk's writings to be most serviceable in courses on the history of the novel, on self-reflective narratives, on methods of comparative studies, and on the theories of worldly cultural literacy.

Writerly is the term conventionally used to describe literary works that point to their origins in already existing writings or that strategically frame themselves within fictitious writings that they create for that purpose. As a student of architecture and a talented painter before he decided to focus his creative energies on writing, Pamuk brought to his writing this self-consciousness that in the visual arts is known as painterly, as opposed to linear. References to chromatics persist in his work, for example, in the titles of a number of his novels—*The White Castle*, *The Black Book*, *My Name Is Red*—and his volume of essays titled *Other Colors*. The frequent focus of his essays on the visual arts reminds us that painting continues to be important to him. His essay in *Other Colors* on the Venetian Renaissance painter Gentile Bellini (1429–1507), "Bellini and the East," demonstrates especially his keen appreciation of the distinction between the painterly and the linear. Painterly, or self-conscious art, as a counterpoint to linear, or mimetic representation, harkens back to a literary duality articulated by Friedrich Schiller in *On Naive and Sentimental Poetry* (1800), a philosophical treatise whose title Pamuk adapts as the title of his 2009 Charles Eliot Norton Lectures at Harvard, published the next year as *The Naive and the Sentimental Novelist*.

Notable in this appropriation is Pamuk's shift from *poetry* to *novelist*, a change that subtly replaces the artist's product—poetry—with the artist himself—the novelist. There is more to be said about this intriguing shift and the significance of Pamuk's comments on Bellini's painting for the novelist's stratagems. Pamuk associates painterly and writerly with the deliberate self-consciousness that Schiller calls "sentimental." Contemporary criticism has characterized the narratives of such writing as metanarratives, connecting their consciously self-reflective virtuosity with postmodernity in literary history (though many ancient texts reveal a self-consciousness about their own performance as texts). Pamuk's essay on Bellini is an eloquent illustration of where the painterly, the sentimental, and the metatextual converge. *Critical ekphrasis* would be an apt characterization of such interarts and cross-disciplinary insight, a hybrid, heterodox mode of apperception and reading that is characteristic of Pamuk's novels and essays. At a key moment in the Bellini essay, Pamuk notes, with regard to a gouache pen-and-ink miniature portrait of a Turkish seated scribe attributed to Bellini and now in the Isabella Stewart Gardner Museum in Boston (Bellini):

> A century ago, in 1905, this painting was still in Istanbul. . . . Years ago, after wandering among the [Gardner] museum's Titians and John Singer Sargeants,

> I found my young painter on a display table in a corner, on one of the top floors. . . . As I gazed down at the painting, the distance between me and it seemed to be the same as the distance between the painter and his blank sheet of paper. I was looking at Bellini's small painting in just the same way that a sultan might, in a private moment, look at a miniature illuminating the thick and heavy book in his hand. I too was gazing downward like the painter in the painting. . . . We see in both the things that define paintings as objects: the edges of the paper or canvas, the painter's pen or brush, and the pensive concentration on the artist's face. (*Other Colors* 317–18)

There is much here to suggest how Pamuk would have us read this image, and a number of noteworthy details emerge in his reading of this work's history. To begin, Pamuk points out that the painting in Boston was still in its native city of Istanbul a century ago. Pamuk doesn't question the attribution of the painting to Bellini. Just as important, Pamuk insists that the painting's central figure is a painter and that his imminent activity is painting or drawing, rather than writing, despite its conventional title, *Seated Scribe.* Furthermore, the frame of reference and Pamuk's lexicon in discussing the work pertain to the art of painting and the history of art, specifically to the self-conscious mode of "painterly" painting. He describes the painting in terms that identify it with what Schiller calls "sentimental," a work that displays awareness of its own making, thus suggesting how he would have us read a work of art, whether a painting, a poem, or a novel.

Teaching Pamuk in the light of this essay, I call this scene of reading and its demonstration "Pamuk's Quintessential *P*s: Place, Position, Pose, Perspective, Predicament." Much of his writing can be read through the five-sided spectrum of this heuristic operation, as can much of modern literature and contemporary artistic production. And while I do not intend to simplify the complexity of the author's work or the intricacies of reading and interpretation, the efficacy of all pedagogy relies on certain structuration founded in the material, especially material that must be conveyed across cultural traditions, historical frontiers, and artistic practices.

The first of the five plosives I term "Pamuk's Quintessential *P*s," *place* comes with its contrapuntal double, namely, displacement, the way his reading of the Bellini *Seated Scribe* begins by remarking on the work's translocation from its native Istanbul to a museum in Boston. The significance of such displacements in human history and cultural patrimony is something to which Pamuk is highly alert, especially as it pertains to the building of museums and their collections. Furthermore, Western classical literature and performance teach us that most works, whether tragedies or epics, start with displacement, what the ancient Greeks called a peripeteia, a turn. Across the world's literatures and other art forms one can observe that beginnings often entail a shift in terms of time, space, value, or meaning.

In Pamuk's case, especially in detective fictions such as *The Black Book* and *My Name Is Red*, the turn that propels the narrative and captures the reader's attention consists of an act of mystery—a disappearance, a murder—and moves through a series of dislocations toward a solution, or the promise of a solution. Perhaps the most demonstrably peripatetic narratives of place and displacement in the Pamuk canon are *The New Life* and *Snow*. These are errant pilgrimages: the narrative of *The New Life*, set across Anatolian way stations, marks the traversal of topographic space and cultural time capsules in the striated history of Turkey, where differing historical worlds coexist in the same times and places. *Snow* is a transnational passage between Germany and Turkey and an intranational passage between metropolitan Istanbul and provincial Kars in far northeastern Turkey. These traversals turn space into place; that is, they become the complex records of culture in historical transformations, revealed to readers as narratives of transformation—narratives that are in constant metamorphosis. Invariably these dislocations find the narrator in a place of writing and locate the readers in a place of reading.

The second *P* is *position*: Pamuk intricately and deliberately positions the elements of his novels. Key factors such as narrator (often a namesake of the author), characters, and reader are strategically consigned to scripted positions that become meaningful in the complex unfolding of the narrative. This is analogous to the way that Pamuk assumes the viewing position of the sultan for whom Bellini painted the *Seated Scribe* as well as the position of the scribe himself. Pamuk choreographically positions and repositions the elements of his narratives, at times subtly—the positional shifts and sleight-of-hand substitutions of doubles designed to elicit double takes from the reader of *The White Castle*—and at times dramatically—as with the position of the cadaver that speaks from the bottom of a well in the opening pages of *My Name Is Red*. No less meaningful is the coital position in the opening scene of *The Museum of Innocence*, a positioning that complicates the innocence of the main characters.

While positions are mobile and subject to characters' actions, a *pose* (the third *P*) is a stationary position whose immobility persists as a transfixed sign. Like a still life, a posed figure is still a life, albeit deliberately arrested by artifice in ways that can seem paradoxical: witness the French term for still life, *nature morte*, which speaks of its object as being born (*nature*) in death (*morte*). Pamuk takes the dialectical tension between the dynamic of innocence (or would-be innocence) and the suspended animation of museum objects and transforms it into a narrative vibrancy that propels the novel. Pamuk's discussion of the Gardner painting gives the reader a key to reading Pamuk himself, and certainly for deciphering the painterly inflections in his narratives. In discussing this essay with students I ask if the depiction and its pose are representational or symbolic. Pamuk, the unremittingly dueling dualist, resolves this either-or question in favor of the representational, inasmuch as he identifies an actual historical subject represented here—a beardless, earringed page of consummate beauty in the court of Mehmed the Conqueror—captured in a pose of imminent invention. But Pamuk equivocates on the symbolic significance of the figure and its pose in the historical context of the East and the cultural aesthetic of the Ottoman court, which the Venetian Gentile Bellini visited shortly after the peace treaty of 1479 between Istanbul and Venice.

Like the painter in a pose that so intrigues the novelist as poser and as poseur, Pamuk, in self-consciously assuming the position he describes before the painting, turns himself into a compelling figure that is simultaneously an enigma and a posturer. In the context of this perennial duality and its dialogical equivocation, the reader given to following Pamuk's prompt is, for example, likely to read the opening lovemaking scene of *The Museum of Innocence*, in which the protagonist playfully enters his beloved "from behind," as narrative representation of an erotic backdoor entry into the potboiler plot of a star-crossed love story. At the same time the reader cannot avoid the symbolic significance of the scene and its historical density—the name of the novel's protagonist, Kemal, announces a new "Kemalism" and has highly symbolic connections with modern Turkish history.

True to their characteristically dialectical form, Pamuk's novels are and are not allegorical. Pamuk's narrative gambit in *The Museum of Innocence*, the lovemaking position, and the very concept of a museum become symbolic of a national history—a family romance, some might say, and most apt for this novel's plot, which includes an erotic entanglement within a family (Kemal and his beloved cousin Füsun). Whether as naive poser who poses difficult questions within the conundrum of national history or as sentimental poseur who is given to obsessively playing the role of national gadfly and devil's advocate, Pamuk performs his role as Turkey's preeminent national writer. Readers countenance the enigmas of the novelist's narrative stratagems and the paradoxes of a national history riven by the competing impulses to slough off its past and to preserve its familial history as a museological object. This struggle has existed at least since the Ottoman reforms of the 1839 edict known as the Tanzimat, and certainly since the founding of the Republic of Turkey in 1923 and the radical restructuring of Turkish society and rewriting of history under Mustafa Kemal Atatürk.

The fourth *P* is *perspective*, key to Pamuk's dual, ambiguous, and ambivalent entanglements. In "Bellini and the East," Pamuk reveals the polar ends of this perspectival duality as "vanishing point" and "recollection." He associates vanishing point with the gaze of the Spanish painter Diego Velázquez, represented as a self-portrait in his 1656 painting *Las Meninas*. The painter's gaze extends beyond the canvas in front of him, into what Pamuk calls "a vanishing point" (*Other Colors* 318). "Recollection," or "recall," Pamuk associates with the gaze of the figure in Bellini's *Seated Scribe*, who looks not past his paper but gazes inward, recalling the collective history he embodies and is about to project onto the pristine sheet. Pamuk dramatizes this perspectival introspection in *My Name Is Red* when he portrays the miniaturists of Herat as blinded so that they could paint from the second sight of recollection. Like his precursors—for example, Ahmet Hamdi Tanpınar (1901–62), who clung to the Ottoman inheritance even as he attempted to synthesize that legacy with European experimental modernism (see *Other Colors* 204–13)—Pamuk reads Bellini's "painter" as a pivotal figure on whom hinges the recollection of the past and the arrival of the future on his white page. Like Velázquez, he has a biperspectival gaze: equivocal inasmuch as he looks to both past and future. The conjugation of these two painterly events—recalling the past and creating the future—in the history of art reflects the practices of Pamuk as a novelist of the East and the West. This is indeed a *predicament*, the fifth *P* and one that Pamuk dramatizes, implicating the reader in the process, just as Velázquez and Bellini do when they have viewers contemplate the depicted artists who are destined to regard in perpetuity their own works-in-process.

Pamuk engages in these performative acts with consummate virtuosity, most often with an ironic stance that presumes the reader's complicity and thus commingles our reading with his writing. This crisscrossing is often staged at the beginnings and ends of his novels. In other words, the opening and closing frames both enclose the novel and frame the reader as accessory to the making of the novel. The would-be enclosing frames operate, ironically, as overtures, or frames that open outward at the beginning or at the end, thus serially perpetuating the concatenation of open-ended, linked narratives. Part of the pleasure of reading Pamuk derives from seeing the author's overture for what it is—and also detecting what it is not. In other words, seeing simultaneously as a naive and as a sentimental reader, one can choose whether or not to be taken in by the framing overture that Pamuk proposes.

Here, for example, is the opening of Pamuk's fifth novel, *The New Life*: "I read a book one day and my whole life was changed" ([Vintage] 3). Part of the newness declared by the novel's title lies in the transformation of the narrator-protagonist upon reading a book in the book he is narrating. The protagonist, in other words, doesn't simply narrate. As the narrator-protagonist of a novel by someone called Orhan Pamuk, he also objectifies a procedure that he narrates as part of his own narration by the writer. This is diegesis—indeed, in keeping with Pamuk's penchant for double dealing, a double diegesis. Readers of *The New Life* partake of the reader-protagonist's fate as they read his novel. This convention originates in Greek tragedy in what is called *methexis*, or the opening up of the theatrical performance to the participation of the audience. Pamuk was probably inspired to use this device by Tanpınar, who recast the classical Greek *methexis* into what he called *terkip*.

The Turkish *terkip* translates as "composition" or "synthesis," a locution and process that Tanpınar makes use of both as an essayist (in "Istanbul" in his volume *Beş Şehir* ["Five Cities"]) and as a novelist (in *Huzur* [*A Mind at Peace*]). *Terkip*, in Tanpınar's pointed and frequent usage, extends from literal synthesis or composition to a process more akin to what is called in Latin *ars combinatoria*, a bringing together of diverse elements. Pamuk refers to this as "recalling" when he describes Bellini, the *Seated Scribe*, the subject's pose, and his own pose in front of Bellini's painting. For Tanpınar the confluence of cultural histories enable Istanbul to perpetually recompose itself as a complex, heterogeneous city, as Pamuk will note in his memoir *Istanbul: Memories and the City*. The most theatrical illustration of this crossing of narrative and performative lines appears in Pamuk's novel *Snow*, where, in a truly dramatic reenactment of classical *methexis*, the so-called fourth wall is shattered by live gunfire from soldiers, which blends the audience's lived social violence with the violence being performed by the actors on stage.

"The new life" in the novel *The New Life*, then, is the tale of the characters' adventures in living and reading and, at the same time, the reader of the novel's adventure in reading. At the opposite end of a narrative thread, here is part of the recursive coda in the final paragraph of *The White Castle* in what would be a closure, but ends as an aperture:

> He sat at our table, and I found my book where I had, as if yesterday, thrust it away sixteen years before; I laid it open before him. He was able to read Turkish, if slowly. . . . Then he turned and gazed blankly out of the window, resting and trying to digest what he'd read. I watched with delight as he looked first at some infinite point in the emptiness, as people do in such situations, at some non-existent focal point, but then, as I had expected, his vision focused: now he was looking at the scene through the frame of the window. My intelligent readers have surely understood: he was not so stupid as I supposed. As I had thought he would, he began to turn the pages of my book greedily, searching, and I waited with excitement till at last he found the page he was looking for and read it. Then he looked again at the view from that window overlooking the garden behind my house. I knew exactly what he saw.
>
> ([Carcanet] 160–61)

There is a reversal in the relation between the reading character, the larger world outside the text that he is in the process of reading, and readers reading the novel. Rather than pulling the reader's world into the narrative, as in *The New Life*, the narrative here projects its character outward beyond its textual perimeter. It does so narratively, of course, constructing a frame that the narration overflows into a confluence beyond its parameters. Two frames become continuous: the frame within the pages of the text and the frame of the window (another perspective) through which the protagonist gazes when he lifts his eyes from the page. *The White Castle* projects its protagonist's reading beyond its textuality and into the landscapes he glimpses when he looks past the page. The narrator, then, ensures that the readers of the novel understand this slippage from one frame (the page) to the other (the window), a slippage that superimposes the two into a continuous landscape. What is being read and what is being seen, along with all the recalled history of that reading and seeing, are conflated. And the narrator puts readers on notice: "My intelligent readers have surely understood: he was not so stupid as I supposed." At the risk of being taken for less than intelligent, readers, like the reading character in the novel, would naturally wish to prove themselves equal to the task of a reading predicament scripted for them.

Pamuk devotes the last of his Norton lectures to tantalizing his audience. The final act (excluding the book's epilogue) is entitled "The Center" (*Naive* 151–78). In this lecture Pamuk presents the ultimate good, the pièce de résistance, to which, he says, all novelists aspire and toward which all readers are led. True to the narrative tradition of peripatetic shifts and unpredictable turns, Pamuk goes on to disclose the illusory nature of this desideratum. He thus leaves novelist and reader in a predicament: a world where the center perpetually recedes, much like the optics of the vanishing point countenanced by the reading character in the novel. In this climactic gesture, the naive and the sentimental become crisscrossed and thereby rendered moot. Pamuk illustrates the reader's predicament on this shifting ground by invoking one of the masters of the novelistic genre whom he often holds up as a model—Leo Tolstoy.

Pamuk begins and ends *The Naive and the Sentimental Novelist* with Tolstoy: "Let me give another example, again from Tolstoy, which deals with the act of gazing out a window and shows how one can enter the landscape of a novel while reading. The scene is from the greatest novel of all time, *Anna Karenina*" (8). This is the episode in which Anna is not reading the book she holds, instead gazing at the snowy landscape outside the train window and reflecting on not reading as she cuts the bound pages of the book. Pamuk concludes his lectures and his book with this remark: "With Anna's gaze, a whole landscape comes to life before our eyes. We must thank Anna, for we enter the novel through this gaze—her gaze—and find ourselves in the Russia of the 1870s. Because Anna Karenina could not read the novel she held in her hands, we read *Anna Karenina* the novel" (178).

This episode is key, but it is by no means a center. It is, however, a peripeteia, a turn that pivots on the ambiguity of the naive and the sentimental, a polarity whose points—in part 1, chapter 29, and in part 7, chapter 31—frame Tolstoy's novel. The world in the text that Anna is not reading and the world viewed from the window of the train are linked, ironically, by the paper knife that cuts the book's pages. Anna holds the pages against the cold glass pane of the window that frames the landscape, a landscape that remarkably becomes like a page that she is engaged in reading. An instrument that normally severs objects, the knife serves to connect the frames of the world in the book and the world that speeds by. And Anna herself becomes the fulcrum of this ironic connection as she presses to her face the blade cooled by the train window.

Arriving at Anna's final act in part 7, the reader realizes just how proleptic are Anna's gestures in the earlier scene. At the fatal moment of throwing herself between the cars of the train rushing by, Anna sees clearly everything in the book she had not been reading in part 1. And, lest we miss the connection between these two episodes, Tolstoy suspends Anna's initial suicidal gesture so that she may also plunge her red handbag under the wheels of the train. This is the same red handbag from which Tolstoy has Anna remove her unread book in the earlier episode. Highly symbolic, Anna carries her baggage, so to speak—her identity and history—in life and in death. And while my students often excitedly inquire whether Anna's unread book might be a certain novel by Gustave Flaubert that twenty years earlier had dramatically and fatally yoked the naive and the sentimental in its also-eponymous protagonist, Madame Bovary, Tolstoy's narrator forecloses on that enticing possibility by telling us that Anna's book was "an English novel." Of course, one should not dismiss the possibility that Tolstoy, like Pamuk would later become fond of doing, is dragging a red herring across the reader's path.

Pamuk's perpetually twined, dialogical, and contrapuntal narratives reveal him to be an inveterate teacher of reading. His narrative illustrations of reading teach readers how to read. And Pamuk's own acts of reading, as a critic and historian of painters, novelists, and poets who have been crucial to his own formation as a writer and as a reader, demonstrate how to read at once naively and sentimentally.

NOTE

[1] This essay quotes from the 2007 Alfred A. Knopf edition of *Other Colors*.

Mapping Pamuk onto the World Literature Syllabus

Erdağ Göknar

My seminar Pamuk and World Literature at Duke University frames Pamuk and his work comparatively, allowing students to make connections between national literary traditions, such as the Turkish, and world literature, or what some have called the "world republic of letters" (Casanova, *World Republic*). As Pamuk's translator, I also wanted to bring discussions of translation—linguistic and cultural—to the classroom. I tell students that the first-time reader of a Pamuk novel goes through an initiation, as the text itself teaches one how to read the conventions of Pamuk's work.

A productive way to teach the seminar is to examine the itinerary of Pamuk's own work. As a starting point, this places us in a specific historic moment (1980) and a specific geography (Istanbul, Turkey). Pamuk's first novel, *Cevdet Bey ve Oğulları* ("Cevdet Bey and His Sons"), was written before and published after the 1980 Turkish military coup, which figures large in all his work as a type of cultural violence that informs literary production. This circumstance leads to a question I present for discussion early in the seminar: what might be the effects of the Turkish military coup (and political violence in general) on Pamuk as a writer?

Before he turned thirty, Pamuk had experienced three military coups—in 1960, 1971, and 1980—that supported an authoritarian legacy of Turkish secular nationalism. The coups formed the political background of his development as an author. The trope of an impending coup d'état and the theme of ongoing political conspiracy shape the plots of most of his novels. *Cevdet Bey ve Oğulları* is set over the 1908–09, 1922–23, and 1960 political upheavals and ends just before the 1971 coup. *The Silent House* is set during the social polarization between right and left in the 1970s and ends just before the 1980 coup. *The White Castle*'s fictional preface, dated 1982, begins in the coup's wake. *The Black Book* and *The New Life* unfold under the oppression of conspiracy and imminent coup. *My Name Is Red*, in a political allegory, pits the Ottoman sultan against a conservative Islamic resurgence, and *Snow* treats the Turkish "coup" as a melodrama and a literary device. In 1997 the military forced the resignation of Prime Minister Necmettin Erbakan of the Islamicist Welfare Party in order to assuage public fears of a politically enfranchised Islam. This so-called postmodern coup inspired Pamuk's *Snow*. As a trope, the coup consequently came to represent a reenactment of the establishment of the nation-state and to function as a metonym for secular, modern cultural revolution.

After *Cevdet Bey ve Oğulları*, Pamuk's novels trace new spatiotemporal itineraries, seeking innovative juxtapositions and greater levels of legibility for his growing readerships. Each novel introduces a new space and time, or "chronotope" (Bakhtin, *Dialogic Imagination* 84–85): seventeenth-century Ottoman Istanbul, 1990s Anatolia, Istanbul's palimpsestic urban spaces, and the intimate spaces of middle-class and bourgeois homes. In these settings one can trace the text's growing awareness of its relation to the national tradition, to world literature, to historical or social realism, to metafiction, or to one or multiple genres. Each of Pamuk's literary innovations conceals a concern of legibility to new audiences—a translational concern writ large. That is, as Pamuk's readership expanded from national to global, his novels became increasingly multilayered, mixing genres and pushing the boundaries of literary form.

My syllabus relies on the critical concept of cultural translation.[1] In anthropology, cultural translation refers to the act of describing to one cultural community how members of another interpret the world and their place in it (Asad). In cultural and postcolonial studies, it refers to the ways in which displaced people negotiate cultures other than their own. *Translation* derives from the Latin *translatus*, meaning "carried across." For anthropologists, foreign cultures are "carried across" to domestic readers through texts, while for cultural studies scholars, the experience of exile and displacement is itself a "carrying across" from one context to another. One can broadly conceive of a Pamuk novel as a medium of cultural translation between national and world literatures.

To underscore this exchange between the local and the global in Pamuk's own work, I turn to a short piece entitled "World Literature" that appears in *Öteki Renkler*, the original, Turkish version of the abridged *Other Colors*. The English version is a reedited volume that excludes some of the more revealing pieces, such as Pamuk's insightful commentaries on the Turkish literary canon. To judge from the editorial choices of the two volumes, Pamuk's self-representation as an author changed in the eight years between the publications of *Öteki Renkler* (1999) and *Other Colors* (2007). The first version represents an author of the periphery, who at one time might have been described as a Third World author. The second version represents a Nobel laureate and a global author of world literature. Pamuk in 1999, perhaps revealing his vulnerability and uncertainty, sees fit to include pieces and interview excerpts such as "Oh, You Who Have Chosen a Path in Life, Your Situation Is So Much Better Than Mine," "We're All Being Followed, but Some of Us Are Being Followed More," "Why Can't We Tell the Story of Our Own Lives?," "Am I an Intellectual, I Wonder?," and "Growing Up with Jews in Istanbul," all of which are excluded from the English edition. Most tellingly and regrettably, the 2007 edition includes none of the sections on the Turkish writers who influenced Pamuk. In a sense, he has conciously removed himself from the national tradition.

Pamuk's critique of world literature was also redacted from the 2007 version. Asking students to speculate on Pamuk's editorial ommissions may spark an interesting class discussion. When Pamuk wrote the piece on world literature, his work had not yet been recognized by international awards such as the International IMPAC Dublin Literary Award (2003), the Peace Prize of the German Book Trade (2005), the Puterbaugh Fellow Award (2006), and the Nobel Prize in Literature (2006), which helped establish his international standing. The piece is written by an author who openly considers himself an outsider and a practitioner of literature from the periphery. In my seminar I use it to indicate the categorical differences between a Eurocentric world literature consisting of the great-books canon and what I call "worlded literature," politically engaged, socially embedded novels contingent on specific localities and subcultures.

The world literature piece reads like notes for the talk Pamuk gave in honor of Weimar, Germany's selection as European Capital of Culture in 1999. The event featured a discussion about world literature in the coinciding 250th anniversary year of Goethe's birth in Frankfurt. Here, Pamuk deconstructs the concept of world literature, in a kind of politicized, quasi-leftist, quasi-postcolonial manifesto:

> World literature? At first the notion sounds attractive, even mysterious. The fraternal order of those who read books! Not the literatures of nations, but the literature of the entire world! This notion immediately delivers us from the authoritative and restrictive demands of national traditions and, with childlike innocence, fosters the fantasy that the literatures of all nations are akin to one another! But over the last two centuries, when we look at influences, borrowings, admiration, the focus of gossip and legend, and the reactions of the press and media, it becomes evident that literature is not just a subtle remembering, but also a cunning forgetting:
>
> Over the last two centuries, nations that have a high literacy rate, boast a love of literature, and take pride in their literature's richness have imposed their own literary forms and styles upon others.
>
> Today's "world literature," particularly the art of the novel, is a triumph of the West. Modernism, which was a reaction to the growing focus of novels on the everyday and the increasing commodification of literature in the nations of the European center, resulted in the rapid forgetting of local and traditional literatures in peripheral nations with low literacy.
>
> The British detective novel (e.g., Agatha Christie; Sherlock Holmes) exemplifies the difficulty of literary forms traveling easily across borders despite advances in communications. This form could not be established in Germany or France, let alone in India and Turkey.
>
> Such failure and lack created a division of labor in the world: while some discovered the identity of the murderer, the meaning of life, the structure of the world and language, and the depths of the human soul, certain others could only have their voices heard if they told stories about poverty, misery, violence, and backwardness.

> As my books get translated into foreign languages, I am confronted with this accusatory question: "Do you write for Turkish readers or for readers around the world?" Behind this question is an extremely suspicious reaction to the literary division of labor in the world. Not to mention a terrifying nationalism that might only be overcome through more exchange, more libraries, a culture of writers who read each other's work, and a rich tradition of translation.
>
> Due to the speed of communication and the high level of readership in the nations of the center, world literature has begun to resemble a kind of national literature: the center imposes its own tastes upon an entire periphery and the periphery can only have its voice heard to the degree that it uses the language of the center.
>
> The approach of writers in the center who write as if they are in the periphery (Faulkner, Bernhard) and those in the periphery who write as if they are in the center (Dostoevsky, Borges) might be able to deliver us from stifling nationalist demands and international stereotypes.
>
> (*Öteki Renkler* 203–04; my trans.)

This sketch outlining Pamuk's critique of world literature is an important preamble to approaches to teaching Pamuk, because it identifies some of the challenges of writing novels in Turkey. Furthermore, it presents literature as a global political struggle. Students should be made aware of each of its arguments and consider whether they agree or disagree and why. For example, Pamuk marries the political and the literary while leveling criticism against the economics of international publishing. He reminds us that world literature includes dominant forms and content. On the one hand, phrases like "division of labor" evoke a leftist critique while "center" and "periphery" recall Wallersteinian world systems theory. On the other hand, nationalism is presented as detrimental to cultural production. The (literary) world is conceptualized as being oriented around a "triumphant West," which is also the fountainhead of modernity and modernism. Pamuk, angry at having been excluded from world literature and at the same time targeted by Turkish nationalists, feels caught between a Western neoliberal ethos and strident Middle Eastern nationalism.

However, in presenting the dilemmas of the novelist writing from the periphery, Pamuk also offers a negotiated solution that is a key to his own work: writing with doubled awareness of both the center and the periphery. This idea can be traced back to one of Pamuk's Turkish literary mentors, Ahmet Hamdi Tanpınar. Tanpınar described cultural borrowing as a kind of synthesis that he termed *terkip*. Tanpınar relies on *terkip*—between East and West, French and Turkish literatures, Ottoman past and Turkish present, Islam and secularism, tradition and modernity—as a literary method, particularly in novels like *A Mind at Peace* (Eronat 42–43). In form and content, all of Pamuk's fiction relies on this principle, which is in essence one of cultural translation. Once they learn how to recognize *terkip*, students are adept at finding examples of it in Pamuk's novels. During class discussions, I teach *terkip* by asking students to discuss passages that they think include hybrid or synthetic elements and perspectives.

Yet Pamuk is doing more than practicing *terkip*: he is "worlding" world literature. But what does his "worlding" involve? Heidegger used the term *in-der-Welt-sein* ("to-be-in-the-world") to describe the complexities of "being in the world" (30). He believed that we are inextricably "worlded": bound up in a complex web of associations and social practices. The idea is that acknowledging worldliness or worlding in literature could emphasize this complex web and signify ongoing, generative, and, above all, contingent processes of existence. By worlding his fiction, Pamuk points to and challenges the exclusions of world literature. He doesn't reproduce the aesthetic form of the European novel but rather produces aggregate, polysemous texts of political violence, history, poverty, modernity, and identity conveyed through Turkish, Ottoman, and Islamic tropes. I use the notion of a worlded literature to point to the ways Pamuk both critiques world literature from the perspective of Istanbul and at the same time participates in its transformation. Pamuk's worlding is political and historical, bearing the scars of idealized projects of modernity in places like Turkey. As such, Pamuk's work bears the traumas of both European colonialism and the Kemalist cultural revolution and reveals the novel to be an incomplete, broken, violated form in which point of view and character are exceedingly unstable. That is, Pamuk's novels transform world literature into worlded literature, which make them difficult for readers familiar with the centripetal forces of world literature yet unaccustomed to the centrifugal forces of worlded literature.

Emily Apter's critique of world literature through the framework of debates on translation is instructive here. In her politically charged *Against World Literature: On the Politics of Untranslatability* (2013) Apter rejects the assumption that everything can be translated into a global idiom of world literature. The book articulates the concept of "untranslatability," the thorny, frustrating notes of dissonance and misunderstanding that establish the texture of translation and cultural engagement. Pamuk's novels often manifest this opacity of untranslatability. They are political, complex, digressive, and nonlinear. They use multiple approaches and intertextual sources, generating rough connections that give rise to exhilaration and exhaustion. His readers should expect passages of untranslatable blackness: frustration, obsession, delay, claustrophobia, irrelevance, and futility. These are traces of the incomplete, ongoing task of cultural translation.

Students new to Pamuk's work should be introduced to the opposing forces in his fiction. On the one hand, canonical Western books shadow each of Pamuk's novels: *Cevdet Bey ve Oğulları* (Thomas Mann's *Buddenbrooks*); *The Silent House* (William Faulkner's *As I Lay Dying*); *The White Castle* (Jorge Luis

Borges's Islamic stories); *The Black Book* (James Joyce's *Ulysses*); *My Name Is Red* (Umberto Eco's *The Name of the Rose*); *Snow* (Fyodor Dostoevsky's *Demons*); *The Museum of Innocence* (Vladimir Nabokov's *Lolita*); *A Strangeness in My Mind* (in part, Charles Dickens's *Great Expectations*). On the other hand, his work sutures each of these works into a broader network of lesser-known Eastern contexts and traditions. Each of Pamuk's novels intertextually alludes to a constellation of other literary works, images, and objects. But they are all also Istanbul novels, and they introduce Istanbul as an emerging global literary city. In his "World Literature" piece, Pamuk hints at how he should be read as an author of worlded literature: at the intersection of Turkish and world literatures as they flow through the urban spaces, relics, and ruins of Istanbul.

Another way to approach Pamuk's literature is through close readings of scenes and images. I draw my students' attention to short passages that reveal Pamuk's cultural logic. Pamuk writes metafictional narratives in which the story of a novel's creation becomes part of the plot; self-reflexively, the novel in the plot is produced through an authorial process of worlding. In this process, writing and novel production are presented as part of the "Order of Écriture" (Farred) in which writer and reader become initiates into a sacred order of textual production, first local and then global. Furthermore, as I argue in *Orhan Pamuk, Secularism, and Blasphemy*, Pamuk places various material and secular tropes alongside mystical and sacred ones. Everyday writing, for example, becomes worship. What emerges is a productive tension based on the tendency toward either cynical deconstruction or obsessive mystification. To broadly convey this paradoxical literary accomplishment, I rely on the shorthand "*din* and *devlet*" (religion and state), a traditional formula for Turkish political authority that I contend is presently also shorthand for Turkish cultural authority. Pamuk's novels, manifestations of the profane and the sacred, are blasphemous because they threaten the strictures of secular and sacred power. Each of the following moments from Pamuk's novels may spark broader discussions about Pamuk's literary innovations and what I term *secular blasphemies*:

The ironic and uncanny scene in *Cevdet Bey ve Oğulları* where Refik, a figure of secular modernity, must perform the ritual prayer in the mosque at his father's funeral; he doesn't know how to, so he fakes it without taking his ablution. This is one of a recurring series of Pamuk's scenes of sacrilege and blasphemy ([İletişm] 213).

The tragicomic scene near the end of *Silent House* where the secular historian Faruk Darvınoğlu happens upon a group of German tourists at a "Turkish night" belly dance show and meditates on the questions of orientalism, identity, and truth in historical (and, by extension, literary) form; in the process, Faruk champions the belly dancer as a heroine of anti-European resistance (290–92).

The preface of *The White Castle*, where the same Faruk Darvınoğlu finds and translates an archival Ottoman manuscript for modern Turkish readers, thereby presciently reintroducing Ottoman Turkish (and Islamic) cultural legacy into the secular modern Turkish present (7–10).[2]

The conclusion of *The White Castle*, where the narrative point of view turns to an unnamed European reader who is reading the manuscript that is the basis of the novel itself. This character is a cameo of unwitting readers placed into Pamuk's text. The last dramatic exchange in the novel is that of the reader looking up to recognize the author, whose text has just questioned all he knows to be true, framed in a window (179–80).

The climactic Borgesian double murder in *The Black Book* that turns a crime of jealousy and vengeance into the blending of a Western Oedipal myth (the death of the author-father Celâl) and the Eastern Sufi quest of Galip's authorial self-discovery, a dramatization of secular Sufism ([Vintage] 439–40).

The elaborate clock described in *The New Life* that combines tropes of *din* and *devlet* through two figures: a turbaned imam who declares, "Allah is Great!" and a clean-shaven secular modern Turk who states, "Happy is he who calls himself a Turk!" This alludes to a combination of Islamic and secular figures working as part of a single apparatus, symbolizing an Islamosecular symbolic complex that drives Turkish literary production ([Farrar, Straus, and Giroux] 87–88).

The "picture of happiness" conjured at the end of *My Name Is Red* that alludes to the Communist poet Nazım Hikmet. The image describes an infant (the "author" Orhan) suckling at his mother's breast presented in the form of a Renaissance Madonna and Child portrayal. The image brings together sacred iconography and the fantasy of socialist happiness and establishes another secular-sacred trope, a dominant characteristic of Pamuk's fiction ([Alfred A. Knopf, 2010] 412).

The moments of scathing, conspiratorial parody of Kemalism and political Islam that run throughout the political melodrama *Snow*: Ka, the left-leaning intellectual, coming to faith; Fazıl, the religious-school student flirting with atheism; the didactic Kemalist play that unfolds as an actual coup; a former Marxist turned Islamic terrorist (Blue) obsessed with recognition from the West; the secular (unveiled) and religious (veiled) sisters who have slept with the same Islamic terrorist; and the guilty pleasure of the compromised author ("Orhan") writing a novel of witness that is also a parody of the secular Turkish intellectual.

In *Snow*, the snowflake icon that maps the experience of Ka in Kars through a sacred poetics of everyday experience. The snowflake, mapping poems Ka receives through a kind of revelation, indicates the fleeting union of individual desire and the divine, which is thwarted by political violence and social pressure ([Vinatge] 260–61).

The parody of bourgeois happiness represented by the obsessed Kemal in *The Museum of Innocence*. Pamuk's notion of the museum-as-novel and the novel-as-museum evokes Tanpınar's observation in *A Mind at Peace* that a novel could be made out of the discarded objects being sold in a secondhand shop or street bazaar (60).

The ironic scene in *A Strangeness in My Mind* where the conservative Mevlut is called up to an apartment to sell boza to a roomful of drunk secular Turks who interrogate him about his life, beliefs, and the rise of political Islam. They are scarcely aware that they will soon be marginalized by conservative AKP politics, which represent Mevlut and his class (21–29).

Finally, I invite students to make other literary comparisons with Pamuk. Students have suggested Borges, Albert Camus, Franz Kafka, Faulkner, Eco, Nabokov, and Gabriel García Márquez, as well as less obvious comparisons with novels such as Arundhati Roy's *The God of Small Things*, Salman Rushdie's *Midnight's Children*, Gao Xingjian's *Soul Mountain*, Cormac McCarthy's *Blood Meridian*, Mario Vargas Llosa's *The War at the End of the World*, Naguib Mahfouz's *Children of the Alley*, W. G. Sebald's *The Emigrants*, Aravind Adiga's *The White Tiger*, Miguel Syjuco's *Ilustrado*, and Andrey Kurkov's *Death and the Penguin*.[3] In an era of literary globalization, these works write back to the dominance of the Eurocentric world literary canon. Through a consideration of these literary exchanges and negotiations, we can better understand how Pamuk's literature is a worlded critique of world literature as much as an example of it, something underscored in his 1999 manifesto. Cultural translation and intertextuality turn the Pamuk syllabus into a Möbius strip of world literature and worlded traditions.

NOTES

[1] My syllabus appears as an appendix to this essay. Works mentioned in the syllabus are listed in this volume's works-cited list.

[2] This essay cites the 1990 Braziller edition of *The White Castle*.

[3] Afridi and Buyze's *Global Perspectives on Orhan Pamuk* also compares Pamuk with Amitav Ghosh (141–55), Mohsin Hamid (9–24), and Italo Svevo (25–43).

APPENDIX

Syllabus for Orhan Pamuk and World Literature

Week 1: Introduction

Who is Orhan Pamuk and why should we read him?

Charlie Rose interview with Orhan Pamuk (13 May 2011)

Week 2: Turkish and World Literature

What is the relation between a national literature like Turkish literature and world literature that is read on a global scale?

Findley, "Introduction," from *Turkey, Islam, Nationalism, and Modernity* (1–23)
Pizer, "Goethe's 'World Literature' Paradigm"
Pamuk, "My Turkish Library"
Casanova, "Literature as a World" and *The World Republic of Letters*
Jameson, "Third-World Literature in the Era of Multinational Capitalism"
Pamuk, *Istanbul*, chs. 1–3
Apter, "Global *Translatio*: The 'Invention' of Comparative Literature, Istanbul, 1933" (*Translation Zone* 41–64) (optional)
Damrosch, *What Is World Literature?* (1–38) (optional)

Journal 1

Summarize the world literature debate by comparing Goethe's concept of "world literature" to Casanova's "world of letters" and Jameson's "third-world literature."

Relying on "My Turkish Library" and the Charlie Rose interview, describe the advantages and disadvantages that Pamuk had as a writer from Istanbul seeking global literary recognition.

Week 3: Darvınoğlu in the Ottoman Archive

What is the significance of Faruk Darvınoğlu, a character who appears in two of Pamuk's novels? Why is the Ottoman archive significant?

Quataert, "Ottoman History Writing"
James, *The Figure in the Carpet*
Pamuk, *Silent House*
Faulkner, *As I Lay Dying* (optional)
Göknar, "Occulted Texts"
Pamuk, *Istanbul*, chs. 4–6
White, "The Fictions of Factual Representation," from *Tropics of Discourse* (121–34) (optional)

Journal 2

Describe how Faruk's meditations on historiography in *Silent House* are potential reconceptualizations of literary form and also of Turkish national identity. The response should refer to Quataert or Göknar.

Read the first twenty-five pages of Faulkner's *As I Lay Dying*. Identify five characteristics (in terms of character, style, point of view, structure, content, or plot) that mark this work as a high modernist novel.

Week 4: Literary Modernism and Literary Orientalism

What is the significance of modernism and orientalism to literature?

Lewis, *Religious Experience and the Modernist Novel*
Lukács, "The Ideology of Modernism," from *The Meaning of Contemporary Realism* (17–46)
Mufti, "Orientalism and the Institution of World Literatures"
Pamuk, *Istanbul*, chs. 7–9
Pamuk, *The White Castle*, preface and chs. 1–5
Steinhart, "The Master-Slave Dialectic"

Week 5: The White Castle

Pamuk, *The White Castle*, chs. 6–11
Almond, "Mystery-Tasting and Abyssality: Ibn 'Arabi and Derrida," from *Sufism and Deconstruction* (89–115)
Hutcheon, "Representing the Postmodern," from *The Politics of Postmodernism* (1–29)
Pamuk, *Istanbul*, chs. 10–12

JOURNAL 3

Describe the characteristics of literary modernism and literary postmodernism by referring to Lukács and Hutcheon. In what ways is Pamuk a modernist as well as a postmodernist?

Summarize Mufti's use of Saidian orientalism to critique world literature. Briefly comment on how an aesthetic and politics of orientalism make Pamuk (in *The White Castle*) more legible in the world literary system.

In what ways is *The White Castle* a commentary on the master-slave dialectic?

In "Melling's Bosphorus Landscapes" (in *Istanbul*), how does Pamuk read visual images of Istanbul as a model for the convergence of Eastern and Western perspectives?

Week 6: Representing the "Author"

What is the significance of the author figure in Pamuk's work? How does this figure change from text to text?

Pamuk, "*The Paris Review* Interview" (*Other Colors* 353–78)
Pamuk, "My Father's Suitcase" (*Other Colors* 403–17)
Pamuk, *Istanbul*, chs. 13–15

Week 7: Borges: Modern and Postmodern

What characterizes the "modern" and the "postmodern" in Turkish and world literatures?

Borges, *Ficciones*
Pamuk, *Istanbul*, chs. 19–21
Almond, "Borges the Post-orientalist"
Pamuk, *The Black Book*, part 1

JOURNAL 4

First, identify three literary characteristics that could be described as Borgesian. Next, trace the appearance of these characteristics in Pamuk's *Istanbul* (up to ch. 21).

Trace the influence of Borges on Pamuk in one chapter of *The Black Book*. Be specific in defining the exact nature of this influence.

What are the main characteristics of literary form and content in the work of authors like Borges and Pamuk that cause them to be ostracized in their own national traditions? (Some basic online research about Borges's literary politics is necessary to respond to this question.)

Week 8: Istanbul and Intertextuality

What is intertextuality and how is it reflected in the urban spaces of Istanbul?

Pamuk, *The Black Book*, part 2
Pamuk, *Istanbul*, chs. 22–27

Week 9: Modernist Istanbul

What characterizes a modernist literary depiction of a city like Istanbul?

Tanpınar, *A Mind at Peace*, part 4
Selections from Derviş et al., *Becoming Istanbul: An Encyclopedia*
Film: Esmer, *Ten to Eleven*
Pamuk, *Istanbul*, chs. 28–33

JOURNAL 5

Scene reading. Read the concluding scene in *A Mind at Peace* between Mümtaz and Suad as a scene of stigmata (the appearance of the wounds of Christ). Explain the various intersections of the secular and the sacred.

Allegorical reading. Read the relationship between the doctor, young intellectual (Mümtaz), and the older intellectual (İhsan) as a national allegory. What do the doctor's last words to Mümtaz ("You're mine, all mine!") signify at the novel's close?

Encyclopedia entry. Pick an object that appears in one of the Pamuk or Tanpınar excerpts. Using *Becoming Istanbul* as a template, write your own encyclopedia entry for this object.

Week 10: Ottoman Legacies

What is the Ottoman legacy and why is it significant to Turkish literature?

Pamuk, *My Name Is Red*, chs. 1–30
Porter, "From the 'Theory of the Two Qalams'" (optional)
Film: Annaud, *The Name of the Rose*

JOURNAL 6

Pamuk's *My Name Is Red* and Eco's *The Name of the Rose* share important similarities. They are historical fictions that center on murders committed in religious contexts. They are also concerned with the production of texts (illumination and scribal arts) and with the way certain books can threaten the status quo. In short, they both focus on themes of authority, tradition, and blasphemy. In your response, describe the function of the secret or absent text in these two works.

Week 11: Sufism: Lover and Beloved

What is the lover-beloved trope and how does it function in traditional Islamic and postmodern literature?

Pamuk, *My Name Is Red*, chs. 31–59
Sells, *Early Islamic Mysticism*
Pamuk, *Istanbul*, chs. 34–37

Week 12: Kafka

What is the significance of Kafka to Pamuk and specifically to *Snow*?

Pamuk, *Snow*, chs. 1–19
Film: Welles, *The Trial*
Documentary film: Şavaş, *Coup/Darbe* (optional)

Journal 7

In what ways does Pamuk rely on intertextuality with Kafka's works to create a political argument in *Snow*?

Week 13: The Innocence of Objects

What is the relationship between object and text in Pamuk's novel *The Museum of Innocence*?

Pamuk, *The Innocence of Objects*

Weeks 14–15: Points of Comparison

Presentations

Journal 8

Summarize two of the main insights you learned in this course.
Assume that there is a "figure in the carpet" of Pamuk's work (see James). What is it?

What Is World Literature? Teaching *My Name Is Red* as the Other Text

Barish Ali

Mapping World Literature

In *The Naive and the Sentimental Novelist*, Orhan Pamuk illustrates the value of a novelist's intense projections upon the world while, at the same time, strongly suggesting that otherness diminishes once we enter the space of a novel:

> What we feel when we open the curtains to let the sunlight in, when we wait for an elevator that refuses to arrive, when we enter a room for the first time, when we brush our teeth, when we hear the sound of thunder, when we smile at someone we hate, when we fall asleep in the shade of a tree—our sensations are both similar to and different from those of other people. The similarities allow us to imagine the whole of mankind through literature, and also enable us to conceive of a world literature—a world novel. But each novelist has a different way of experiencing, and writing about, the coffee he drinks, the rising of the sun, and his first love. These differences extend to all of the novelist's heroes. And they form the basis of that novelist's style and signature. (29)

This is an instructive observation in a world where we continue to be presented with dichotomies that reduce relationships to self and other, East and West, "axis of evil" and ally. For Pamuk, the power of the novel lies in its ability to "provoke a search for a center which we can also naively project upon the world" (27). Even novels written far from the literary centers of the world—outside London, Paris, and Vienna, for example—are pushing toward the center of a global reader's imagination; for Pamuk this is where the novelist's wisdom can be found.

The purpose of any course in world literature, in my view, is for students to understand how writers differentiate familiarity from unfamiliarity and pass between the two. Students will come to recognize that anglophone literature is not the center of the literary world—literature connects readers from diverse cultures and increases readers' consciousness about the transnational flow of cultural production. Literature should shock; it should compel us to shift our perceptions of the globe, of our literary maps. This is the implicit goal of my world literature courses.

In the past decade there have been a number of studies on reading world literature in a North American context. Among the most important are two books by David Damrosch, *What Is World Literature?* (2003) and *How to Read World Literature* (2008). Damrosch argues that world literature is not an "infinite, ungraspable canon of works but rather a mode of circulation and reading, a mode that is as applicable to individual works as to bodies of material, available for reading established classics and new discoveries alike" (*What* 5). I'd like to draw two points from this: first, that texts travel outside their linguistic and historical contexts; and second, how world literature can be read globally. It is difficult to map individual works onto a world literature course and achieve harmony among them.

Other teachers have recognized the challenge of developing a new conception of world literature. In "World Literature and Global Theory" Vilashini Cooppan discusses her approach to designing a world literature course at Yale. She suggests that any such course can follow two directions; one territorializes while the other deterritorializes:

> A representative reading of the terrain of world literature would introduce particular works as embodiments of national sensibility, examples to be assimilated into the compass of worldly knowledge. Alternatively, we can conceive of the curricular map less in the mode of territorial specification and acquisition than in that of defamiliarization and displacement. Any map presents the global as a local utterance, for any attempt to represent "the world" inevitably bespeaks the mapmaker's own placement. To change a map, then, is to change not only what we look at, but also the very place and premises from which we look. (26–27)

Cooppan's notion of reading a defamiliarized map is striking in its similarity to what Pamuk says about the novel and its writers: "The history of the novel is the history of human liberation: by putting ourselves in others' shoes, by using our imaginations to free ourselves from our own identities, we are able to set ourselves free" ("In Kars"). Both Cooppan and Pamuk suggest an idea of deterritorialization that is not merely geographical; rather, it is a decentering of identity. Hence the significance of reading from the perspective of multiple narrators, human and fantastic, in *My Name Is Red*—narrators that circulate, like the gallivanting gold coin who learned from one of its owners that "there was no place on Earth where a coin couldn't go" (103).[1] As soon as I hand students the syllabus my goal is to decenter their positions as subjects, in part by fleshing out the ideologies that shape cartographic constructions.

Mapping My Name Is Red *onto a Non-Western Literature Course*

At the State University of New York, Buffalo State College, a mid-sized liberal arts college, we have two world literature courses. Both are junior-level courses narrowly limited to post–Second World War literature: World Literature after 1945 examines literature from at least two continents, though in the past it has been taught with an emphasis on continental Europe and South America; Non-Western Literature after 1945 is strictly non-Western.

I have taught *My Name Is Red* in world literature courses and in a course on modern European literature, positioning it in each course as the other text—essentially as a wild card. *My Name Is Red* can stand as the most Eastern among Western texts and the most Western among non-Western texts. I say this fully aware that it is a cliché to claim that Pamuk straddles Eastern and Western literary traditions. In fact, Pamuk's geographical hybridity is what makes him marketable to Western readers. This is exemplified by Pico Iyer's quotation on the cover of Pamuk's *Other Colors*: "Deeply human and engaging. . . . [Pamuk] has become one of the essential writers that both East and West can gratefully claim as their own."[2] Perhaps it goes without saying that the so-called East-West question figures strongly in class discussions of Pamuk in both courses, if only as a way of destabilizing this dichotomy.

In what follows, I outline some of my central preoccupations and challenges when teaching *My Name Is Red* in my non-Western literature course. In this course, we read Pamuk's novel after watching Gillo Pontecorvo's film *The Battle of Algiers* and after reading Assia Djebar's *Fantasia: An Algerian Cavalcade*, Emile Habibi's *The Secret Life of Saeed: The Pessoptomist*, Naguib Mahfouz's *Arabian Nights and Days*, Tahar Ben Jelloun's *This Blinding Absence of Light*, Tayeb Salih's *Season of Migration to the North*, and Marjane Satrapi's *Persepolis*. This course is narrowly focused on literature from the Middle East and most of the texts are novels. My course World Literature after 1945, by contrast, includes poems, plays, memoirs, and novels. (The two world literature courses are complementary: students often take both because the courses fulfill the college's English-degree requirements for non-Western and world literature.)

Informed by Cooppan's deterritorializing approach, on the first day of my non-Western literature course I bring in a page from Hergé's *Tintin in the Congo* (1930–31) in which the child journalist points to a map in front of a class of African children and declares, "My dear friends, I will speak to you today about your fatherland: Belgium!" (my trans.). I ask students to think about what the image and language imply and what it means when Milou, Tintin's dog, silences the young students by complaining that "two of them are chattering." I continue introducing the contentious cartographic terrains of the course by having a student read from the beginning of Jamaica Kincaid's memoir "On Seeing England for the First Time" (1991), which is a reflection on the author's education in colonial Antigua. Kincaid recalls that the teacher's demand to "'draw a map of England' was something far worse than a flat-out declaration of war" (34). I pair this with Jacques Derrida's *Monolingualism of the Other*, which begins with his recollection of learning to "draw the coast of Brittany" with his eyes closed in school in French Algeria but learning nothing about North Africa (44).

My goal is for these examples to convey the idea that maps are arguments, propositions, and gridlines of power and that literature can help us unravel their agendas—or at least understand how writers around the world navigate this grid in their writings. As Damrosch points out, "Works rarely cross borders on a basis of full equality; if the classics and masterpieces long dominant in world literature have typically enjoyed high prestige and authoritative weight in their new homes, the power relations are often reversed when noncanonical works come into North America today" (*What* 24). The question, then, becomes how to bring a translated, non-Western text into a North American context; this is no easier with Pamuk's books even though the author has imported himself into the United States by giving seminars, lectures, and interviews—he has been visible, available, and translatable. The character Enishte Effendi in *My Name Is Red* is faced with a similar task: importing the Sultan's secret book of miniatures into Venice (a parallel that is not lost on my students).

By the time the class reads *My Name Is Red*, the idea of Eastern otherness has been dispelled quite a bit. Students are always quite surprised to find that Marji, the Iranian protagonist of *Persepolis*, is not so different from themselves: she listens to pop and metal, has house parties, flirts with boys, and so on. Such a representation doesn't resemble the "axis of evil" they've learned about. Likewise, students find that the narrator in Ben Jelloun's *This Blinding Absence of Light* knows much more about American films than he knows about *The Arabian Nights*. When we reach *My Name Is Red*, Pamuk helps me emphasize once again that there is not always a rigid divide between East and West.

Reading and Representation: Teaching My Name Is Red

On the surface, certain elements of *My Name Is Red* seem isolated from contemporary politics: the murders that surround the Sultan's secret book of miniatures, the book's controversial combination of Ottoman and "Frankish" (the term the Ottoman characters in the novel use to refer to the West) artistic styles, the violent encounters between art and religion, and the use of multiple narrators to report these events—including a coffeehouse storyteller who pretends to be a gold coin, a dog, a tree, and the color red. Students find it refreshing to read a book that is both a murder mystery set in the past and a doctrine on Ottoman aesthetics, especially given the predominantly political tones of the other readings in my course. The miniaturists in *My Name Is Red* struggle to create art in a society that considers figurative art to be forbidden by its religion; a discussion of questions surrounding representation is an effective way to guide students through the cultural and aesthetic issues in the novel. In other words, my primary goal is to enable students to see how the various questions related to representation interact with one another in Pamuk's novel. I use three approaches to achieve this goal. First, I promote discussion about the vexed question of painting as a metaphor for representation. I direct students to the linguistic impossibility—narration by a corpse—that opens the first chapter and the narrator's contention that "if the situation into which we've fallen were described in a book, even the most expert of miniaturists could never hope to illustrate it" (5–6). We discuss what it means to read a novel, constructed entirely of words, about an illustrated book. Second, I show how questions of representation in the novel open up another layer of debate surrounding Eastern and Western painting styles. This lengthy discussion helps students understand the broader didactic nature of the text. The debates among the miniaturists can enlighten students about the interconnectedness of literature, art, and ideas and how they relate to the decentering of the East-West theme that the course underscores. Third, I provide students with models for engaging in discussion-based textual analysis. Effective pedagogical entry into the first two points is impossible without close readings. The following sections present these three approaches in more detail.

Painting as a Metaphor for Representation

Before I engage in any close reading, I provide a concise overview of the novel's historical context. Following the cartographic theme of the course, I display a map of the Ottoman Empire, emphasizing that in the sixteenth century the empire had a foothold on three continents: Asia, Europe, and Africa. I also show replicas of Ottoman miniatures and images of real miniatures.

With the text and the images at hand we embark on a discussion about painting and representation. Students will inevitably bring up the opposition between words and images; we then discuss how this dualism relates to ekphrasis, which I define as "the verbal representation of visual representation" (Mitchell 152). When my students have a visual reference in place and an awareness that the novel uses only words to talk about painting, I'm in a better position to ask them about the problem at the heart of the story: the degree to which Ottoman art should be open to Western influence. I then shift my focus to my second goal: to explore how representation in the novel is inseparable from the debate surrounding Persian versus Renaissance perspectival forms of painting. Students continue to discuss ekphrasis—or representation more generally—even as the conversation takes up issues surrounding Eastern and Western ways of painting and seeing.

Representation and the East-West Debate

By foregrounding ekphrasis in the discussion of *My Name Is Red* and by recognizing that most of the novel's narrators reflect on their own aesthetic approaches to painting, I provide students with a new perspective on the East-West question. Initiating students into the text with maps and paintings helps to provoke responses that are both political and aesthetic. In "A Selection from Interviews on *My Name Is Red*," Pamuk claims that the East-West question is merely "lurking somewhere in the background": "All of my books are made from a mixture of Eastern and Western methods, styles, habits, and histories, and if I am rich it is thanks to these legacies. My comfort, my double happiness, comes from the same source: I can, without any guilt, wander between the two worlds, and in both I am at home" (*Other Colors* 264). I assign this short article in class, but not because I want students to favor authorial intent in their analyses. And though the novel's author-figure Orhan (revealed as the writer of the story at the end of the text) encourages readers to reconstruct Orhan Pamuk's life from the pages of the novel, I warn students not to fall into this trap and get too intimate with the author, especially because Pamuk's "double happiness" belies the crisis at the heart of the text. This crisis is voiced late in the novel by the *meddah*—the storyteller—when he dresses in drag to explain what would make him happy: "My fickle heart longs for the West when I'm in the East and for the East when I'm in the West. . . . I only want to amuse myself frontside and backside, to be Eastern and Western both" (354). Something sinister lurks behind this forbidden desire: the storyteller, an outlaw of social change, is murdered by a mob—his tongue cut out—almost as soon as he utters these words. I fall back on this moment to ask questions about the storyteller's desire to experience multiple perspectives at once. By the time I get to this point, the novel's third murder, I want to be able to ask my students why this unity of representation, which is the real struggle of the artists in the novel, is unattainable.

To examine this question about unity of representation, we look at how the murderer's divided self reflects the division between Turkish and Frankish styles. Appropriately, and perhaps ironically, it is a mongrel that explains these opposing perspectives in the opening pages of the novel: "In the lands of the infidel Franks, the so-called Europeans, every dog has an owner. These poor animals are paraded on the streets with chains around their necks. . . . Dogs who roam the streets of Istanbul freely in packs and communities . . . are beyond the infidels' conception" (14). This is the first passage the class studies, because of its remarkable familiarization and defamiliarization; the text becomes a beast fable, but the beast mocks the reader: "I'm a dog, and because you humans are less rational beasts than I, you're telling yourselves, 'Dogs don't talk.' Nevertheless, you seem to believe a story in which corpses speak and characters use words they couldn't possibly know" (11). The dog offers an alternative to the kind of knowledge offered by Western reason.

As the various narrators draw the reader into the text, the performative impossibilities that open up the narrative to the world compel students to also think critically about their own complicity in the murder mystery. I then bring their attention back to the map at the front of the novel and proceed to discuss the book of miniatures commissioned by the Sultan. It is important to point out the intended audience of this collection of miniatures: it is created precisely to cross a border that separates two great empires. The book celebrates the Sultan's life and the power of the Ottoman Empire but also, produced in the forbidden Frankish style, serves as an "olive branch extended to the Venetians" (110). Students are quick to point out one of the central preoccupations of the text: many of the miniaturist painters resist the intrusion of European styles and sensibilities into the Ottoman court. Here the class reflects on the East-West question, and I am careful not to present this proposed cultural exchange as a celebration of multicultural unity. Even as the novel navigates the cultural interactions between Europe and the Ottoman Empire, these interactions represent two hegemonic ideologies brought in conflict by two imperial figureheads, the Ottoman sultan and the Venetian doge. But, again, the multiple narrators of *My Name Is Red* provide many perspectives. A student usually points out that the phenomenon of the Sultan's book of miniatures—wherein marginal people, objects, and animals acquire presence and color and voice—is very similar to Pamuk's own literary strategy in *My Name Is Red.* If students don't bring it up, I mention that Pamuk's narrative model follows that of his own coffeehouse storyteller, who explores several types of discourse by giving voice to sketches from the Sultan's book.

The discussion of signature and style provides opportunities for students to discover other perspectives. Close reading is essential for students to understand the function of signature and style in the narrative. Through this discussion I want to stress to students that the course is not simply about exposure to different perspectives; the course is meant to critically examine how other cultures approach difference and otherness. The murderer who is suspicious of—yet drawn to—Western styles makes an excellent example of the complexity of cultural interactions.

Models of Close Reading and Discussion-Based Textual Analysis

It is challenging to get some undergraduates to analyze passages and talk about representation in Ottoman miniatures, if only because many of the ideas the passages introduce are positioned well beyond or against Western conceptions of authorship and art. For example, statements in *My Name Is Red* such as "painting is the act of seeking out Allah's memories and seeing the world as he sees the world" (79) and "the art of perspective removes the painting from God's perspective and lowers it to the level of a street dog" (160) go against conventional Western ideas of visual representation. Yet such passages can lead to fruitful discussion, especially if read alongside moments in the text where Western concepts are ridiculed by Pamuk's characters who see individual style in illustration as a defect.

I ask students to identify passages where style is at the forefront of the miniaturists' debates and then discuss the aesthetic and cultural tensions that the passages raise. Since it's impossible to ignore the "whodunit" aspect of the novel, students invariably point to the murderer's announcement that style would reveal his guilt: "What was venerated as style was nothing more than an imperfection or flaw that revealed the guilty hand" (18). We discuss the question of style at length and the significance and meaning of bringing Venetian style and sensibility into the Ottoman miniaturist tradition. For instance, we look at the moment when the murderer asks Enishte Effendi, the character in charge of preparing the Sultan's secret book, "what is the essence of 'style'? . . . Should style distinguish a good artist from others or not?" Enishte replies that "style is the result of years of disagreements, jealousies, rivalries and studies in color and painting" (167–68).

Students have approached the question of style in a number of ways. One student, who wrote about the relation between cultural identity and artistic style, argued that Pamuk exemplifies the ideologies espoused by Enishte since he is an Eastern writer who, by virtue of being a novelist, positions himself in a Western literary tradition. Pamuk says as much about himself, but the student went on to argue that there's a significant difference between Pamuk as a modern writer and the miniaturists in his novel: Pamuk's technique and style are inseparable from his cultural identity; the miniaturists, however, are not permitted to paint with the same sincerity because their own style—and therefore their own identities—are threatened and destroyed by their culture.

Another student, Elizabeth Staniszewski, wrote: "Prior to reading this text I never gave much thought to the possibility that perhaps an artist is not really an individual—or a true artist—if he is taught from birth that putting pieces of oneself into one's work is something to be frowned upon or even punished." Another student argued that "characters in this book cannot balance adhering to old tradition and taking inspiration from Western culture. It is hard for the miniaturists to achieve a balance because most characters want a style, but are taught that the best painters are imitators. It's difficult to understand why wanting a style is bad. Even Black says at the end of the text, 'Everybody secretly desires to have a style.'"

As these passages illustrate, students often discuss why Pamuk's illustrators have difficulty negotiating Eastern and Western artistic methods—why the radical artists are attacked when they insist on innovation and style. At the same time, students recognize that traditional Ottoman art was itself a product of innovation, having resulted from the meeting of Persian, Arabic, Chinese, and Hindustani styles of painting. This contradiction reflects Pamuk's own philosophy of writing: his refusal to be bound to a national sensibility.

My Name Is Red *and History*

Part of the joy of teaching *My Name Is Red* has to do with how Pamuk transcends ideological and aesthetic divisions between East and West. On another level, the pleasure derives from negotiating two other aspects of the novel: the detective story (popular entertainment) and the story of the miniaturists (cultural history). When teaching world literature, one must navigate between what Damrosch calls a "total immersion and an airy vapidity" (*What* 22). This is one of my own pedagogical conundrums: how much history belongs in a world literature course?

My Name Is Red, the only historical novel on my list, intensifies this problem. Readers must have an understanding of Ottoman history as well as some sense of modern Turkish history: the Kemalist reforms, debates about secularism and political Islam, Turkey's own war against the Kurdistan Workers' Party (PKK), and Turkey's European Union candidacy. An understanding of the changes that transformed Turkey from a multilingual, multiethnic empire to a monolithic nation-state is an essential part of reading Pamuk's novels. I present a montage of this Ottoman map and students are assigned activities to help them understand the historical context of all the texts on the reading list.

But even without a comprehensive contextualization of Turkish history, students can still appreciate and comprehend Pamuk's signature and style. The novel teaches that a signature in a work of literature, like a signature on a painting, merely helps to identify the presence of an author; but style is a secret mark that is woven throughout the text. Determining authorial intention is often a shaky proposition: the author may contradict himself from one interview to the next, so we take some comments as true and completely dismiss others. Pamuk has been almost too forthcoming in talking about his own work. I therefore warn my students to acknowledge the author—who, in addition to interviews and lectures, playfully plants his signature throughout his novel—but not to embrace him the way Shekure embraces her son Orhan.

Style is harder to see than signature, but it can reveal so much more—such as guilt. Indeed, the murderer thinks his style is so well concealed that he challenges the reader: "Try to discover who I am from my colors and my words, as attentive people like yourselves might examine footprints to catch a thief" (17). This is also Pamuk's challenge to readers: examine his footprints to see not only how he and his characters are projected onto the world but how, like the counterfeit coin, we too can interact with the world. By the end of the semester

I hope my students have learned to bring this approach to reading other authors of world literature as well.

NOTES

[1] This essay quotes from Erdağ M. Göknar's translation of *My Name Is Red* published by Vintage Books in 2002.

[2] This essay quotes from the 2007 Vintage Books edition of *Other Colors*.

Reading the End of Empire: Teaching *Istanbul* with Two Ottoman Memoirs

Carolyn McCue Goffman

Orhan Pamuk's *Istanbul: Memories and the City* (2005), Halide Edib's *Memoirs* (1926), and Selma Ekrem's *Unveiled: The Autobiography of a Turkish Girl* (1930) all deal with complicated social and personal transitions in elite families during the last years of the Ottoman Empire and the first decades of the Turkish Republic. Teaching the three memoirs together places Pamuk's memories of his home and city in dialogue with similar depictions in Edib's and Ekrem's memoirs. Pamuk's concerns with his Turkish identity and the Ottoman past echo the end-of-empire anxieties in Ekrem's memoir, which deals with Islam, the First World War, and the Allied occupation of Istanbul, while Edib's autobiography describes personal and political struggles in the late Ottoman Empire. This essay recommends specific chapters from Edib's and Ekrem's books to be read alongside Pamuk's *Istanbul.* I use this approach in literature-based, interdisciplinary undergraduate seminars on imperialism and nationalism, in which we address literary depictions of historical themes. Edib and Ekrem are accessible writers whose mix of history and personal narrative illuminates the late-Ottoman intellectual milieu, from which Pamuk can claim direct descent; the texts also show that Pamuk's anxieties about social class, religion, nationalism, and the West are firmly rooted in Turkey's Ottoman past. Edib's work emphasizes her hopes for Turkey's future and provides a starting point for understanding Ekrem's and Pamuk's ambivalences and uncertainties; Ekrem's memoir describes her struggle for personal freedom in tandem with the end of the empire and the rise of the Turkish Republic. The Istanbul homes and families of Pamuk, Edib, and Ekrem are sites of similar political, religious, educational, and domestic anxieties at different moments in the twentieth century. By comparing these three authors, students will better comprehend the historical threads that absorb Pamuk. Just as Pamuk weaves his family's story into the city's past, Edib and Ekrem show how Istanbul, in both its private and public spaces, transformed around them as the old empire became the new republic. I discuss Pamuk's *Istanbul* in relation to the following chapters: from Edib's *Memoirs*, "My Educational Activities, 1913–14" and "Educational Work in Syria"; from Ekrem's *Unveiled*, "The Shadow of Fear," "Going to Jerusalem," "The Black Tcharshaf," "The Death of Old Stamboul," "Black Bread and Paper Dresses," "Turn to the East and to the West," and "My American Venture."

Pamuk relates his central idea, Istanbul's *hüzün*, or nostalgic melancholy, directly to the city's Ottoman past, visible in the buildings and landscape. Edib and Ekrem similarly connect their personal lives to public events and places that surround them. For Pamuk, Istanbul's "grand houses" are now in ruins, "mere shadows of this destroyed culture" (49–50).[1] By contrast, Edib and Ekrem live in still-grand Istanbul houses from which they carefully, sometimes fearfully, negotiate the public and private spaces of late-Ottoman Istanbul. Edib's central trope is the divided home: the harem and *selamlık* (respectively, the women's and men's sections of a house) are at the heart of her troubled childhood memories; in her adulthood, new houses replace the traditional Ottoman homes. Ekrem's central metaphor, as her title suggests, is the veil, which represents not only her personal grievances at restrictions on Muslim girls but also the shroud cast on the city by the sultan's surveillance, the First World War, and the Allied occupation. All three writers, inhabiting the same city at different times, echo one another across the century in their anxieties about Turkish identity, the lure of westernization, and the stresses of nationalism.

Pamuk's narrative concerns the rapidly vanishing remains of Ottoman Istanbul in the second half of the twentieth century, the power of the Western gaze, his own family history and conflicts, his family's spiritual apathy, and the *hüzün* that colors his own and others' experience of Istanbul. Creating a working definition of *hüzün* is a good focal point for student discussion: students must parse the associated meanings of melancholy and nostalgia. Pamuk writes, "for me, [Istanbul] has always been a city of ruins and end-of-empire melancholy" (6), and he realizes that he loves the city "not for any purity but precisely for the lamentable want of it" (320). His nostalgia is not for a "golden age" (320); instead, he is irresistibly and pleasurably drawn to both the city's beauty and its loss.

The ambivalence of nostalgia can also be approached by comparing Ekrem's description of her family to Pamuk's description of his. The Pamuk family, with its complicated oscillation between energy and stagnation, is a less successful version of Ekrem's family. Ekrem's parents are affectionate with each other, intellectually companionable, and don't follow the Ottoman tradition of inhabiting separate parts of the house. As a child Ekrem hears them regularly discussing frightening political events. Pamuk's parents, in contrast, are estranged and bitter, their unhappy marriage obvious to everyone. Ekrem's father was a prominent Ottoman official, under surveillance by the sultan's spies and in danger of being accused of a fictitious crime. Pamuk's father is running the family business into the ground. But despite the families' differences in character and the fifty years that separate them, they share a similarly elite social status and a strong commitment to westernization. They also share a deep ambivalence about the encroaching provincialism of Anatolia, which brought to Istanbul (in both Ekrem's and Pamuk's times) a more conservative Islam and people who, as long-established Istanbul families like the Pamuks secretly feared, might be more authentically "Turkish" than themselves.

While Pamuk in 2005 and Ekrem in 1930 both invoke nostalgia for the Ottoman past, Edib, in contrast, firmly rejects nostalgia and keeps her gaze on the future, looking back as a patriotic historian with a mission to show Turkey's inevitable path to modern statehood. The following background on Edib sets up the themes that the reader encounters in *Istanbul* and helps students understand her political position. Edib (1885–1964) was the daughter of a prominent secretary in Sultan Abdülhamit's court and became a famous heroine of the Turkish Republic. She was the first Muslim Turk to receive a bachelor's degree from the American College for Girls, the school that Ekrem would attend during the First World War and the sister school to Robert College, the high school Pamuk attended in the 1960s. During the Allied occupation of Istanbul after the war, Edib's political activism put her in danger of arrest by both the British and the sitting Ottoman government. During the Turkish War of Independence she served as a close adviser to Mustafa Kemal Atatürk and, despite her personal reticence and modesty, she delivered stirring speeches, wrote articles for the Turkish press, worked as a field nurse and a soldier in the military, and represented the Turkish cause to the world by writing in English for the foreign press. However, Edib and her husband, Adnan Adıvar, took issue with Atatürk's autocratic methods of governance. In 1924 they went into exile when an opposition party they helped to found was closed down and its leaders accused of sedition. Adıvar was cleared of the charge in 1926, but the couple chose to live abroad until 1938, the year Atatürk died. Edib published her memoir in two volumes in England in 1926 (*Memoirs of Halide Edib*) and 1928 (*The Turkish Ordeal*). *Memoirs*, the work under discussion here, is aimed squarely at a Western audience: she corrects orientalist views of Ottoman women, advocates for the modernization of women's status in marriage and politics, and promotes democratic, secular ideals. Edib represents herself as an observant Muslim and seeks a balance between secularism and respect for religious tradition and observance. Her descriptions of her personal life are sometimes sentimental, her dry irony a little heavy-handed, but her values are clear. She is a secularist, asserting that the new Turkish nation will prosper if it promotes religious tolerance, gender equality, and universal education. Anticipating a skeptical, Western reader with orientalist prejudices, she declares that the new Turkey will be as modern, civilized, and progressive as any other nation.

As Pamuk divides *Istanbul* between his personal memories and depictions of the city by artists and writers before him, so Edib divides her narrative between the private and the public, applying, as Sibel Erol writes, the symbolism of the divided home to her own work, creating a "harem" section in the book about her personal growth and a "selamlık" section to depict national events in Turkey (Introduction xv). In contrast to Pamuk's fascination with the *hüzün* of Istanbul, Edib acknowledges and then dismisses her own reluctant nostalgia for the old ways of the harem. She condemns the separation of the sexes but respects the traditions of her beloved, elderly female relatives. One particular scene vividly demonstrates her feelings. At the height of her political and writing career,

Edib was "constantly out for lessons and lectures," and in the late evenings, when "the noisy little house slept and left me quiet in my room," she devoted herself to her writing (353). However, she felt guilty when she did not have time to visit with her Granny, who, seeing Edib busily working, would walk "back to her room with a sadness which spoiled my work, even kept me awake with remorse" (354). Edib notes the gulf between herself and Granny, who is "much shocked by the new women. Their talk, their walk, their dress, and their general aspect hurt her. She felt lonely, like a stranger in a world where she felt she had stayed too long, like a visitor who has outstayed his welcome" (353).

Granny represents the old harem life, which, in part because of Edib's efforts, is rapidly disappearing. Edib does not regret its loss, but she acknowledges some nostalgia for times past, writing that even she "must have had some secret longing" for "the old houses with the wisteria, the spacious rooms with many windows, and the blazing lights of Istamboul seen through clean white curtains" (354). Edib's new house, with its "chairs and heavy curtains and the little rooms," distresses Granny, but Edib writes that this new home has "helped me to stand on my feet at a moment when I was broken physically and spiritually" (354). Edib uses these images of old and new houses to convey a turning point for herself and for the Ottoman Empire, capturing at once an optimistic vision of the future of Turkish women and an anticipatory nostalgia for a past that has not yet disappeared. After Granny suffers a stroke and loses her speech, Edib lovingly cares for her, seeing her as the last of her kind: "She called me with her eyes. . . . I ran and laid my cheek against her cheek. That wonderful clean and personal perfume, which only the old women of her class and generation had, penetrated me" (356–57). Edib, clear-minded about her purpose, recognizes and then gently puts aside her nostalgia.

Edib and Pamuk similarly reflect the social and gender roles appropriate to their historical moments. For Edib, nostalgia must be acknowledged and then discarded to create a modern Turkey. Pamuk, however, chooses to absorb himself in melancholic nostalgia for a past that seems utterly lost. These two responses toward the Ottoman past introduce useful talking points for students as they work to define *hüzün*: What parts of the past does Edib cherish? What parts does she reject? Why does Pamuk need the past? What is lacking in his present moment, both as a character in his memoir and as writer of the memoir, that the past can supply?

In contrast to Edib, Ekrem (1902–86) is more concerned with personal, rather than political, freedom. Ekrem was the granddaughter of the Ottoman poet Namık Kemal and the daughter of an important Ottoman official who served as governor of Jerusalem and of the Ottoman-controlled Greek islands of the Aegean, which included Rhodes and Lesbos, during Ekrem's childhood (Ekrem 150). *Unveiled*, published in the United States in 1930, opens just before the 1908 Young Turk Revolution and concludes in 1920s America. The title highlights the veil as a familiar symbol of Ottoman womanhood, and the text shows how veiling is connected to class, religious, and national identity. For Ekrem, veiling symbolizes not only the restricted life of Ottoman women but also the fear of the sultan's spies and the social upheavals of the secularist movement, the last a theme that Pamuk also addresses. Ekrem's ambivalence about contemporary events extends to the idea of *kısmet* (fate); in her veiled Ottoman world, where surveillance dominates, she fears mysterious powers that can control one's life. Only when she settles in America as an unveiled young woman does she finally say that she can escape the force of destiny.

Even as a child Ekrem is frightened of Sultan Abdülhamit's network of spies: "Spies—the very name threw dread into my heart. Did I not hear my mother saying that the very walls had ears?" (9). To her young mind, spies and God are always watching: "The words Allah and fate silenced me. Allah was a power even more supreme than my parents I had been told. A power that saw all and heard all" (39). Ekrem's childhood is marked by concealment, secrecy, and the power of fate, and she yearns to "unveil" herself, literally and figuratively, to escape the cloak of secrecy and fear that she senses around her.

In Ekrem's Istanbul, veiling and unveiling become both public and private acts. Wearing the veil is a public performance undertaken for an audience. But Ekrem also shows how intensely personal the act is: she describes the feel of the veil, the way the world appears from behind the veil, and, most alarmingly, the way people whom she loves are altered when they are veiled. When her older sister puts on the "tcharshaf," or veil (*çarşaf* in modern Turkish), she becomes "[a] stranger to me now, a slim black bundle whose dark veiling cast over me a shadow, a shadow that seemed to grow mammoth and extend its clutches over my life. . . . How could she smile from this black prison that cut the air and sunshine from her and the glint of her headful of golden hair from us?" (178). Veiling transforms a sister into a stranger, and makes the familiar frightening. The safety of sisterhood is changed by conditions that Ekrem cannot control.

Veiling is important to Pamuk as well. Students who have read *Snow* will recall the girls who choose suicide rather than attending school with uncovered heads. But why is veiling so abhorrent to Ekrem in 1918? Students can examine this historical moment, during and just after the First World War when Christians in Istanbul celebrated the Allied occupation of the city. Ekrem describes her sudden awareness of "non-Turkish people" in the city: Greeks, Armenians, and others, including family servants and classmates at the American College. Hope came from "Moustapha Kemal" and his "new young power" in "Asia Minor," the land of real "Turks" (280–81). Suddenly Ekrem aligns herself with Anatolia and seems to see herself as a real "Turk": but what has that identity come to mean? For all three writers what it means to be Turkish is a primary concern.

Pamuk certainly shows that the question of Turkishness is a source of anxiety for the Pamuk family. Fifty years after Ekrem looks to "Asia Minor" for Turkey's freedom, the Pamuk family feels its own claim to being Turkish is threatened by the more religious, less secular citizenry. For Pamuk, as for Ekrem, the feeling is connected to both the private and public domains and to issues of secular identity. As does Ekrem, Pamuk focuses on the safety of domestic space and the peril of public streets. The young Orhan has access to his mother's private feminine world, but he can also enter the public masculine domain of Istanbul's neighborhoods. To the little boy, the streets seem mysterious and frightening: "Accustomed as I was to the semidarkness of our bleak museum house, I preferred being indoors. The street below, the avenues beyond, the city's poor neighborhoods seemed as dangerous as those in a black-and-white gangster film" (34). For Pamuk, the "pervasive melancholy" (29) of the streets evokes not only the loss of Ottoman identity but also the slippage of his family's class privileges, losses exacerbated by Turkish middle-class secularism, its seeming rejection of Islam, and the embrace of westernization. For Pamuk, religion is something practiced by the "maids" in head scarfs who work in the family building and by the local tradesmen and workers who attend prayer at the mosque. His family feels both superior and fearful in its secular disdain for religious observance, and the young Pamuk worries that "one day the poor might use their special relationship with God against us" (177).

The Pamuk family's fear of the religious lower classes is not unique to their time. Ekrem also fears the poorer, more openly religious classes, a fear justified by her actual experiences on the street, where passersby loudly demand that she and her sister cover their heads. Ekrem describes a day when her sister had boldly "thrown back" her veil on the street, and Ekrem "heard angry voices" in her ears: "'To what days are we left? Women going about open to the world? Hey, hanım, do you want your daughter to go to hell? Cover her face! . . . It is the like of you who bring ruin to this nation! Imitating the Christians, showing your face!' the hodja screamed out" (180–81). The "hodja" (a religious teacher) represents the male voice of the Ottoman establishment, a voice that Ekrem fears and resists her whole life.

Ekrem's stories of public outcries against unveiled Muslim girls show class and ethnic tensions emerging as the Turkish Republic rose from the defeated Ottoman Empire. Such tensions appear more submerged in Pamuk's work, where the street may have an underlying menace but is less likely to threaten people who look westernized. In Ekrem's time the influences of the West, like a girl's hat, are seen as challenges not only to the Islamic heart of the Ottoman Empire but also to Muslim Turkish male supremacy. Men on the street, undeterred by the girls' class status, assume a male authority over all Muslim women, as Ekrem witnesses: "'Your children are wearing hats as the Christians do. Are you not a Muslim?'" (194); "'Are they [Ekrem and her sister] Turkish? . . . They are Turkish and wearing hats. The world is turning upside down'" (211); and "'Our hodja effendi was right, he said this was the end of the world, that women would go out in the streets. . . . Ah, these newly sprung people, their heads filled with European ideas, they will be the ruin of us yet'" (212). Clearly, a female's head covering was a potent symbol of political and social change and a catalyst for reactionary response. For the young Ekrem, these frightening attacks blurred the boundaries between the personal, domestic world and the public, religious, political world. Moreover, the hodja invokes the "nation," meaning the ethnic group of Muslim Turks of which Ekrem is a part. Can Ekrem be both Turk and secular, as she wishes? What does the veil signify at this moment before the birth of the Turkish Republic, and what does it signify in Pamuk's secular, mid-century moment?

Pamuk's narrative describes similar correlations between secularism and social class half a century later. In his family, westernization and secularism are marks of class ascendancy: one cannot be both religious and of the educated middle class. For the Pamuk family, the rejection of religion creates a gap in daily life that the child puzzles over and the adult Orhan tries to fill. Forty years after Ekrem struggles to wear a hat in public, secular clothing has become the norm on the streets of Istanbul. Secularism for mid-century Turks is a stand against economic backwardness and an attempt to claim the advantages of the West. But in this self-styled progressiveness Pamuk discovers a loss, symbolized by the decaying buildings of Istanbul and the declining fortunes of his family. He writes that "in the secular fury of Atatürk's new Republic," home was "cleansed of religion" and "became as empty as the city's ruined yalıs," the old wooden summer houses on the Bosphorus (179–80). By mid-century secularism has taken hold forcefully. As a child Pamuk learns about religion from members of the lower classes, not from his own family members, who linger uneasily on the edge of belief, "like those godless bourgeois families of Europe who lack the courage to make the final break" (179). He writes, "it was left to the maids to fill in the void (and satisfy my curiosity—if God didn't matter, why did they build so many mosques?)" (180). As a child, he sees the "foolishness of superstition" and confuses childhood "nonsense" rules, such as "[n]ever put your left foot first," with religious practices, such as tying pieces of cloth on the sheikhs' *türbes* (180). The young Orhan puzzles over these acts but fails to find satisfactory answers in his stolid, secular home.

While Edib's and Ekrem's families in the 1900s and 1910s practice Islam and maintain a respectful tolerance of older family members' traditional practices, the Pamuk family disdains "superstitious" behaviors and defines its own secular and class identity in opposition to a religious one. Pamuk's family "reduced religion to a strange and sometimes amusing set of rules on which the lower classes depended; having stripped religion of its power, we were able to accept it into our home as a strange sort of background music to accompany our oscillations between East and West" (180). The Pamuks refuse to regard themselves as Muslim, but they are far from comfortable with their secularism. Pamuk describes a comical family scene: his grandmother and her friends would refuse to fast for Ramadan, but at dusk, the time for religious observers to feast, "they would eye the table as hungrily as if they, like the ordinary Muslims who made up 95 percent of the country, had gone without food since dawn" (181). Pamuk's family feels the loss of a faith but is so fearful of losing elite status that it can define secularism only by opposing religion: there is no room for the tolerance practiced by Edib. To the Pamuk family, religion is an obstacle to success, and the young Pamuk understands from the "high-handed ridicule" directed at the lower class that "religious people" not only paid a price for their faith, but because of them the "dream of a modern, prosperous, westernized Turkey was more difficult to achieve" for everyone (182).

Student discussion may focus productively on ways in which the Pamuk family's attitudes toward religion are both a continuation and a distortion of the secularism practiced by Ekrem's family. Ekrem's grandmother and other older female relatives faithfully perform their religious duties, but her immediate family, like others of this educated class, saw westernization as the only possibility for Turkey in the twentieth century. Students can pursue the connections between westernization and secularism in relation to these writers: Why does secularism seem to preclude Islam in Pamuk's 1960s, but not in Edib's 1920s?

While Atatürk's leadership epitomizes the ideological move to the West, the Pamuk family's ambivalences and internal crises demonstrate the complex social difficulties that developed in the ensuing decades. Indeed, Pamuk suggests that the turn to the West seems incomplete or even misdirected, and, by the mid-twentieth century, the practice of secularism and its accompanying devotion to westernization have, at least in the Pamuk family, become rarefied and sterile, their original purpose obscured. The Pamuk family's secular ideology seems to Pamuk to be as blind as any religious one: "Although everyone knew it as freedom from the laws of Islam, no one was quite sure what else westernization was good for" (10). Four decades earlier, however, Ekrem claims that westernization saves her in both small and large ways. On the streets of Istanbul she inverts the act of veiling and eludes criticism for it by dressing and speaking like a foreigner. Since no one rebukes European women for going about unveiled, Ekrem cuts her hair short, wears a hat, and speaks only French or English in public. People might safely judge her, she writes, to be an "eccentric American left in Stamboul by mistake"; in any case, she "could not be Turkish" (269). This cultural cross-dressing, even as it displays her determination to be an independent female, demonstrates her ambivalence about her identity as both Turk and Muslim. Students may consider whether Ekrem's appropriation of Western dress foreshadows Turkey's future secularization and, indeed, the conflicted attitudes of the Pamuk family.

Ekrem eventually moved to the United States, where she could "wear a hat" and where "everyone found work" (290). Away from Istanbul, Ekrem, with unintentional irony, built her career on re-creating a vanished Ottoman past by writing books about Turkey for children and nostalgic articles about "old" Turkey for the *Christian Science Monitor*. The concluding sentences of *Unveiled* look ahead to this future and her own unresolved ambivalence: "My life would be a seesaw, now touching Turkey, still carrying in its meshes the fragrances of the East, still reflecting as in a pool the slow beauty of centuries that had gazed therein, and then falling to America, the young and breathless West, the builder of centuries to come, creator of the swift beauty of action" (320). The idea of nostalgia is clearly important here, and students might consider whether Ekrem's nostalgia for the lost empire is a new expression of elitism. Does the privilege of harking back to lost glory days give her a particular status as an elite ex-Ottoman and as an author? How does her nostalgia differ from Pamuk's *hüzün*?

Pamuk, unlike Ekrem, does not deny his ambivalent feelings about the Ottoman past; rather, his memoir shows his attempt to understand his past and present, his family's westernization, and his own Turkishness. Ekrem escapes to the United States, but Pamuk chooses to stay rooted in Istanbul. He writes, "I've accepted the city into which I was born in the same way that I've accepted my body. . . . This is my fate, and there's no sense arguing with it" (7). In contrast, Ekrem, in her new life in America, rewrites both her destiny and her past. If *Unveiled* condemns the Ottoman regime's repression of women, Ekrem's later writings celebrate vanished family structures that were based in the separation of household into harem and *selamlık*. Indeed, her contact with the new Turkey was brief, and her choice to live in the United States until her death suggests that she was comfortable writing about the vanished past from a distant place. Edib, for her part, accepts her role as a missionary for the new Turkey. She concludes her *Memoirs* by looking forward, not backward, and unambivalently declaring that Turkey is part of the West: "[h]ow the new era began" will be "the tale of one of the greatest epics of modern Europe!" (472).

While Edib in 1926 confidently anticipates a strong, secular Turkish nation, she also, sometimes unconsciously, hints at lingering tensions about nation, gender, and religion that Ekrem and Pamuk will later describe. Ekrem, writing in America in 1930, remains fixed behind a veil of nostalgia for the past that she was so eager to escape. While Ekrem defies the "fate" of her religious, national, and gendered identity by leaving Turkey to search for a fate that was "acclimated to America" (304), Pamuk embraces the Ottoman past and the twenty-first-century Turkish present through the patina of melancholy. In 2005 Pamuk highlights the beauty and sadness of Istanbul's *hüzün*, the remnant of lost glory and a marker of present emptiness. Reading these three authors in conversation with one another provides vivid historical and social context for students and instructors and helps readers see Pamuk's writings as part of a continuum of the end-of-empire experience in Turkey.

NOTE

[1] This essay quotes from Maureen Freely's translation of *Istanbul: Memories and the City* published by Vintage Books in 2004.

The Discourse of the Other in *Snow*

Esra Mirze Santesso

I should start by admitting a few things about myself: I am Turkish, I grew up in Istanbul at a time when the veil was banned by the constitution, and I have had the opportunity to interview Orhan Pamuk a couple of times. In many ways, these things mark me as an insider: I am able to appreciate the local nuances of Pamuk's problematization of Turkish identity and I have benefited from conversations with the author himself. Of course, being an insider does not necessarily provide me with a reliable, unfailing perspective, a point I make at the start of class discussions about Pamuk's *Snow* in my upper-division courses The Novel after 1900 and Contemporary World Literature.

First, I encourage my students to think about the implications of being an outsider, one of the central concerns in *Snow*. The protagonist, Ka, grapples with his outsider status in Kars, a remote, forlorn border town in eastern Turkey. As soon as he arrives in the decrepit city—which suffers from staggering unemployment and a growing suicide rate among so-called headscarf girls—he is marked as an outsider because of his background as an educated, middle-class, secular journalist from cosmopolitan, booming Istanbul. In our initial discussion, my students quickly infer that Ka's ideological position is shaped by his urban identity. The locals believe that Ka's metropolitan affiliation impedes his ability to represent and give a voice to the headscarf girls; as a secular urbanite, Ka simply cannot contextualize the hardships imposed on young Muslim women. His cultural and political separation from the veiled women, in other words, obfuscates his ability to comprehend their predicament: "[f]or girls like that, a suicide wish is a wish for innocence and purity" (124).[1] At the end of our discussion, my students recognize that the tension between urban and rural identity hints at an irreconcilable ideological gap: for the rural inhabitants, the veil is a form of resistance against a repressive state regime that has forsaken religion for the sake of modernization; for the secular urbanite, the veil represents antisecularism and is regarded as an emblem of Islamism, which wants to replace the constitution with the laws of sharia. This initial discussion allows the students to step into the shoes of the protagonist and to think about their own positions as outsiders unfamiliar with the culture and politics of the region.

While Ka initially suffers from the community's distrust and feels ostracized, his outsiderness eventually serves as an advantage in capturing the stories of the "suicide girls" (10). To put it differently, if Ka's goal is to truly understand the plight of these women, then his position as an outsider affords him various opportunities he can capitalize on as a reporter. This line of thinking echoes the

Bakhtinian form of "creative understanding" that requires estrangement as a condition for empathy:

> In order to understand, it is immensely important for the person who understands to be located outside the object of his or her creative understanding—in time, in space, in culture. For one cannot even really see one's own exterior and comprehend it as a whole, and no mirrors or photographs can help; our real exterior can be seen and understood only by other people, because they are located outside us in space, and because they are others.
>
> (*"Speech Genres"* 7)

In my course on the novel, I regularly assign essays by Bakhtin in order to explore the genre and to reflect on the way Pamuk uses this particular medium (arguably imported from the West) to address ideological tensions unique to Turkish politics. In particular, I turn to "Response to a Question from the *Novy Mir* Editorial Staff" (*"Speech Genres"* 1–9) and "Discourse in the Novel" (*Dialogic Imagination* 259–422) to explore ideas about how language represents various ideological commitments. The first essay is especially useful in complicating the insider/outsider binary: as Bakhtin argues, critics should aspire to detach themselves from personal biases by creating a distance between self and subject matter—an exercise that essentially emulates the outsider's perspective. With this in mind, my students start to see Ka's outsider gaze not as a disabling perspective but as a more objective and perhaps authentic account of events that can produce a balanced reading of a politically vexed crisis. But can an outsider become an insider? Ironically, such distancing may very well pave the way for cultural reintegration. Ka thinks about his journey to Kars as "an attempt to step outside the boundaries of his middle-class upbringing, to venture at long last into the other world beyond" (18). Students soon discover that what Ka desires from contact with the local community is some sort of redemption: to reconnect with his roots, to develop a sense of belonging to a nation from which he has been alienated, and to help to put an end to political and ideological partisanship and fragmentation. In other words, his journalistic inquiries are a means for him to capitalize on his outsiderness in order to gain an insider's wisdom.

My classes are usually composed of a mix of relatively cosmopolitan urbanites and sometimes less confident rural students. I ask students how they see themselves in relation to academia and to mainstream culture more generally. I also encourage them to apply the insider/outsider binary to campus life; we consider the possibility of sororities, fraternities, honors programs, and racial and religious clubs as places where membership is required to gain access. The discussion reveals that everyone is always a potential outsider. Then, we imagine strategies for turning outsiderness into an empowering position—as Ka hopes to do—and discuss the notion of thinking as an outsider as a key to a deeper understanding of seemingly closed-off issues and inaccessible controversies based in partisanship.

After this initial discussion of the idea of outsiderness as a route to reacculturation and understanding, I introduce other related ideas that are central to the novel: empathy, otherness, translation, and political theater. In an interview, Pamuk articulates the reason he has become a writer: "It is a challenge and duty of literature to understand the passions of anyone" (Smith). At this point I introduce Bakhtin's "Discourse in the Novel" to discuss how the novel as a genre is invested in the notion of polyvocality: Bakhtin's theorization of heteroglossia, the capacity to represent various and conflicting perspectives within the novel, further eludidates *Snow*, which Pamuk describes as his "first and last political novel" (Göknar, *Orhan Pamuk* 183). Indeed, the desire to feel empathetic compassion, especially toward those who hold unfamiliar or unpopular opinions, drives *Snow*'s plot; as Pamuk's characters come to represent various ideological positions (through heteroglossia), the author's attempt to humanize—rather than demonize—these opposing advocates becomes apparent. I often quote Carlos Fuentes to demonstrate the novel's inherent desire to explain otherness by switching skillfully between different forms of language: "The novel is born from the very fact that we do not understand one another, because unitary, orthodox language has broken down. . . . Impose a unitary language: you kill the novel, but you also kill the society" (qtd. in Rushdie 420). This sentiment is prevalent in Pamuk's work. In many ways *Snow* is a novel about building tolerance in a society fragmented by ideological wars: "How much can we hope to understand those who have suffered deeper anguish, greater deprivation and more crushing disappointments than we ourselves have known? Even if the world's rich and powerful should ever try to put themselves in the shoes of the rest, how much would they really understand the wretched millions suffering around them?" (259). The first entry point to the text, then, is to acknowledge *Snow* as a work that aims to create an empathetic connection between insiders and outsiders, between opposed characters as well as between characters and readers. To achieve this aim Pamuk takes advantage of the genre to provide a dialogic forum where antagonistic viewpoints are explained and explored both within and outside the narrative.

This dialogic exploration includes the readers: reading is a way of experiencing a new world vicariously and of allowing one's passions to be influenced by empathy. Class discussion about literature as empathy helps renew a sense of curiosity about a text that is for some students almost impenetrable in its foreignness. Gradually students understand that leaving the certainty of their own biases for the sake of entering into a new frame of mind allows them to forge empathetic ties with characters and to participate in the creation of the novel. I often allude to Salman Rushdie—another author I like to include in my course on the novel—and his discussion of "secret identity" that generates from a symbiotic relation between the reader and the writer. As Rushdie writes, "What is forged, in this secret act of reading, is a different kind of identity, as the reader and writer merge, through the medium of the text, to become a collective being that both writes as it reads and reads as it writes, and creates, jointly, that unique work, 'their' novel. This 'secret identity' of writer and reader is the novel form's greatest and most subversive gift" (426). As my students begin to develop their literary empathy and embrace otherness, I encourage them to work at translating the text into their own realities, an exercise I elaborate below.

Because my students might be uninformed about Turkish cultural and political life, I try to help them overcome their initial anxieties about the text. I argue that a more accurate understanding of the other often requires unlearning personal biases that come from orientalist attitudes. Starting the discussion with an admission of ignorance or bias unburdens my students, as they come to view their unfamiliarity with the subject matter not as a handicap but as a basis from which to build a dialogue between their own culture and a foreign one. We begin by openly discussing their image of the Muslim, and students admit to having certain prejudices and fixed ideas; unflattering images of Muslims tend to flood the discussion. Students' ideas about Islam and the figure of the Muslim tend to be uniform and uncomplicated, and therefore they are often surprised to hear about tensions within Muslim states regarding the role of religion in public life. To start, I chart a spectrum of subject positions that summarizes the various forms of religious affiliations under the general umbrella of Muslim. Indeed, *Snow* contains a meticulous depiction of the full range of Muslim characters—secular, moderate, practicing, pious, conservative, fundamentalist, radical, extremist: there are pious believers who fear "fall[ing] under the spell of the West" (78); there are political Islamists who seek power by exploiting religious sentiments ("we've fallen into this destitution because we've wandered off the path of God" [26]). There is also a firm distinction between moderate secularists who are "prepared to live" alongside the Islamists "as long as [the Islamists] don't use intimidation or force to make Westernized women wear scarves" (148) and fanatic secularists "who detect . . . a political motive every time [they see] a covered woman in the street" (22). This nuanced portrayal of characters allows my students to recognize that subject positions cannot be reduced to a single identity. In other words, they learn about the complexities of simplistic labels by unlearning their own orientalist biases—which generally they did not know they possessed.

The basic ideas of orientalism continue to be helpful when we delve deeper into the hijab debate, which drives the main plot of *Snow*. Arabic for "curtain" or "cover," *hijab* describes the practice of devout women in Muslim societies covering their hair and neck as a sign of modesty. Student opinion is divided regarding the practice: many find it difficult to understand why a piece of clothing would be banned in a wide range of spaces; for others, the headscarf unquestionably represents patriarchal repression, and banning it seems logical. Their reactions echo the divided opinions of academics: critics such as Bernard-Henry Levy have argued that "the fight against the veil is for the liberty of women and therefore for human rights" (qtd. in McGoldrick 13). Fran Hosken has gone even further, equating the veil with violent criminal offenses against women such as "[r]ape, forced prostitution, polygamy, genital mutilation, pornography, beating of girls," or simply identifying it as a "violation . . . of basic human rights" (qtd. in Mohanty 66). The opposing side, however, views the modern veil as a symbol that has been reappropriated as an emblem of female empowerment. Miriam Cooke contends that young Muslim women are embracing the veil to assert their agency; most Muslim women put on the veil as a marker of a collective subjectivity, expressing their will to participate in the *umma,* the global community of believers (92).

I approach this highly controversial phenomenon not as a matter of personal expression (as it is usually regarded in Western feminist discourse) but as an expression of political will. My students gain a greater understanding of the political context by learning that in 1982 a Turkish Higher Education Authority decree banned the headscarf in public places. This pronouncement was supported by the Supreme Administrative Court, which asserted that "beyond being a mere innocent practice, wearing the headscarf is in the process of becoming a symbol of a vision that is contrary to the freedoms of women and the fundamental principles of the republic" (qtd. in McGoldrick 134).

Snow enters the headscarf debate within this political frame, presenting veiled women as occupying a feminist position: "it has to do with wanting to control our bodies. . . . For girls like that, a suicide wish is a wish for innocence and purity" (124). Those who oppose the veil signal backwardness: "it was very popular with Westernizing state officials eager to free women from the scarf and other forms of religious coercion" (147). But, of course, Pamuk's literary prowess comes from his ability to invoke this recognizable binary, only to problematize its reductionist logic: "the real question is how much suffering we've caused our womenfolk by turning headscarves into symbols—and using women as pawns in a political game" (43). Such contextualization helps students not only to appreciate the complexities of the issue but also to recognize the author's investment in larger political debates, including questions about democracy and civic rights: What is at stake when a state committed to secularism and democracy limits the rights of Islamic fundamentalists who support the desecularization of civic life? My students gradually come to realize that while the veil may be both a marker of difference and a sign of tolerant multiculturalism in the West, in the East it has more immediate and profound ramifications—to the extent that many see it as a threat to the democratic and secular structure of the state. At the same time, as a political symbol the veil dehumanizes Muslim women, making women who wear headscarves instruments of ideological propaganda. Regardless, the veil, the quintessential orientalist emblem of Muslim female subjectivity, transcends the private sphere and enters the ideological sphere.

It should be clear that I focus my class around two seemingly contrasting phenomena: empathy and otherness. Students more readily grasp otherness, particularly when discussing a community that they have never encountered. Recently, in an attempt to cultivate more responses of empathy and to ground our classroom discussions in actual experience, I took my students on a field trip to a mosque. Students observed the dynamics of a faith-based community in their own city and experienced firsthand what it means to be a Muslim minority in Atlanta. They followed the mosque's rituals—they took off their shoes at the entrance, were separated by gender, listened to the imam's Friday sermon, and observed the prayer. Female students were especially intrigued by the idea of putting on the headscarf: for some, this was a way of experiencing the life of the other. The interactions they had with mosque officials introduced them to the idea that Islam, far from being the cohesive, consistent political organization they imagined, is, like Christianity, about finding answers to personal and moral queries. After this experience, as they continued to read *Snow*, they thought about the politics of identity in new ways: while religious affiliation may not be a contentious component of identity in the West, where it is predominantly confined to the private domain, Pamuk's characters—religious or not—find themselves haunted by Turkey's Islamic past and unable to let go of religion for the sake of modernization.

The class next addresses questions of translation—both literal translation of the text and translation as the adoption of a new cultural filter. Much has been said about translation as a text's second life; by this point in the semester, students in Contemporary World Literature are familiar with David Damrosch's arguments about translation: "works of world literature take on a new life as they move into the world at large, and to understand this new life we need to look closely at the ways the work becomes reframed in its translations and in its new cultural contexts" (*What* 24). The translated text, now potentially able to speak to multiple audiences, experiences a sort of rebirth as it moves from a national readership to a global one. More important, the translated text enters a "contact zone," where meaning is reconfigured (Pratt 36). If *Snow* is ultimately a book about silence—that is, a lack of dialogue between political factions in Turkey, between the East and the West—then the translated *Snow* provides a means to overcome that silence, as the afterlife of the text opens new possibilities for global exchange. In this manner, translation becomes a form of "transculturation," a term coined by Fernando Ortiz to describe a process of metamorphosis resulting from cultural interaction (102). Establishing the translated text as a contact zone between East and West (no matter how problematic such broad categories may be) energizes students to overcome their anxieties as outsiders and to think about meaning defined not by monocultural expertise (Turkish culture) but as a collaborative, cross-cultural process. This is an empowering position for students: they employ transculturation as a way to launch their own interrogations of identity. Returning to the example of hijab, I point out to them that while the veil might be a political problem specific to a Muslim country, the reasons behind supporting or banning it are informed by liberal and feminist ideas that act as pillars of Western society. On one hand, it could be argued that an equal, liberated woman should have the right to choose her clothing; on the other hand, it could be argued that an equal, liberated woman should be protected against patriarchal rituals that force the veil upon her. Translating the Turkish dilemma to the larger debates about liberalism and feminism is precisely what I mean by transculturation.

Finally, I ask students to interrogate the relation between truth and performance, specifically theatrical performance—a question literally manifested in a scene that blurs the lines between reality and fiction (Mirze). In *Snow*, a coup is carried out by a frustrated actor, Zaim, who believes that the Islamists need to be wiped out in order for the people to continue on with the Kemalist project of modernization. Taking matters into his own hands, he stages a military intervention at a time when the eastern border town of Kars has been disconnected from the rest of the nation due to heavy snowfall. But Pamuk has a twisted sense of humor: the coup is mistakenly viewed as a patriotic performance rather than a genuine political intervention. The audience at first cheerfully applauds the players, who are actually military personnel. And when a solider opens fire, the audience assumes it is part of the plot: "Nuray Hanım . . . was full of admiration for the beauty of the theatrical effects, rose to her feet . . . to applaud the actors" (160). In order to communicate the gravity of the moment, Zaim is forced to interject and announce that "[t]his is not a play—it is the beginning of a revolution" (157). Nevertheless, the dumbfounded crowd cannot grasp the implications of the revelation and continues to treat Zaim's proclamation as part of a text. Only when more people are killed and wounded by overexcited soldiers does the crowd start to clue in. Pamuk's points about the audience's misreading are poignant: the public is so accustomed to bellicose rhetoric that they fail to recognize real violence; when dialogue is replaced by constant noise, all meaning is silenced, and action is interpreted first and foremost as mere performance. At this point I try to demonstrate the blurring of reality in popular films such as *Inception*, *Vanilla Sky*, and *Avatar*. By showing the disconnect between experience and truth, I reiterate the point that there are always insiders (who are privy to knowledge) and outsiders (who misread signs)—yet neither of these positions are privileged, since knowledge can be elusive, and misreadings may clear the way for alternative interpretations and become instrumental in redefining truth. This openness to misreading is another strategy I use to help students overcome the fear that their outsiderness will result in an embarrassing moment of misconstruing the text: if the text itself is open to the idea of misreading, then misreading must be a legitimate exercise for its readers to indulge in.

For a final assignment, I have my students watch *Axis of Evil*, a comedy tour featuring four Arab American stand-up comedians. I invite students to think about this comedy show as political theater, to reflect on the relationship between humor and stereotypes (especially those associated with Muslims), and to examine the way these stereotypes are referenced but also debunked by each performer. I assign students a short paper contrasting Pamuk's narrative with the comedians' "texts," focusing on the strategies each uses to address politicized, staged representation. I ask them to think about the position of the speaker and the burden of representation: that is, how do these insiders (the dramatists in *Snow* and the comedians in *Axis of Evil*) develop tactics to speak with outsiders and how do they correct outsiders' misconceptions?

In many ways my approach to teaching *Snow* attempts to situate the text within world literature rather than presenting it solely as a product of Turkishness, which automatically opens up possibilities for transnational reciprocity. In Bakhtin's words, the novel's strength lies in its ability to transform us: "in place of our tedious lives we are offered a surrogate, true, but it is the surrogate of a fascinating and brilliant life. We can experience these adventures, identify with these heroes; such novels almost become a substitute for our own lives" (*Dialogic Imagination* 32). To make *Snow* their own, students need to feel comfortable with foreignness and recognize that while the novel might be invested in the exploration of Turkish national identity and the way it dithers between modernity (inherited as part of Kemalist ideology) and tradition (attachment to Islam), it is simultaneously an examination of global trends that juxtapose secularism with Islamism. Subsequently, students begin to think about canonization and the way meaning is constructed in the messy in-between spaces of transnational exchange rather than within neatly delineated national borders. Pamuk makes this point repeatedly by resisting the idea of identity as uncomplicated and redeemable. I read students one of Pamuk's responses from my interview with him:

> All sorts of description and clarification of a given identity, all sorts of attempts to define a group, a tribe, a nation and pinpoint its identity, I think, are vain and, most of the time, serve very conservative political needs. I write my novels addressing both the national reader and international reader, and to both I would say that our national identities are fabrics designed to suppress rather than free us or liberate us. . . . [Journalists ask] whether Turkishness and Europe are contradictory, I say no, I don't think so. [Sometimes] I think "this is Turkishness" and then I think "this is Europe" and I don't think there is much difference. (Pamuk, "Implementing" 178)

Pamuk himself is invested in the idea of transcending national borders to enlarge his audience and to challenge the notion of Samuel Huntington's "clash of civilizations." Therefore, locating the text within the paradigm of world literature allows students to identify the plurality of the audience as well as the duality of the narrative, which oscillates between Eastern and Western, secular and religious, national and global.

While teaching *Snow* can be challenging, a key for success lies in communicating to students the goals of the novel genre and of literature in general. In *Snow*, before his untimely death, Ka is able to forge a bond with the inhabitants of Kars through literature; he composes a poem about snow that captures the emotional complexity of the town amid political upheaval. Although Pamuk is suspiciously silent about this poem, preferring not to reveal it directly to his readers, he is evocative about its impact on the community. One character describes Ka as a "modern-day dervish": "You've withdrawn from the world to devote yourself to poetry. . . . Just as I've decided to trust you, you've decided to trust me" (76). Ka wins the trust of the community by distancing himself from his own ideological biases and embracing a plurality of experiences—just as readers learn to trust Pamuk as they confront their own ignorance and naiveté and enter another part of the world through the power of literature.

NOTE

[1]This essay quotes from Maureen Freely's translation of *Snow* published by Vintage Books in 2005.

TEACHING PAMUK
IN DIALOGUE WITH WORLD LITERATURE

The Transmission of Pamuk; or, The Sound of *Silent House*

John Limon

Teaching Silent House *in a Course on Faulkner and His Influence*

I have taught the works of Orhan Pamuk in three undergraduate courses aimed at literature majors: one called Faulkner and His Influence, one called The World Novel, and one simply called Orhan Pamuk. I will begin this essay by discussing how I teach *Silent House*, Pamuk's second published novel, in the Faulkner course, because the Faulkner-Pamuk connection is crucial even to the other two courses. A course devoted to world novels might be organized by pairing writers whose common techniques suggest unexpected affinities across distant cultures. And a course specifically focused on Pamuk's career might usefully contemplate his long-standing attention to issues of apprenticeship and influence. These issues lead inevitably back to Faulkner. A goal of all three courses is to explore how premodernity bleeds into modernity, and modernity into postmodernity; what gets clarified for readers is how societies such as Pamuk's and Faulkner's exist simultaneously in different epochs.

In a course on Faulkner and His Influence, students inevitably observe that, like *As I Lay Dying*, *Silent House* features multiple narrators. In each book, one of these is an old woman, a family matriarch: in Faulkner's novel, when the dying Addie finally narrates, she is medically dead; in Pamuk's, the dying Fatma shares in the narrating from the start. In both, the matriarch's bedroom resembles the antechamber to a grave. Each woman wishes to carry a family secret, an infidelity in her marriage, to the grave with her. These secrets explain much to readers but conceal essential facts from the novels' characters.

In this course students notice the astonishing degree to which Pamuk repurposes *The Sound and the Fury* for the scaffolding of *Silent House*. Or not astonishing: Pamuk was asked by the *Paris Review* if he had ever been as radically affected by a book as Osman, the narrator of Pamuk's novel *The New Life*, whose "whole life was changed" by reading one (*New Life* 3).[1] Pamuk answered: *The Sound and the Fury* (*Other Colors* 363).[2] Both *The Sound and the Fury* and *Silent House* are largely narrated by three males: three brothers in Faulkner's novel, two brothers and a cousin in Pamuk's. There is in each book a sister, Caddie in Faulkner and Nilgün in Pamuk, who suffers as much as those who narrate but is not entrusted with the narrative. The youngest brother in Faulkner, Benjy, and the cousin in Pamuk, Hasan, commit confused assaults on women that are inadvertently incestuous. In both books the eldest and most literate brother, Quentin in Faulkner and Faruk in Pamuk, is self-destructively preoccupied with the passage of time. And in both books, the most furious brother, Jason in Faulkner and Metin in Pamuk, is obsessed with the impossibility of earning enough money; the Southerner eventually sells the family house, while the Turk begs his grandmother to sell her house to finance an escape to the United States. Jason and Metin both have catastrophic car trouble that symbolizes their failure to deal with modernity as represented by modern women.

In the Faulkner course, students may discuss how Faulkner's prolonged ambition to name one of his books *Dark House*—the rejected, more intelligible title of *Light in August*—is almost fulfilled by Pamuk's *Silent House*. Connecting the two titles begins with a question: What are the social, literary, and metaphysical meanings of a house? We can divide this question to reorganize what we have considered so far. There are contradictory spatial or boundary issues. What does it mean for a house to open out to an infidelity? What does it mean for a house to enfold incestuous desire? There are contradictory temporal issues. What does it mean for a house to persist for generations? What does it mean for a house to resemble a grave? In *Light in August*, a woman is killed in her family home; in *Silent House*, a woman is attacked outside her family home but dies in it. The array of themes recalls Edgar Allan Poe's "The Fall of the House of Usher," in which the patrimonial house is the home of floating incestuous desires, untimely death, and mistimed burial. Faulkner adapts the monovocal gothic Romantic tale for his polyvocal modernist novel. The remainder of this essay will look at what Pamuk adapts from Faulkner's modernism for his postmodernist novel.

Teaching Silent House *in a Course Centered on Orhan Pamuk*

Pamuk wrote two novels prior to *Silent House*, one of them unpublished. He considers his first published novel, *Cevdet Bey ve Oğulları* ("Cevdet Bey and His Sons"), a translation of which has not yet been published, as juvenilia (*Other Colors* 362). Therefore, a course called Orhan Pamuk must orient itself differently from the Faulkner course: *Silent House* would not be positioned as a belated Faulknerian novel but as the first authentic Pamuk novel. Even so, the Faulknerian influence cannot be avoided. If *Silent House* is the first term of Pamuk's mature career, it anticipates what is perhaps his magnum opus thus far, *My Name Is Red*—and both novels, in the Faulknerian manner, have multiple narrators, some of whom speak posthumously.

The most fruitful approach to the Faulkner-Pamuk entanglement is not to locate it on the biographical outside of Pamuk's oeuvre but to recognize that apprenticeship is a theme on the narrative inside of his oeuvre. *My Name Is Red*, usefully paired with *Silent House* in a Pamuk course, is centrally a meditation on the relation between master and apprentice and a general theory of cultural transmission. Readers learn that influences enter Ottoman art from everywhere: Venice, Persia, China, India. Pamuk would not be the first Turkish artist to adapt a foreign technique; appropriation is a customary aspect of Turkish art. And *My Name Is Red* also includes an internal story of apprenticeship—or rather, two.

First, *My Name Is Red* suggests that Ottoman apprenticeship is less concerned with the modesty of artists in training than with the murderous, homoerotic competition for the master's favor. But there is a second, antithetical, heterosexual transmission story, which begins with the competition for Shekure, a young widow with two children, one of whom is named Orhan. At the end of the novel we learn that its existence and its form, which consists of many first-person narratives mysteriously inscribed, have depended on the telling of the story by Shekure to Orhan. We are led to believe that the transmission from mother to child can best be metaphorized as a scene of nursing. The formation of an artist may be conceived masculinely, Oedipally, as a murderous, phallic competition for the techniques of representation, or femininely, maternally, as an imbibing of immediate oral bliss.

These transmission stories alert us to seek in any Pamuk novel the metastory of its own existence. In *Silent House* a generation from the central family of the novel is absent: Fatma, the family matriarch, is the grandparent rather than the parent of Nilgün, Metin, and Faruk. Their father and mother are dead. Faruk, a historian who resembles Pamuk in self-conscious melancholy, seems as impotent as his polymathic grandfather to complete a manuscript such as the novel he inhabits. In the presence of what may be considered Pamuk's first masterwork, we are given almost no transmission story at all to explain its existence. The world in which the novel is set, the world of the Turkish bourgeoisie, is a society of orphans, literally or (in the case of the friends of Metin) morally. We can eventually locate a muted transmission story in the book, but as an approximation we infer that Pamuk in his first mature novel describes his contemporaries as a lost generation. That much he has in common with Western modernists as opposed to Ottoman miniaturists. Pamuk imagines himself as a writer in a parentless cohort of siblings, much like the declining family he imagines in *Silent House* but paradoxically energized by historical rupture.

Silent House *and World Modernism*

Is it a certainty that Pamuk, like most of his orphaned modernist fraternity, should be judged and analyzed as a novelist? Franco Moretti invites us to think of twentieth-century modernism—poetry, drama, and prose alike—as essentially epical, though he considers James Joyce's *Ulysses* to be the only success in registering the incoherent stimulations of world capitalism. Faulkner, according to Moretti, measurably retreats from the ideal desultory epic in *The Sound and the Fury*, which begins in Benjy's desultory mind, then falls back to a slightly less desultory mind, then to a clear (if crazed) mind, then to third-person objectivity (*Modern Epic* 171–73). Moretti returns to Faulkner in his chapter on another of Faulkner's descendants, Gabriel García Márquez, in which Moretti locates *A Hundred Years of Solitude* more or less halfway from *Buddenbrooks* to *Ulysses*; he considers Márquez's novel a too-charming placement within a narrative of the temporal incoherencies of the world capitalist system. The charge against *Buddenbrooks* is that it is as centripetal as a maelstrom: "In the hundred years of the family saga, . . . history has become longer, and the space narrower. Because *Buddenbrooks* is not, as is often said, a novel on 'Germany,' but on Lübeck—and perhaps not even that, but on the House of Buddenbrook." Moretti adds that "[h]ouses again, and a narrow region, are the sites of the Faulkner cycle" (*Modern Epic* 237).

Is the world of *Silent House* as narrow as Mann's or Faulkner's are alleged to be—a housebound failure to register the disordered world at large in an epic? One might learn from "The Fall of the House of Usher" that even the massive solidity of an ancestral mansion is no protection against the miasma surrounding it. Looking farther back, to the House of Atreus of Greek tragedy, we note that doomed houses always look inward incestuously and homicidally and outward homicidally and promiscuously. Physical houses and dynastic houses, even when proof against light or sound, cannot preserve family homogeneity, which always begins to resemble tabooed incest, against the hybridizing world. For example, the correspondent dark houses of isolates Joanna Burden and Gail Hightower in *Light in August* cannot exclude the emblem of all conceptual, racial indistinction, Joe Christmas. Nor can Pamuk's silent house exclude the "midget" Recep, who is unclassifiable insofar as he is a relative of the Darvınoğlu family but is treated by them as its servant (and by strangers as subhuman). There is another analogy: Recep, inexplicably devoted to holding the Darvınoğlu family intact, is also the book's equivalent of Faulkner's Dilsey, the only integral figure of the disintegrating Compson family. Moreover, the incestuous desire in *Silent House* is mainly expressed by Recep's nephew Hasan, the family patriarch Selâhattin's illegitimate, lower-class grandson, whom the family wishes to exclude from the house. If both *The Sound and the Fury* and *Silent House* concern the continuities of a house, the house that continues includes figures who represent both the castellated domestic walls and their fissure: in *Silent House*, a centrifugal figure (a by-product of promiscuity) holds the house together; a centripetal figure (propelled by incestuous feelings) breaks the house apart. Only a united house can fall; only a house divided against itself can stand.

A class discussion could address whether these familial complexities are conservative in effect: how have the racially and socially excluded been enlisted (like Dilsey and Recep) as the only protectors or, like Hasan despite himself, as idolaters of the aristocratic pretensions of their bourgeois masters? The books will appear to some students to be socially naive if the poor characters' loyalties to their "betters" are made to look unproblematically virtuous in the cases of Dilsey and Recep or primordial and fated in the case of Hasan. But there is another way to read the dynamic: both Faulkner and Pamuk are visibly concerned with the contradictions of their social worlds. Both books reflect the exploitative yet unsustainable labor practices of their respective societies: almost no productive work is done by Compsons and Darvinoğlus. This is the point of the reprise, in both books, of the Greek dramatic or gothic, Romantic trope of the family curse. In Pamuk's book the curse gets passed down in the male line from grandfather to father to eldest son, inherited as alcoholism and futile literary or political ambition. Mutually exacerbating, drinking and writing leave the family exposed to financial ruin.

Thus the dreams of the Darvınoğlus, dreams of Western democracy and science, have destructive consequences for the family. Not that the novel favors autocracy and orthodoxy: the novel is dialogic. And another Western import, American technology, which Moretti takes as the true source of magic realism in *A Hundred Years of Solitude*, creates no marvels in *Silent House*. Just as *As I Lay Dying* puts into relation a nearly prehistoric Southern family and modern technology by means of the Graphophone, so does *Silent House* register the influx of American technology and popular culture by way of the frequently tracked itinerary of an Elvis record. Readers experience the magic of the Graphophone by proxy, but never hear about the Elvis record being played; the record represents the uncompensated disenchantment of Turkey's affluent, bored children.

Or perhaps that puts the matter of magic too simply. There is magic in *Silent House*, but it is paradoxical and exists in the mind of the deceased grandfather, Selâhattin. Selâhattin's dream was to single-handedly bring to Turkey a half millennium of Western modernity at once—humanism, science, empiricism, Enlightenment, democracy, secularism, industry, technology—in the form of an encyclopedia that, however, he cannot finish. He is akin to Virginia Woolf's Mr. Ramsay in *To the Lighthouse*, whose advancement of Western thought terminates at the letter *Q*; Selâhattin's encyclopedia ends at the letter *O*. One paradox of Selâhattin's dream is familiar: science and technology are expected to provide all the miracles of the lapsed supernatural. Another paradox is stranger. The source of Western wonders, Selâhattin declares, is death: "there is no such thing as God and heaven and hell, there's only one thing after death, only what we call Nothingness. . . . Nobody in the East is aware of this. And that's why we've been oppressed for hundreds, thousands of years" (*Silent House* 296). Death enables freedom from agents of traditional power: husbands, dictators, gods. The catch that enervates Selâhattin's dream is that he is thus enchanted by disenchantment itself. This is the original paradox of Pamuk's career-long meditation on the relation of East and West. Selâhattin's vision of Western technology materializes in the generation of his grandson Metin and Metin's friends in the form of motorboats and fast cars. The acknowledgment of absolute death is not what produces the wonders and freedoms of technology; the banalities of technology produce the seductiveness of death. That is the fate of magic realism in *Silent House*.

Teaching Silent House *in a Course on the World Novel*

The likeliest courses to include *Silent House* would have titles like World Literature and The World Novel. What turns literature global? In Moretti's sense of world literature, European and American texts are ranked by their success in displaying the effects of world capitalism; more commonly, the rubric selects works that are produced anywhere in the world and whose forms transgress national boundaries. We can hazard one generalization about the lowest-order taxonomic gesture of the latter undertaking: in contemporary scholarship on global novels or on world modernism, authors are typically admitted onto the world literature ark in pairs.

There are at least two opposed reasons for this matchmaking. In one of the canonical books on world norms of canonization, Pascale Casanova's *The World Republic of Letters*, all modern writers who do not write from cosmopolitan centers face an identical problem—how to become recognized in Paris (or lesser cynosures like London, Barcelona, or New York). Writers removed from the metropolitan centers of literary prestige pair with each other in search of solutions. Faulkner is Casanova's climactic example: he is credited with showing a series of writers, "from the West Indies to Portugal and from South America to Africa," how to attain "the Greenwich meridian [Paris modernism] without in the least denying their cultural heritage" (338). Faulkner is superior to Joyce insofar as he "is recognized by authors from rural countries with archaic cultural structures" (338). He is paired with, among others, Rachid Boudjedra in Algeria (342–44).

The World Republic of Letters is relentlessly focused on centers; even Faulkner is said to teach writers how to be true to their rural, archaic cultures—while appeasing Paris. By contrast, the essayists in *Geomodernisms* tend to decenter the map of modernism. Two representative essays from *Geomodernisms* could be assigned to epitomize the decentering: if T. S. Eliot is paired with Langston Hughes, it is not a case of London tutoring Harlem in how to appeal to European literary gatekeepers; if E. M. Forster is paired with Arundhati Roy, it is not to analyze Roy's solicitation of the metropolitan imperial center (Doyle and Winkiel 262–80, 245–61). While *The World Republic of Letters* is centered on advanced European temporality as if on the Greenwich meridian, *Geomodernisms* is spatial, proposing conceptual mappings by way of the geographical. A simple comparison of the two books would begin with their antithetical conceptions of modernism: in Casanova, modernism is a function of modernity in its pursuit of a disenchanted, abstract, universal, specialized freedom; in *Geomodernisms*, pervasively, modernism is a rebellion against modernity, in search of global relief from its abstract aridity.

Neither book captures the relation of Faulkner and Pamuk. Faulkner could hardly enable Pamuk to discover the literariness of Pamuk's "rural" or "archaic" society; Istanbul is neither, and Pamuk is rather more cosmopolitan than Faulkner was. Nor does Pamuk show western European and white American writers something that is more spiritually, culturally, or corporeally vivacious than their own societies. The relation of Faulkner and Pamuk begins with the similarity of their respective relations to the pasts of their defeated worlds: each writer lives in the aftermath of the catastrophe of his culture's historical ambitions, though accomplished for centuries in the case of the Ottoman Empire and never achieved in the case of the Confederacy. As much as Fatma in *Silent House* resembles Addie in *As I Lay Dying*, her more significant literary relation may be to another grandmother, Damuddy, who is dying out of sight in *The Sound and the Fury*; dying with Damuddy is her memory of the antebellum South, as Fatma's memory of Ottoman Turkey dies with her. (In *Silent House*, the matriarch dies loudly and furiously. In *The Sound and the Fury*, the matriarch dies silently.) The similar historical disorientations of the two cultures will allow teachers to make a connection between them that is not merely a case of unilateral soft power. Both novelists describe belated, abrupt, ambivalent confrontations with modernity; neither ascends to it or escapes from it. Comparing Faulkner with Pamuk puts into relief some of the key features of *Silent House*, where Pamuk defines his place in political history by way of his place in the history of the novel as a genre.

Though I have likened Faruk and Quentin—both are literate, melancholic, past-obsessed, and self-destructive—Quentin is not identified as a writer. Nor is Darl, the equivalent figure in *As I Lay Dying*. But Faruk is, and this points to Pamuk's postmodernist inclination: within his book is an image of the book. Faruk's desire to read history as pure facts, not stories, is the conceptual crux of Pamuk's novel. Though Pamuk the novelist is distinct from Faruk the Baconian historian, the full extent of Pamuk's sympathy with the Baconian's fetishism of the artifact will become clear in *The Museum of Innocence*: Pamuk's fetishistic protagonist in that novel does not want memories of the past; he wants the past. In another way, Pamuk stays attached to Faruk's dream—Faruk returns as the historian of the more or less postmodernist fiction *The White Castle*, a book whose global postmodern pedigree is established by its formal descent from Julio Cortázar's "Axolotl," another verbal Möbius strip.

The past of *The Museum of Innocence* is personal; the past of *Silent House*, *The White Castle*, and *My Name Is Red* is the Ottoman Empire, always conjured at a moment of intersection with the West. More precisely, the Ottoman documents studied by Faruk in *Silent House* do not make reference to the West, but the pure empiricism of his research, culminating in skepticism about stories per se, produces in the novel a sense of a return to the origin of that genre in Europe as described by Michael McKeon (23–128); in the novel we can feel simultaneously the pressure of the Ottoman and the European seventeenth century. Early modern science produced in European philosophy an empiricism that would undo itself as skepticism. Insofar as McKeon's book is about the correlations of epistemology and politics, progressive empiricism gives way to conservative skepticism (265–70). Though Faruk is not tempted by the reactionary politics of the friends of Hasan, Faruk's sister's Marxism seems to him simply another dubious story about the relevance of past to present; his own past detaches from the present as a materially interconnected world that Faruk prefers not to narrate but to inhabit detail by detail. *Silent House*, in short, is self-conscious in the ungrounded, postmodern way by being self-conscious in the way of epistemologically unsettled early modernity, when the novel form was invented. When Faruk returns to the collected works of Pamuk in *The White Castle*, in which he introduces the manuscript he is credited with having discovered in the Gebze archive, he frames the magic realism of that narrative with a residue of historical skepticism.

Teachers of *Silent House*, whether or not they are teaching a class familiar with Faulkner, must raise the question of its division of thirty-two chapters among five narrators. At a minimum, instructors will want to allude to Bakhtin's "dialogic imagination," the imagination of living, authority-leveling, past-unsettling contradiction. Classes trained in theory should read the essay "Epic and Novel"

(*Dialogic Imagination* 3–40). Yet one aspect of the competitive narration differs from Faulkner to Pamuk, and so it requires special justification. Almost all the narrative segments of *Silent House* are, at moments, addressed to specific individuals. For example, Fatma addresses many of her remarks to her late husband; Hasan addresses many of his to Nilgün. For what purpose does Pamuk play this variation on the dialogic Faulknerian technique? By what mechanism can we imagine the arrival of these narrative segments at their intended internal audiences?

These questions must be raised within an inquiry into the modern novel and the novel as a genre. Here is one possible beginning. In *As I Lay Dying*, it is impossible to account for the characters' narrations on the pages of the book: it is easily proved that we cannot be in the presence of actual writing by characters, of transcribed speaking, or of transcribed thinking. This is true in *Silent House* as well, except that Pamuk intervenes (in the English translation but not in the original Turkish text) by titling each section in the third person (for example, "Recep Goes to the Movies") before turning the narration over to that character, who then narrates something, somehow, and addresses part of that narrative to someone. Is this a kind of postmodern co-optation of the epistolary novel? If so, we circle back to the novel's incipience to discover the epistemology of a kind of literary Baconianism: a justification of the novel as the historical recovery of artifacts—assembled, captioned, but otherwise untouched by the historian.

We are returned, possibly, to the historian Faruk's world, but we cannot rest there. As McKeon might have predicted, there are two kinds of authors in *Silent House*, in generic competition, just as novels as a genre, as McKeon learns from Bakhtin's "Epic and Novel," are scenes of generic competition (McKeon 11; Bakhtin, *Dialogic Imagination* 3): one author, Faruk, whose naively antifictional historicism leads him to a debilitating skepticism about all narrative, and another, called Orhan, who, in an aside by one of Metin's bourgeois friends, is said to be "supposedly writing a novel" (*Silent House* 288). That is the entirety of Orhan's appearance in the book: it is either true or fictional that he is writing a work of fiction. He is not imbibing the story from his mother like the historically earlier or bibliographically later Orhan; we have no idea how he overhears what goes on inside the silent house. There can be no adequate transmission story because those who are on the inside of the house are inadequate to the polyphony of its story, which also means that we cannot imagine any of them admiring a protean novelist enough to entrust the family chronicle to his care. The absence of a storytelling mother on the inside of the novel keeps it from being nearly as incest-ridden as, say, *As I Lay Dying*; *Silent House* does not have a mother at its center, nurturing its continuous maturation by way of an unbroken maternal bond. It has no center.

But if the novel Orhan is writing is the one we are reading, the question of his own credentials is moot: he is making the story up, placing himself omnisciently on the story's inside. The novel he is writing is located, by way of Faruk, at the empirical-skeptical epistemological crisis of the genre's origin; by way of the Faulknerian experimental polyphony, at the modernist moment of the genre; and by way of Pamuk's self-reference, at the postmodern end of the genre. In these ways *Silent House* thematizes its own status and indexes its own schizoid historical identity. Is *Silent House* any kind of realism? Here is its realism: Pamuk writes a novel that is only possible if the Turkey he inhabits is the temporally skewed Turkey he describes, at once early modern, modern, and postmodern. From the quadrilateral of possibilities he assembles for contemporary Turkey (Marxist, nationalist, Americanized, nostalgic), there emerges a cultural form that was invented to speak dialogically for a silent house divided against itself: in the case of *Silent House*, communism against capitalism, nationalism against internationalism, the present or future against the past. If the novel in question manages to exist, it must exist realistically. (This is the ontological proof of the reality of Pamuk's book.) World literature describes a world in which world literature is possible: that circularity is the beginning of a way to read literature and the world by way of world literature.

NOTES

I'd like to thank David Damrosch for stylistic and organizational help and Sevinç Türkkan for stylistic, organizational, and factual help in the writing of this essay.

[1] This essay quotes from the 1998 Vintage Books edition of *The New Life.*

[2] This essay quotes from Maureen Freely's translation of *Other Colors: Essays and a Story* published by Alfred A. Knopf in 2007.

Unpacking Pamuk's Library: A Print-Cultural Dialogue with World Literature

B. Venkat Mani

> My dazzled eyes could no longer distinguish the world that existed within the book from the book that existed within the world.
>
> —Pamuk, *The New Life*

> Successful book covers serve as conduits, spiriting us away from the ordinary world in which we live, ushering us into the world of the book.
>
> —Pamuk, "Nine Notes on Book Covers," *Other Colors*

Pamuk's dialogue with world literature has garnered an incredible volume of critical interest. However, the author's engagement with the materiality of books has been neglected. Many of his essays focus on the medium and the act of reading and on the acquisition and collation of rare and new books in Turkish and from other literary traditions.

In this essay I discuss how Pamuk's novels and essays can be taught to deepen students' knowledge of and interest in library and print-cultural histories, especially when framed through the story of the worldwide circulation of his texts in translation. Pamuk's works reflect the dual nature of the book as an intellectual artifact and a material one. Instructors, by paying attention to this duality, can direct students to questions about the material production of literature, the creation of readerships within and beyond national boundaries, and to histories of the uneven circulation of literatures, especially those originating outside Euro-American metropolitan locations. A print-cultural approach—a mode of critical reading that engages with the materiality of book production and circulation (Mani, *Recoding*)—to Pamuk's texts can draw students' attention to the transformative moment of books and libraries—from physical to digital objects—that marks our current period (Mani, "Breaking"). Such an approach can also open questions of accessibility and acquisition, propriety and appropriation, as well as inheritance and inhabitation of creative traditions in Turkey and Europe, which form the critical core of Pamuk's work. Most important, working through print-cultural aspects of Pamuk's writings can assist in confronting an important challenge when teaching world literature in a Euro-American setting: namely, the essentialization of non-Western literatures as mostly oral and traditional, and therefore bereft of the advancements in literacy and social modernity that are assumed to be the sole privilege of Western literatures.

Pamuk's Novels: World Literature and Its Turkish Circulation

In the *Cumhuriyet Dönemi Türkiye Ansiklopedisi* Arslan Karnaydağ reports that Ibrahim Mütferrika set up the first printing press in Turkey in 1729; the first published book was an Arabic-Turkish dictionary (2824). The earliest available data on Turkish books reveals that of 1,530 books published in 1934, 308 were works of literature. By 1958 the total number of published books had more than doubled, while the share of volumes published in literature had tripled: of 3,925 published volumes, 905 were works of literature. Of 7,479 books published in 1973, 1,373 belonged to the field of literature. By 1984, of 7,224 books published, 1,300 were identified as literature (2832–33). These figures acquire a new shade of meaning when compared with the number of works translated from Turkish into English during the last century or so. As Saliha Paker and Melike Yılmaz document, the number of works of Turkish literature translated into English increased from three in the third decade of the twentieth century to twenty-seven in the first decade of the twenty-first century. The total number of Turkish literary works translated into English is much lower than the number of Euro-American literary works translated into Turkish. Paker and Yılmaz focus mainly on translations between English and Turkish; however, expanding the field to translations to Turkish from languages other than English demonstrates the same pattern. According to statistics available through UNESCO's Index Translationum, between 1948 and 2014 there were 7,006 works classified as literature that were translated into Turkish from all world languages. The British children's book author Enid Blyton leads this list with ninety-seven works, followed by the romance author Barbara Cartland with seventy-eight. In the same period only 2,047 Turkish literary works were translated into other world languages. Pamuk tops the list with 318 works, followed by Yaşar Kemal with 242 and Nazim Hikmet with 130 ("Index"). The complexities of the politics of translation in Turkey are beyond the scope of this essay.[1] But it is important to note that the amount of time between the publication in Turkish of a work by Pamuk and its translation to English keeps getting shorter: *Beyaz Kale* (1985) was published as *The White Castle* in 1990; *Kara Kitap* (1990) was published as *The Black Book* in 1994; an English translation of *Istanbul* was published within months of its Turkish publication in 2005.

Scholars have pointed out that the internationalization of Pamuk's novels coincides with a new interest in the translation of Turkish literature and marks a shift from an interest in *köy edebiyati* ("village literature"), such as those of Yaşar Kemal, to the urban novel with themes of contemporary politics and clashing secular and religious values, as in Adalet Ağaoğlu's highly successful *Curfew* (1984) (Seyhan; Paker; Esen, Preface). While this is correct, three other reasons explain Western publishing houses' interest in Pamuk's works: each of his novels sells approximately two million copies within months of publication; his interventions in contemporary culture, within and outside Turkey, are thematically sensitive and sometimes controversial; and his aesthetic innovations and unorthodox use of language have long been debated in Turkey. Covers of Pamuk's novels in Turkey carry excerpts of reviews published in *The Guardian*, *The New York Times*, *Le Monde*, *Die Zeit*, and others. Coverage of Pamuk in the Turkish language press in Turkey and Germany includes commentary on the purported compromises the author has made on aesthetic and political grounds to suit Western readerships. Such commentary appeared in the Turkish daily *Hürriyet* ("Pamuk Alman") as well as in letters by Turkish-German readers to editors of *Die Zeit* and the *Frankfurter Allgemeine Zeitung* ("Welt"; "Friedenspreis für Schriftsteller") following the conferral of the Deutsche Friedenspreis in 2006 ("Friedenspreis für Pamuk"). Notably, no Turkish government official attended the Friendenspreis ceremony ("Applause"). In the Anglo-American press, however, Pamuk has become somewhat of a native informant, similar to the treatment of Salman Rushdie by the press in the late 1980s and early 1990s. D. M. Thomas's review of *The New Life* described Pamuk as a "carpet-weaver gone blind," and Margaret Atwood's review of *Snow* described the novel as the Turkish take on the clash of civilizations, thereby essentially ascribing secularism to the West.

Pamuk has worked against such misunderstandings, not only in speeches, interviews, and essays but also in his fiction. Pamuk's first novel, *Cevdet Bey ve Oğullari* ("Cevdet Bey and Sons"), is in dialogue with non-Turkish literatures. The structure of the novel intersects with the most famous family saga in German, Thomas Mann's *Buddenbrooks*. Its characters are well acquainted with literature in French, which was the language of education and upward social mobility for the Turkish feudal elite in the late nineteenth century as well as for the revolutionary generation of the early twentieth. Cevdet, the protagonist, tells Seyfi Pasha, a feudal official in the service of Sultan Abdülhamit: "Monsieur, [j]e lis Balzac, Musset, Paul Bourget . . . " (62).[2]

The epigraphs in Pamuk's novels map the international circulation and network of his ideas. In *The White Castle*, a Turkish mistranslation from Proust becomes the epigraph, as Faruk, the implied narrator and the alleged translator of the manuscript from old Turkish into the modern idiom, recounts the relationship between a Turkish nobleman and his Italian captive in seventeenth-century Istanbul. The story of the troubled journalist Galip in the stagnant political atmosphere of late 1980s Istanbul becomes central to *The Black Book*, which includes an epigraph for each chapter, ranging from citations from the *Encyclopedia of Islam* to Lewis Carroll's *Alice in Wonderland.* Citations from the Qur'an initiate the reader into the world of *My Name Is Red*, which depicts multiple centers of book production: Baghdad, Kandahar, and Isfahan, among others. Ahmad Hamdi Tanpınar is read alongside Charles Baudelaire and Edward Said in *Istanbul.* As for *Snow*, Robert Browning, Stendhal, and Joseph Conrad make initial appearances, while Fyodor Dostoevsky, Anton Chekhov, Ivan Turgenev, and Franz Kafka cast long shadows over the narrator, Orhan. In all these novels, the narrator reads and reports on his readings, directly addressing the reader of the novel. Other texts populate the narrative or are presented as epigraphs. As poetic borrowings become central to Pamuk's works, books—real and imagined, published and not—become part of the story and the act of storytelling.

Pamuk's novels ask readers to consider the parameters of what is shared and what is perceived as unshared. A parallel consideration of the power differentials created by the uneven contours of commerce and the circulation of books as readable objects suggests the question of shared reading—as a practice, as a strategy, but also as a space. What constitutes the shared space of reading? How does an attention to the materiality of literature help us understand the contested nature of literature as shared property? These questions are central to my teaching of Pamuk's works in translation, which I include in undergraduate courses on world literature framed through oral and print-cultural histories of the circulation of literary works. In the following discussion, I approach these questions first through *Snow* and *The New Life*; then I turn to Pamuk's essays on books and reading.

Halfway through *Snow*, a young Kurdish activist "whose mother's brother lives in Germany" makes the following statement: "All I'd want them to print in that Frankfurt paper is this: We're not stupid, we're just poor! And we have a right to want to insist on this distinction" (275).[3] The young man is debating a political statement—to be sent for publication in the *Frankfurter Rundschau* —that he would cosign with an Islamic fundamentalist, an ex-socialist, and a Kemalist secularist. This gathering of ideologues, which includes Ka, the protagonist, takes place in Hotel Asia in the city of Kars in the aftermath of a political play. Entitled *My Fatherland or My Headscarf*—an allusion to Namık Kemal's 1873 *Vatan yahut Silistre* ("Fatherland, or Silistra")—the farce turns into a political tragedy. During the last act, local police officers shoot people in the audience to suppress fundamentalist reactions.

As the debate continues, the Kurdish activist, reflecting on Europe, makes an untimely statement about literature: "When they write poems or sing songs in the West, they speak for all humanity. They're human beings—but we're just Muslims. When *we* write something, it's called ethnic poetry" (279). The activist presents a longer history of the West's domination of the non-West, which motivates readers to question their relation to the text. The operative claim that one has the right to insist on distinctions leads to a consideration of other related rights: the right to insist that the world is full of distinctions, the right to assert that there are inequities caused by the role of capital, the right to be taken seriously, the right to inform another human community of these distinctions. The Kurdish activist registers these rights, even as he bitterly acknowledges the lesser status ascribed to the creative tradition to which he belongs. There is a cosmopolitan obligation—the obligation to question the very normativity of equity as a norm—that the Kurdish activist wants to be relayed to the world. Such a cosmopolitan obligation is cast in terms of colliding communities of readers and their opponents, within and beyond the national space, through the politics of books.

Pamuk's novel *The New Life* includes one of the author's most prolonged engagements with books and print culture. A line from Novalis's *Heinrich von Ofterdingen* serves as an epigraph to the novel, in which the embattled relations between local versus national and global versus cosmopolitan surface through the tragicomedy of a controversial book, first mystified and mythologized and then parodied by the narrator. Osman, the protagonist, is in search of the author of an anonymously published book, also called *The New Life*. His search leads him to the private library of an Uncle Rıfkı, a railroad engineer, which contains "translated works of Dante, Ib'n Arabi, and Rilke from the world classics series published by the Ministry of Education . . . translations of Jules Verne, Sherlock Holmes, Mark Twain" and many others (256).[4]

The New Life starts with Osman's confession of total transformation: "I read a book one day and my whole life was changed" (3). The readers (admirers) of the book authored by Rıfkı recognize its multiple social lives, and for them, life, book, and world become inseparable. The book's detractors fear its social impact. Their self-proclaimed leader, Dr. Fine, is in an all-out battle against printed matter, and considers Gutenberg to be "one of the pawns of the Great Conspirator [Satan]," who "outstripped the production of the industrious hand, the patient finger, the fastidious pen" (107).

If *The New Life* narrates the search for readers of a book, in *Snow*, the narrator Orhan takes the readers to two far-flung libraries, one in the city of Kars, and the other in Frankfurt, as Orhan investigates the murder of the protagonist, Ka. The library in Kars is full of "five or six students . . . also a handful of retired government officials . . . [who] had probably come here to escape the cold in their houses" (214). The only book mentioned in that library is "several old volumes of *The Encyclopedia of Life*" (214). As for the Frankfurt library, the narrator comments on the heterogeneous group of patrons: "Inside were the types you always find in such libraries: housewives, old people with time to kill, unemployed men, one or two Turks and Arabs, students giggling over their homework assignment, and all other manner of stalwarts ranging from the ranks of the obese, the lame, the insane, and the mentally handicapped" (252). Unsurprisingly, this library is Ka's public refuge from the isolation he experiences in his decrepit, tiny apartment. It is the last place Ka visits before he is murdered on the street; readers visit it with Orhan during the forensic investigation associated with the murder. Orhan, while opening copies of collections of poetry in the English section of the library, "shed[s] tears for him [Ka] and for the years he'd wasted away in this library" (252). Ka's reading comprises poetry by W. H. Auden, Browning, and Samuel Taylor Coleridge. Checkout slips bearing the signature of the exiled

Turkish poet identify his temporary possession of volumes from the Frankfurt library—indeed of his poetic borrowings. There is little to be owned in the exiled subject's life, one that is characterized by borrowed time, space, and, as the novel emphasizes, the materiality of intellectual stimulation.

The balancing act between two worlds and the uneven trajectories of circulation of literatures from non-Western peripheries into Western centers accompany Pamuk beyond his novels. His nonfiction writings engage with questions of access to books and creation of readerships. This is particularly evident in several essays published in the collection *Öteki Renkler*, many of which are included in its English translation, *Other Colors*.

Pamuk's Essays: Books, Readers, and Worlds

First given as a speech in Weimar in 1999 at a celebration of the 250th anniversary of Goethe's birth, "Dünya Edebiyatı" ("World Literature"), one of the most fascinating essays in *Öteki Renkler* (which, however, doesn't appear in *Other Colors*), serves as a preface to Pamuk's readings of books in his private library: Laurence Sterne's *Tristram Shandy*, Dostoevsky's *Notes from the Underground*, and others. Pamuk begins with prudent uncertainty: "World literature?" he asks, calling the term at once "thought provoking" and "mysterious." By associating world literature with "a high brotherhood of those who read books" and "the whole world's literature" and a "global fraternity of literature," Pamuk at once diagnoses authority and naiveté in the term. The initial skepticism quickly gives way to a confident investment in world literature. Listing "influences, borrowings, and infatuations" of the last two centuries, which are central to his novels, Pamuk declares: "literature is as much a delicately constructed memory as it is a subtly constructed forgetting" (*Öteki Renkler* 203).[5]

Resonances of constructed memory and constructed forgetting are found in the seven brief points that follow Pamuk's introductory remarks. Each point touches on compelling issues that have reached center stage in recent academic discussions of world literature: literacy, readership, the importability of literary forms such as the novel, power hierarchies and ensuing tensions that form and inform connections between linguistic and literary cultures of the geopolitical centers and the periphery, divisions of literary labor between Western and non-Western writers, the dangers of popular international trends in the age of electronic media, and, finally, language, authorship, and the construction of target readership in translation. In sum, Pamuk identifies all the ingredients that constitute the idea of world literature, while simultaneously providing a critical agenda for engaging with such a grandiose idea.

Pamuk's mention of the emancipatory potential of world literature from restrictions of national literary demands makes his discussion of world literature easy to compare with Goethe's *Weltliteratur* (1936), in which Geothe declares the meaninglessness of the term *national literature* and encourages the approach of world literature (Eckermann 94). In addition, Pamuk's attention to the commercialization of literature and the unprecedented proliferation of international trends, as well as the specific invocation of a "division of literary labor," situates Pamuk's thoughts in the vicinity of Karl Marx and Friedrich Engels's ideas on *Weltliteratur*. As is well known, Marx and Engels situated world literature in the cosmopolitan consumption of goods caused by the worldwide circulation of capital (71). However, Pamuk's speech is hardly a simple continuation of these earlier discussions. While Goethe and Marx and Engels anticipate the arrival of world literature in the future, Pamuk's account of the present circumstances of world literature confronts the historical sedimentation of 250 years that divided the world and literary labor into geopolitical centers and peripheries.

The crucial turn in Pamuk's speech comes toward the end, as he approaches the question of translation through the translations of his own works and his imagined and target readership—Turkish and worldwide. In this "frequently posed question," Pamuk diagnoses a frightening nationalism, a recourse to which he finds in "influences, libraries, writers who read each other, and a rich culture of translation" (*Öteki Renkler* 203). Through the explicit mention of libraries, Pamuk points to a different possibility of imagining spaces of literary exchange in the larger landscape of world literature. His reflections end with Faulkner and Borges—writers who, in his opinion, defy the limitations of central and peripheral affiliations—in order to reemphasize world literature's potential to rescue authors and readers from national demands and international trends (204).

Pamuk's insertion of libraries between "influences" and "writers who read each other" serves as an apt point of departure to think through particular moments that energize constructed memory and constructed forgetting. The fifteen essays in the section "Books and Reading" in *Other Colors* document Pamuk's acts of reading and collecting. In "How I Got Rid of My Books," Pamuk describes the rearrangement of his library in the aftermath of the two earthquakes that hit Turkey in 1999. In a passage reminiscent of Walter Benjamin's "Unpacking My Library" (*Illuminations* 59–67) Pamuk writes:

> That my library should conspire in the earthquake's wrath, that it should confirm and dignify its message—this frightened me, and the apocalyptic intimations made me angry. The same thing had happened during the aftershocks of the previous weeks. I decided to punish my library. . . . This was how, with a strangely clear conscience, I picked 250 books from my shelves and disposed of them. (*Other Colors* 107)

As is well known, Benjamin's essay invites his readers to join the chaos of a library that is dispersed in crates and on the floor, a library that has not taken its expected form: an orderly arrangement of books on display. Benjamin associates this dispersed disorderliness with the chaotic energy associated with the passion for book collecting. While Benjamin's essay thrives on such chaotic energy, Pamuk fears the disorder that might be caused by a natural disaster. Similar to Benjamin, for whom dialectical tension between dissemination (*Zerstreuung*) and accumulation (*Sammlung*) becomes central to the personal library, for Pamuk collection contains an act of de-collection.

Nonetheless, and unlike Benjamin, Pamuk takes the opportunity to comment on the culture of reading and collection in Turkey. Pamuk's suspicion of a "global community of readers" in his essay on world literature becomes more emphatic in the essay on his library, in which he reflects on the status of reading in Turkey. Pamuk does not wish to "praise it [his library] in the manner of one who proclaims his love of books to let you know how exceptional he is," for he admits that he still lives "in a country that views the nonreader as the norm and the reader as somehow defective" (*Other Colors* 107). The figure of the reader as a deviation from the norm seems to inform Pamuk's passionate "like and dislike" of books (108). The rest of the essay focuses on de-collection—editing the library, the "thrill of degradation" of a book that no longer has a place on his shelves. From "a Political Confession, a Bad Translation, a Fashionable Novel" (108) to "Turkish literature . . . by half-witted, mediocre, moderately successful, bald, male, degenerate writers between the ages of fifty and seventy" (109), decollecting (not merely unpacking) reshapes Pamuk's library. And as he states, "I'm not ashamed of the book itself, I'm ashamed of having once accorded it importance. . . . My library is not a source of pride but of self-revenge and oppression" (109).

Thoughts about assigning and rescinding importance to books quickly transform into larger reflections on the evaluation of non-Western literatures in global literary traffic. Reading as part of the formation of the self is key to Pamuk's reflections. In "On Reading: Words or Images," he states: "Between the ages of sixteen and twenty-six, reading was central to my efforts to make something of myself, elevate my consciousness, and thereby give shape to my soul. What sort of man should I be? What was the meaning of the world? How far could my thoughts stretch, my interests, my dreams, the land I could see in my mind's eye?" (110). This formation of the reader's self as a function of his or her location in the world emerges as "bliss-in-seclusion," which Pamuk asserts is essential for him as a reader and as a writer. Pamuk mentions bliss-in-seclusion in great detail in his Nobel Prize acceptance speech, "My Father's Suitcase": "When a writer shuts himself up in a room for years on end to hone his craft—to create a world—if he uses his secret wounds as his starting point, he is, whether he knows it or not, putting a great faith in humanity." In this speech, two inherited libraries—his father's library of 1,500 volumes and the suitcase that contains his father's writings—transform into an inhabited library that Pamuk draws on as he pursues his career as an author. The inherited library, of course, is also a bifurcated library, with books from the Turkish tradition whose importance in the reading culture of Turkey was later replaced by well-known Western works, especially in the light of the cultural reorientation under Mustafa Kemal Atatürk:

> In the same way, there was a world literature, and its center, too, was very far away from me. Actually what I had in mind was Western, not world, literature, and we Turks were outside it. My father's library was evidence of this. At one end, there were Istanbul's books—our literature, our local world, in all its beloved detail—and at the other end were the books from this other, Western, world, to which our own bore no resemblance, to which our lack of resemblance gave us both pain and hope.

This hierarchical division between Western and non-Western literatures, created primarily through a perceived inherent superiority of Western literary works, becomes central to Pamuk's reading (and rereading) of *The Thousand and One Nights*. In the essay "To Read or Not to Read," Pamuk credits Antoine Galland with the introduction of *The Thousand and One Nights* (*The Arabian Nights*) to the European literary readership but also notes that the recognition of the work as a literary masterpiece in the Eastern world came only through its recirculation via Paris, "because we live in a culture that had severed its links with its own cultural heritage and forgotten what it owes to India and Iran, surrendering itself to the jolts of Western literature" (*Other Colors* 120). Moreover, as he admits, "young Turks like me who considered themselves modern viewed the classics of Eastern literature as one might a dark and impenetrable forest" (121), a feeling that he was able to overcome only slowly, as he learned to appreciate the "shape, proportions, passions, . . . [and] back-street flavor" of *The Thousand and One Nights* (122).

But it is not merely the shape, proportions, and passions of a work of Eastern literature that Pamuk seeks to promote in his novels and nonfiction writings. The tensions inherent in perceived notions of West and East—derivative modernity of the West and traditionalism of the East; enlightened, rational Western discourse and mysterious, emotional Eastern discourse—are at the heart of Pamuk's work as a writer. His writings on books, readers, reading, and libraries become extensions of the tensions, differences, and inequalities that he perceives when non-Western literatures are compared with Western literatures. Instead of a lopsided promotion of the superiority of non-Western literature, he engages with the complex reception of non-Western works of literature, working through his own prejudices as a reader who is historically and geoculturally situated.

In "What Is the History of Books?," Robert Darnton states that "books belong to circuits of communication that operate in consistent patterns" (206). As

Pamuk's writings on books and libraries reveal, the consistency of those patterns is historically conditioned, culturally determined, and politically charged. The functioning of circuits of communication is also dependent on socioeconomic and historical factors. Reading Pamuk's works with an awareness of print-cultural histories can augment students' understanding of the political stakes of the assumed hierarchies of Eastern and Western literatures. A focus on the books and libraries in his novels and essays can reveal that books are not mere vessels of printed matter and libraries are not mere collections of books. Due attention to cultures of literacy can refute the nativist culturalism of characters such as Dr. Fine in *The New Life*, who denounces books as instruments of a "Great Conspiracy" of the West. As Orhan, the narrator of *The New Life*, claims, "So it was that as I read my point of view was transformed by the book, and the book was transformed by my point view" (6).

NOTES

[1] See Gürçağlar.

[2] This essay quotes from the 1982 edition of *Cevdet Bey ve Oğullari.*

[3] This essay quotes from Maureen Freely's translation of *Snow* published by Alfred A. Knopf in 2004.

[4] This essay quotes from Güneli Gün's translation of *The New Life* published by Vintage Books in 1998.

[5] Translations from *Öteki Renkler* are mine. Quotations from *Other Colors* are from Maureen Freely's translation published by Alfred A. Knopf in 2007.

Border Crossing with *The Black Book*: Overcoming Spatial, Cultural, and Linguistic Distances

Didem Havlioğlu

After I posted the final grades for my Islamic Literatures course at İstanbul Şehir University in 2012, my student Abdullah visited my office. As I prepared to explain his grade, he announced that he wanted to work more on the paper he wrote on Orhan Pamuk's *The Black Book*. It is always a pleasant surprise to see a student expanding the limits of our classroom. His paper eventually became one of three published articles that evolved from the class's reading of *The Black Book* (Karabaşoğlu; Karakaş; Özyürek).

The Islamic Literatures course in which I taught *The Black Book* took place over two semesters at the University of Utah and İstanbul Şehir University. My intention for teaching the novel as part of the series of courses, which was designed to introduce the Islamic canon and literary aesthetics since the advent of Islam, is to bring our historical investigation to the literary culture of today. The novel not only provides grounds for discussion of "the Islamic," aesthetics, and literary history but also problematizes binaries such as Eastern/Western, secular/religious, classical/modern, and national/global.

A vehicle for talking about issues related to world literature and the novel genre, *The Black Book* is also an exciting puzzle for students. It tells the story of an artist's unique quest, similar to that of Stephen Dedalus but from the Eastern part of the world. Pamuk has admitted that he found his literary voice with *The Black Book*, and we cannot help but wonder how this quest of an artist is different from the ones we witness in the modern West (Gülsoy). Tracing the making of an author in his own literary history is a fruitful practice for students of comparative literature.

Nevertheless, *The Black Book* is a challenge to read in a college classroom. Its dense narrative, which has been internationally acclaimed in academia, can be an obstacle for students. Another challenge is the novel's affinity with the wide range of world literature, in particular with classical Islamic texts, which unfortunately are still peripheral for the overwhelmingly Eurocentric literary world. Accordingly, my approach to teaching *The Black Book* is historical and aims to lay the ground for our discussions with the literary history of Islamic literatures. During class discussions and through a survey I conducted after students' initial encounter with the novel, I identified some factors that prevent students from understanding the multiple layers of the novel. Interestingly, students both in North America and Turkey reported similar difficulties, which can be described as experiencing the novel as distant from their own backgrounds. For instance, students had difficulty identifying critical details necessary to understanding the close connection between the visual background and narrative structure of the novel; neither the students in North America nor the ones in Turkey were familiar with the 1970s Istanbul depicted in the novel. In addition, the North Americans had never been to Istanbul and the Turkish students were born and raised in different parts of the city. In other words, the distance between the students and the narrative was multidimensional: between Salt Lake City and Istanbul, between various neighborhoods of Istanbul, and between the time of the novel and the present.

In this article I share three major discussions I developed to overcome spatial, cultural, and linguistic distances between my students and the novel. Before I review the three discussions, I address the student profiles in both countries and then explain my contextualization of *The Black Book* among the primary texts of my Islamic Literatures course.

The students' academic background in North America and in Turkey was similar. In North America they were comparative literature majors who had already read works of world literature by James Joyce, Marcel Proust, Doris Lessing, Fyodor Dostoevsky, and Vladimir Nabokov. Almost all of them had a command of a second language. Most of them knew little about Islamic literature—let alone Turkish literature—though some had lived in the Middle East. The students in Turkey, in contrast, were Turkish literature majors. The curriculum of the Turkish literature program at İstanbul Şehir University is designed with a comparative approach: the Islamic Literatures courses are taught parallel to Modern Literatures courses and both are mandatory. The average class size is about twenty students, which includes three to five visiting students from Europe. Most of the students were born and raised in traditional Turkish Muslim families in Istanbul.

Although I teach the Islamic Literature courses in English in Turkey, I encourage students to read the texts in their original language if they are able to and to incorporate their perspectives into our class discussions. I chose Maureen Freely's English translation of *The Black Book*, which is more faithful to the original text. I discuss issues of reading in translation in detail below.

I select readings that prepare students for *The Black Book*, including those that discuss the Islamic and Ottoman literary background of the novel (Moran, "Üstkurmaca"; Kim, "Mürşid"). A further note about the course name, Islamic Literatures, and its scope: *Islamic* connotes neither a Third World literature nor a national affiliation; it signifies the religion and its effect on every aspect of the culture. My course discusses the cultural aspects of Islam in literary texts, but it is not affiliated with religious studies per se. Marshall Hodgson's term *Islamicate* would be appropriate (59), but I do not want to risk losing prospective students who may shy away from the course because of the unfamiliar term. Instead, by making the literatures of the title plural, I hint at the many Islams in various times and places and the diversity within the tradition, including in the religion.

By the time we read *The Black Book*, students have read extensively in Islamic literatures. The course opens with David Damrosch's *How to Read World Literature* in order to gain familiarity with problems and terminology. We read the classic debate between Fredric Jameson and Aijaz Ahmad to situate the concepts of Islamic and Third World literature. After laying out the theoretical background, we start reading literary texts from the pre-Islamic period. We discuss the spiral narrative structure of *The Arabian Nights*, storytelling for survival and healing, and the interconnectedness of words and sexuality. The second group of texts focuses on the story of Joseph. We compare its telling in religious texts—the Qur'an and the Old Testament—and its retelling in literary versions such as Şeyyad Hamza's *The Story of Joseph* ("Koran"; "Old Testament"; Hickman). The readings present the narrative transformation of a story across centuries, religions, and languages. We also discuss the concepts of beauty and love and their relation to spirituality in the context of the story of Joseph. The third group of texts concentrates on the Sufi traditions of Islam. We start with a selection from Louis Massignon's writings on Mansur al-Hallâc, Farid ud-Din Attâr's *The Conference of the Birds*, and a selection of Jalal al-Din Rûmî's poetry (*Rumi*). We examine allegory and intertextuality as common literary tools in the Sufi tradition. This section ends with the Mevlevî Ottoman poet Şeyh Galip and his poem *Hüsn ü Aşk* (*Beauty and Love*), along with a commentary on the text by Victoria Holbrook in *Unreadable Shores of Love*.

Alongside *The Black Book* I suggest further readings, such as Pamuk's memoir *Istanbul*. I also recommend Nüket Esen's edited volume *Kara Kitap Üzerine Yazılar* as needed. Each of the following sections describes discussion sessions I have devised to help students overcome the various forms of distance—spatial, cultural, and linguistic—that they perceive between themselves and the novel.

Spatial Distance

The novel is set in 1970s Istanbul, which plays a significant role in its major motives and themes, such as the feeling of loss and the personal association with the urban past. The way the city is depicted spatially in the novel closely relates to the novel's spiral narrative structure. I introduce a discussion that helps students to visualize and contextualize the Istanbul of the novel in order to close the gap—geographically and temporally—between students' experience and the text.

The discussion opens with the following question: Would you like to take a walk with the protagonist, Galip, through the backstreets of Istanbul? Galip is an upper-middle-class man who was born and raised in the bourgeois neighborhood

Nişantaşı. My students in North America commented that Galip would not be a perfect tour guide, as he stays primarily in his neighborhood, but it would still be interesting to see the city from his perspective. They compared Galip's alienation and isolation to that of Franz Kafka's Gregor Samsa. Students in Turkey likewise commented that it would be interesting to visit Galip's Istanbul, as most of them feel like foreigners in his neighborhood.

The first activity in this session aims to help students visualize Galip's Istanbul. I project a map of Istanbul, and the students' task is to find each neighborhood depicted in the novel. I break them into groups and assign each group different sections of the novel. They need to find the neighborhood and place names, such as Nişantaşı, Bosphorus, Süleymaniye, Bakırköy, as well as the City-of-Hearts apartments, Alâaddin's shop, Bedii Usta's mannequin shop, and the mosques. To visualize the era, we look at Ara Güler's photographs of Istanbul from the 1950s through the 1970s. We compare pictures of today's Nişantaşı shops, which feature luxury brands such as Armani and Cartier, with the description of Alâaddin's humble shop.

In the novel Istanbul is a geographical place as well as a subtext that sets the mood of loss and melancholy. The points we have identified on the map show a small area with tangled circular streets. Likewise, the buildings, such as the City-of-Hearts apartment with its dark airshaft and the minarets with spiral stairs, reflect both the circular narrative structure and the feeling of loss. Seeing the maze-like streets and the unique layout of buildings helps students understand how Pamuk uses physical space to set the atmosphere.

Each space in the novel has a historical significance for the narrative. For instance, the City-of-Hearts apartment—which alludes to Land of the Heart in Şeyh Galip's poem—stands for Galip's personal history (130).[1] The Bosphorus, as it appears in Celâl's column entitled "When the Bosphorus Dries Up," discloses the city's history of thousands of years (16). Celâl reveals the hidden treasures buried at the bottom of the Bosphorus, such as Byzantine coins and a bandit's car wreck. The juxtaposition between personal and collective histories unravels Galip's vulnerability in a giant city where his inspiration is lost.

During our discussion of the city space a student brought up a passage that takes place when Galip leaves his neighborhood and goes to Bakırköy, at the far western side of the city: "During the long journey, Galip began thinking it was not Istanbul he saw flowing past his window but another city altogether" (123). Galip's alienation from this neighborhood represents the literal and metaphorical limits of his world. While looking for his wife, Rüya, Galip crosses the borders of his neighborhood; the more he discovers about his city, the more he learns about himself.

The next exercise helps students link the city map to the narrative structure of the novel. I ask them to make another map, but this time as an outline of the novel. They usually come up with two columns, one for Galip's story and another for

Celâl's writings. We compare the novel's narrative structure with our previous readings and identify its resemblance to the circular structure of *The Arabian Nights*, which is mentioned occasionally in the novel. In both *The Black Book* and *The Arabian Nights*, the structure serves the purposes of the narrative, creating a circular motion and the feeling of being lost. For instance, Shehrazad entraps the king not only with her body but also with her web of words, telling him an unfinished story every night to distract him and gain time. Likewise, the web of Istanbul streets, echoed in the narrative structure, sets the mood of loss as Galip searches for his missing wife. The discussion sessions on spatial distance proved that visual materials and relevant exercises help acquaint students with the city and eventually relate it to the narrative and the overall themes of the novel.

Cultural Distance

One of the main themes of *The Black Book*, the making of a writer, is layered with cultural background that is embedded in the literary works mentioned in the novel. Since Islamic literatures take the center stage in the narrative, my students are prepared to pick the clues. However, to grasp the deeper levels of the novel students need to compare the literary works they have already read with *The Black Book* and identify their common aesthetic tools. The objective of this discussion is to help them connect the clues and red herrings of the puzzle presented in the novel. We start with the following question: How would you categorize *The Black Book* as a literary genre?

Our first discussion revolves around the novel form and its traditional association with Western literary history. If the novel is a Western genre, *The Black Book*'s distinct affinity with Islamic literary history makes it an unusual novel. Although it appears to be a detective fiction or a love story, considered within Islamic literary history it is the quest of an artist in search of his inspiration. The clues to this identification are found in abundant references to other literary texts, such as Şeyh Galip's allegorical poem *Hüsn ü Aşk* (*Beauty and Love*), which is also seemingly a love story. In his introduction to *Hüsn ü Aşk*, the poet Galip explains that he wrote the narrative poem to mark his place as the last representative in the literary genealogy of Mevlevî poets that starts with Attâr and Rûmî. Similar to Şeyh Galip, Pamuk's protagonist Galip follows his predecessor Celâl and his writings as guides in his quest.

The main assignment in this section is to make a list of books and authors mentioned in the novel. When students pay close attention to such details, they recognize that the epigraph of chapter 33 contains a significant clue: "'The mystery I took from the *Mathnawi*' Sheikh Galip" (397). This line establishes the literary link between Rûmî, Şeyh Galip, and Pamuk, and offers an entry point to the deeper meanings of the novel. I ask the students to go back to Şeyh Galip's *Hüsn ü Aşk* and find the line in the poem. Then we recall Holbrook's discussion of intertextuality in Sufi literature (32). The epigraph is extracted from the following lines:

> I spied new design in that treasury
> I found that cache, and I spent it freely
> I took its secrets from the *Masnavi*
> I stole, but I stole common property
> Now you, too, endeavor to understand
> Come, steal that pearl, spend it at your command! (Holbrook 35)

Şeyh Galip connects his literary genealogy to Rûmî's *Mesnevî*, and declares that he stole "common property." Şeyh Galip refers to literary history as common property and to poetry as its craft. By referring to *Mesnevî* without naming Rûmî, Galip makes use of *telmih*, a common Ottoman literary practice. This rhetorical device allows poets to create tight narratives and practice word economy. Sometimes a sentence or even a word serves to call to mind another text or a set of texts. *Telmih* is an allusion or reference but also a reminder that each text is meaningful in relation to others; as an aesthetic practice *telmih* assumes a collective memory of texts that is shared by poets and their audiences. Moreover, it adds to the enjoyment of reading. According to Al-Gazâlî, "pleasure is a form of cognition" and it is based on collective memory (qtd. in Behrens-Abouseif 23). Seen in these terms, the cultural distance students experience is related to time difference and the loss of collective memory. Although they become familiar with Islamic literatures in this class, they find the connection of Islamic texts to the secular novel unusual. This discussion can naturally lead to another consideration of the terms *Islamic* and *modern*.

Reflecting on the overt symbolism of the character names such as Galip (as Şeyh Galip) and Celâl (as Celâleddîn Rûmî), the class realizes that Pamuk not only makes reference to literary works but also suggests an organic link between his characters and major personas within the Islamic literary tradition. This becomes particularly clear as we pay attention to the nature of Galip and Celâl's relationship through writing. While Galip searches for his lost wife, he also, by reading Celâl's columns, searches for his inspiration, and in the end he begins writing Celâl's columns. In terms of modern aesthetics, which values individual creativity, Galip's losing himself and adopting Celâl's persona might seem unusual. But in Islamic Ottoman aesthetic terms, Galip is legitimately stealing (or inheriting) Celâl's literary persona, a natural part of the process of becoming a writer.

This discussion prepares students to solve the puzzle at the heart of the novel. It was challenging for students to contextualize fresh information on Islamic literature in *The Black Book*, but it was ultimately rewarding when they were able to write their own reflections.

Linguistic Distance

The objective of the discussion on language and translation is for students to understand Pamuk's use of Turkish to construct the story as well as the way the author's language is treated in translations. For this discussion we compare our main text, Freely's translation of the novel, with Güneli Gün's translation.

First, I give a brief lecture on Pamuk's use of Turkish. In addition to the significant meanings of the character names such as Galip, Celâl, and Rüya (Turkish for "dream") and the place-names such as the City-of-Hearts ("Şehr-i Kalp" in Turkish), Pamuk uses Ottoman Turkish, that is, Turkish inflected with Arabic and Persian words and constructions. Moreover, he transliterates these names to emphasize the Ottoman features, such as the accents in the names Celâl and Alâaddin. When Pamuk published *The Black Book* in 1990, Ottoman transliteration was rarely used in modern Turkish.[2] However, from the first decade of the twenty-first century the use of accents saw a revival as a consequence of neo-Ottomanist movements. In 1990, when *The Black Book* was published, Pamuk's critique of the republican cultural revolution was significant in its own right, separate from the romantic, revivalist ideas associated with today's nationalist neo-Ottomanism. I point students to further reading, such as essays by Reşat Kasaba, Çağlar Keyder, and Yeşim Arat (Bozdoğan and Kasaba, 15–36, 37–52, 95–113), which offer deeper understandings of the implications of Turkish modernity.

For our comparative readings of the two translations of *The Black Book*, I assign students the first chapters and ask them to compare the use of diction and spelling in the light of my lecture. My goal—Damrosch calls this "reading intelligently"—is to distinguish translators' strategies "to mind—and mend—the gap between then and now, here and there, another language and our own" (*What* 84). Students recognize each translator's adjustment to accommodate Pamuk's nuanced use of language. Freely adds sentences in the English text, such as "A was for *at*, the Turkish word for horse" to make the meaning clear and remind readers that they are reading a translation (5). Gün's version also makes adjustments, to explain linguistic points such as the strategic use of transliteration in the original. Gün transliterates some of the names: Celâl becomes "Jelal" in her translation. It is as though Gün wanted to hint at the connection between the character's name and the English transliteration of the name of the poet Jalal al-Din Rûmî. Freely, whose translation more closely follows the original, does not change the spelling of the major characters' names. Obviously, translating names and their symbolic and instrumental roles is a critical choice translators must make. Freely places the meaning of "Rüya" as "dream" in parenthesis (8). Sevinç Türkkan discusses the issue of translating names with a number of examples from Gün's text. For instance, Gün resolves the issue of names by including a whole new sentence: "It hadn't surprised him that Rüya meant dream; but later, when they began figuring out the secondary meanings of the names, they were astonished to find in a dictionary of Ottoman Turkish that Galip meant 'victor' and Jelal 'fury'" (qtd. in Türkkan, "(British) Reception" 45).

A comparative discussion of the two translations of *The Black Book* allows students to recognize necessary adjustments made to the text. The exercise encourages them to pay attention to detail, to develop skills for reading translations, and to recognize each translator's strategies to overcome linguistic distances. Moreover, the discussion on the use of language in the translations adds another perspective to their understanding of the narrative in the context of world literature. Students who read the text in Turkish had the opportunity to compare the original to the translations.

Teaching *The Black Book* in North America and Turkey in the context of Islamic and world literatures offers an opportunity to teach across space, time, and language. The most crucial part of my course planning was the selection of the readings. Readings allowed students to gradually get acquainted with Islamic literary history so that when they read *The Black Book* they could make connections among the texts and actively participate in discussions. Some students, like Abdullah, took up the challenge of the novel, while others were overwhelmed with the intensity of our readings and discussions. The novel requires all the attention one can willingly give. Even though the course allotted three full weeks to the novel, we did not have sufficient time for in-depth comparative readings with other literary works. The final papers were eye-opening for me. Some papers chose to focus on a single motif, such as the dream as literary inspiration or the mirror as a reflection of reality. Some others tried experimental readings, such as the novel as a *shehrengiz* (a city thriller in Islamic literature) or as a Sufi transcendental travelogue. After reading these creative final papers, I began to think that a student conference, allowing students to comment on one another's ideas, might be a constructive way to conclude the course. Overall, reading *The Black Book* was a rewarding experience for me and for my students. We learned how to stretch our limits of reading a novel by engaging the concepts of Islamic literature and modern aesthetics.

NOTES

[1]This essay quotes from Maureen Freely's translation of *The Black Book* published by Vintage Books in 2006.

[2]In the wake of the language reform in the first half of the twentieth century, the use of accents on vowels was avoided, as it was considered a residue of Ottoman Turkish.

The World as Book: Teaching *The New Life* Intertextually with Dante, Borges, and Calvino

Delia Ungureanu

Orhan Pamuk's novels have a twofold appeal in teaching the world and its literature in the age of globalization. They make sophisticated use of the narrative techniques of the Western tradition of the novel, even as they decenter these techniques by approaching them from an oblique perspective. Pamuk's novels take on different meanings when read in a Turkish context and in a global context. *The New Life*, Pamuk's fifth novel, sold 200,000 copies in only two months in Turkey—its title, coincidentally, resonated for the Turkish audience with a political reform that was just being implemented, but it was equally a book consciously written as a work of world literature. Intensely engaged with major Western precursors, *The New Life* can well be taught in a world literature context with the instruments provided by the writer himself: the Western intertexts that Pamuk identifies as the literary tradition that informed his writing. In this way, we can understand Pamuk as a writer from the periphery of world literature by measuring his distance from the major centers of novelistic production and his creative defamiliarization of the novel form known to Western readers.

Reader-reception theory has shown that we understand and appropriate a new fictional world by reading it through our horizon of expectations (Jauss) and against our dispositions of reading (Iser). *The New Life* repeatedly evokes three precursors—Dante, Jorge Luis Borges, and Italo Calvino—through which a class can learn about broad processes of intertextual creation, canon formation, and center-periphery relations. These writers can also elucidate Pamuk's novel in particular.

For a graduate class, the terminology proposed by Hans Jauss and by Wolfgang Iser can help students understand better that the reading of world literature is shaped by the target culture in which the reading is performed. Also useful is Heinrich Plett's article "Intertextualities" from his book *Intertextuality* (3–29). Plett's specialized terminology shows structurally the nature of the dialogue between texts, probing how reverential or how ironic they are toward the tradition they are engaging with. An undergraduate syllabus might consist largely or entirely of primary texts and eschew theoretical readings, but it can be helpful to begin discussion by framing the twofold character of Pamuk's novel within the world literary market today, as proposed by Pascale Casanova in her influential book, *The World Republic of Letters*. She identifies contemporary "world fiction" as works that are capable of becoming best-sellers because they display patterns that respond to our horizon of expectations for such works, combining elitist narrative techniques with marketable form. Today world fiction employs all the successful recipes of nineteenth-century popular fiction: the adventure novel, detective novel, love story, travel novel, and, best of all, a novel made of and about novels (237).

In Casanova's terms, the world author is one who is conscious of a book's destiny on a global market, and Pamuk is no exception. *The New Life* is particularly interesting in this respect, as it directly thematizes issues of circulation and the effect of a foreign work on its readers—particularly on the novel's hero, Osman. The novel doesn't identify the book that changes Osman's life, but we can see its effect on him as he makes a journey to find the gaze and light that guided him throughout the book. Only at the end of *The New Life* do we infer that the book Osman was reading is the very book we've been reading. By the end the world text has come to comprise virtually all possible texts and readings. Within this theoretical frame both undergraduate and graduate classes can address Pamuk's dialogue with Western literature, following two major issues that *The New Life* outlines: understanding the book as a way to experience the world in a nutshell; and bridging spatial and temporal cultural distance through universal themes of existential appeal, such as the mystical love relation that Pamuk takes up from Dante's *Vita Nuova*.

The World in a Book: Globalism and World Vision

To address the issue of the world book as a larger-than-life experience, it is helpful to frame it within the author's theoretical position-takings:

> [T]hey reproach me for my lack of life experience, they say that my books are made from other books and not from reality. So what? And, in the end, if the story of Osman at the start of *The New Life*, when he's living with his mother, is literally my story, what does that matter? What matters is the distance, the difference, finding one's own voice; a book has to render the globality of a world vision. Of course, we never succeed, we always hope that we'll be able to write that book which reminds us of the whole world, we hope and we fail.
> (Pamuk, "Orhan Pamuk: Un écrivain"; my trans.)

Pamuk's engagement both with the West and with Turkishness and Middle Eastern identity should be approached through his contact with Western written culture. As he confessed to Horace Engdahl, permanent secretary of the Swedish Academy in 2006, Pamuk experienced the typical anxieties of a peripheral writer when confronted with powerful cultural centers like London, Paris, and New York. Living in New York in the late 1980s, while his then wife was studying at Columbia University and he was still a young writer with no international reputation, Pamuk reflected on the distance from his home culture, and he began asking identity questions within a global frame: "It was then that I understood that the Turkish cultural road and identity should only be a sort of ultra-Occidentalism" (Pamuk, "Interview with Orhan Pamuk").

So the notion of home was born abroad for Pamuk. In New York he discovered the old Sufi texts that had been eclipsed by the Turkish linguistic and cultural reforms of the 1920s, which he read together with postmodern Western writers, whose world vision he saw as similar. In his interview with Engdahl, he remarked, "I began to read old Sufi allegories, old classic texts of Islamic mysticism, Sufi texts . . . with an eye on Borges and Calvino, who taught me to look at literary texts as structures that have metaphysical qualities." Building on Pamuk's suggestion of the importance of these predecessors, a course can effectively explore these relations through a comparative close reading with Dante's *Vita Nuova*, the most obvious intertext for *The New Life*, together with Calvino's *If on a Winter's Night a Traveler* and Borges's short story "El Aleph." All three texts seek to encompass the entire world through their structures while they address problems of memory, reading and writing, and the world. Further, they engage with love as a global theme and with reading as an experience that can bridge spatial, temporal, and cultural distance. We see in these works that intertextuality involves the heart as much as the mind.

Introducing the Comparison

I open the conversation with a visual representation that functions as a common denominator to frame the four writers. To introduce Dante it is useful to offer students a medieval visual representation. As Douwe Draaisma writes, the miniatures and marginal drawings that accompanied medieval manuscripts "were more than a simple alternative for words; they were intended to do what is implicit in the etymology of 'illustration,' illuminate the text, so that it could find its way more easily into memory" (33). A visual way into the comparing of texts is particularly apt for Pamuk, a former painter, and can provide an added connection if *The New Life* is taught together with *My Name Is Red* or *The Museum of Innocence*.

To connect *The New Life* with Dante's *Vita Nuova*—similarly preoccupied with memory and reading—it is effective to use an iconographic representation of the world as the memory of books or the world as the Book of Books. In the eighth-century *Codex Amiatinus*, we see the prophet Ezra transcribing a passage from the Bible in his own book: the left-hand page shows an already written text, whereas the right side is a blank page on which Ezra is poised to write ("Ezra"). Behind Ezra stands a cabinet showing a neatly arranged set of similar books whose position in the background next to Ezra's inclined head suggests that they are the objectification of his memory. As Draaisma argues, a book—and, by extension, a library—was a common metaphor for memory in medieval Europe (32). Memory is here understood as a library that stores the knowledge of the past. Here it functions as a good visual representation of Pamuk's memory of the world writers whom the author references explicitly or obliquely. The world enclosed between the covers of a book is also a metaphor that brings together the Judeo-Christian tradition and the Sufi tradition, so it's a good starting point for understanding Pamuk's novel as a dialogue between the West and the East. This image can introduce the comparison between the opening and closing of Pamuk's *The New Life* and Dante's *Vita Nuova* ("The New Life"), which are both constructed symmetrically around the metaphor of the book of memory. For a graduate class this idea can be framed through a more specialized understanding of the representation of memory in the late Middle Ages, as in Thomas Aquinas, illustrating the medieval tradition of the history of the book: "Books stood at the beginning and end of his memory. The fact that this memory finally became a metaphorical book, constantly filling and enriching itself, 'as page is added to page,' was a tribute not only to Thomas, but also to the book" (Draaisma 32).

Dante's book opens with the image of the book of memory, written by God, from which he transcribes; the moment of revelation triggers the writing: "In that part of the book of my memory before which is little that can be read, there is a rubric, saying *Incipit Vita Nuova.* Under such rubric I find written many things, and among them the words which I propose to copy into this little book, if not all of them, at least their substance" (*New Life* 3). Pamuk opens his novel with Osman reading the novel that reveals to him his life in a nutshell from that moment until his death. It's as if Osman can look into the memory of the whole universe and see his life: "the book worked its influence not only on my soul but on every aspect of my identity . . . my mind barely aware that I was reading, and my whole life was changing as I read the new words on each new page" (3).[1] Like Dante, Pamuk frames his novel with the image of the universe as a book in which the narrator sees his own death, and the novel's end is foretold at its opening, where we read that "[s]omewhere in the final pages, I wanted to say I too had come up with the same ideas. It was much later, after I had been totally overtaken by the world the book described, that I actually saw death appear in the half-light before dawn, radiant as an angel. My own death" (6). Dante closes his autobiography by announcing his intention to write the *Divine Comedy*, made possible by this new life that opens up when his book ends: "it was given unto me to behold a very wonderful vision: wherein I saw things which determined me that I would say nothing further of this most blessed one, until such time came as I could discourse more worthily concerning her. . . . [I]t is my hope that I shall yet write concerning her what hath not before been written of any woman" (*New Life* 86–87). Symmetrically, Pamuk returns in the final passage of his novel to the dazzling light of the opening, the narrator anticipating his new life that begins with death, which coincides with the ending of the novel that we, along with Osman, are reading: "my eyes dazzled in amazement and fear, just as I had once looked into the incredible light that surged from the book, I would be instantly transported into a new world. I knew it was the end of my life. And yet I had only wanted to return home; I absolutely had no wish for death, nor for crossing over into the new life" (*New Life* 296).

Pamuk's opening and closing pages suggest the author's understanding of globality, when Osman sees in the dazzling light the major scenes that will be repeated throughout the book as he searches for his beloved:

> In the light that surged from the book into my face, I was terrified to see shabby rooms, frenetic buses, bedraggled people, faint letters, lost towns, lost lives, phantoms. A journey was involved; it was always about a journey. I beheld a gaze . . . a tender gaze that had long been free of guilt and blame . . . the book must be, of course, about me. Someone had already imagined my ideas and put them down. (5–6)

It is useful to compare this compression of a total world into an infinite series of superimposed images to Borges's "El Aleph," where the narrator sees projected onto a single point the whole universe, including the universe that we're reading:

> I saw in a desk drawer (and the handwriting made me tremble) obscene, incredible, detailed letters that Beatrice had sent Carlos Argentino, saw a beloved monument in Chacarita, saw the horrendous remains of what had once, deliciously, been Beatriz Viterbo, saw the circulation of my dark blood, saw the coils and springs of love and the alterations of death, saw the Aleph from everywhere at once, saw the earth in the Aleph, and the Aleph in the earth and the earth in the Aleph, saw my face, my viscera, saw your face, and I felt dizzy, and I wept, because my eyes had seen the secret, hypothetical object whose name has been usurped by men, but which no man has ever truly looked upon: the inconceivable universe. (*Collected Fictions* 283–84)

The representation of the totality of the universe that both Pamuk and Borges explore points back to the last pages of the *Divine Comedy*. This major intertext may be more successful with a graduate class because it requires more specialized knowledge of the medieval Catholic theology and cosmology that Dante, Pamuk, and Borges are all engaging with. Dante's Empyrean becomes in Pamuk the infinite light of the angel of love and is epitomized in Borges's Aleph. Interestingly, the images contemplated by Dante as he sees the Empyrean already appear as bound together in a single volume, which is this world:

> I saw how it contains within its depths
> all things bound in a single book by love
> of which creation is the scattered leaves:
> . . . .
>
> so did I strive with this new mystery:
> I yearned to know how could our image fit
> into that circle, how could it conform; . . .
> the Love that moves the sun and the other stars. (*Divine Comedy* 392–94)

The representation of the world's globality and the tracing of the universe's structure can also be discussed with Calvino's *If on a Winter's Night a Traveler.* Calvino understands globality as literature woven intertextually. The book inside his book leads to other invented novelists; it is a book made of book openings that feed into one another. Calvino's novel is made of alternative stories: the story of reading his own novel and those interconnected with it and the love story between the reader ("you") and a girl named Ludmila that ends in marriage, unlike the open-ended book that they try to read throughout the novel: "I am becoming convinced that the world wants to tell me something, send me messages, signals, warnings" (54). In both Calvino's and Pamuk's texts, the book becomes the reader's journey to identify the fragments that make up the structure of the world. Osman's repeated experiences of traveling by bus, watching movies, and searching for the lost gaze of his beloved—like Beatrice's eyes guiding Dante's journey—are another way for the reader to experience the world.

For graduate students, the discussion may be supplemented with theoretical texts that focus on literature's effect on readers and their experience of the world. Umberto Eco's *Six Walks in the Fictional Woods* speaks about literature as framing an uncontrollable, meaningless world in order to make sense of it. Another useful theoretical text is Iser's *The Act of Reading*, which shows how texts change readers' points of view and orientations and create desires rather than gratify them. The formative and educational value of books that open up a universe would be an ultimate contextualization for what works of world literature can do.

Love and Its Effects

Books that are heavily dependent on intertextuality, like *The New Life*, often focus on the circulation of texts and their effect on readers. In Pamuk, as in Dante, reading can spark falling in love. Class discussion on the theme of love provoked by reading can be prompted by visual imagery, for example, Dante Gabriel Rossetti's *Paolo and Francesca da Rimini* (Rossetti), which illustrates the famous passage in canto 5 of Dante's *Inferno* in which Francesca describes the start of her ill-fated romance with Paolo:

> We were reading one day, for pleasure,
> of Lancelot, how Love beset him;
> we were alone and without any suspicion.
> . . . .
> When we read that the yearned-for smile was
> Kissed by so great a lover, he, who will never be
> separated from me, kissed my mouth all trembling.
> Galeotto was the book and he who wrote it:
> that day we read there no further. (93; 5: 127–38)

Through this visual counterpart, students can address the theme of love within the larger discussion of experiencing the world through books, as well as the effects of reading.

"El Aleph" provides a further way to approach the theme of love in *The New Life* in dialogue with Dante, because Borges openly takes Beatrice as a model for his character Beatriz. Neither Pamuk nor Borges limits themes to national boundaries, engaging instead with the whole tradition of world literature. To find our way into the theme of love as a dialogue between Pamuk, Borges, and Dante, we can first compare how Pamuk and Borges theorize universal themes in relation to local specificity. Borges's essay "The Argentine Writer and Tradition" uncovers his thoughts on the subject:

> What is Argentine tradition? I believe that this question poses no problem and can easily be answered. I believe that our tradition is the whole of Western culture, and I also believe that we have a right to this tradition, a greater right than that which the inhabitants of one Western nation or another may have. . . . [W]e must believe that the universe is our birthright and try out every subject; we cannot confine ourselves to what is Argentine in order to be Argentine because either it is our inevitable destiny to be Argentine, in which case we will be Argentine whatever we do, or being Argentine is a mere affectation, a mask. (425–27)

In a similar vein, Pamuk remarked to Judy Stone that "I'm tired of being a Turkish writer, in a sense. What I do is fiction. I sometimes feel I don't belong to any country. If I belong to a republic, I belong to a republic of literature" (Pamuk, "Turkish Writer").

Pamuk and Borges teach us not to fixate on local color and national specificity. As Borges ironically remarks in his essay, "The Argentine cult of local color is a recent European cult that nationalists should reject as a foreign import. . . . [W]e can believe in the possibility of being Argentine without abounding in local color" (423–24). Being Turkish didn't prevent Pamuk from engaging, in *The New Life*, with writers as diverse as Dante, Novalis, E. T. A. Hoffmann,

Borges, and Calvino, just as being Argentine didn't prevent Borges from engaging, in "El Aleph," with texts as different as *Hamlet*, the *Vita Nuova*, the *Divine Comedy*, and *The Arabian Nights*. Locally specific themes may fail to resonate with distant audiences or may suffer in translation, but a theme like life-changing love transcends local particulars to address humanity at large. As Pamuk says, "[Y]ou're writing something in your loneliness, but then there's a secret or unexpressed belief that it will address the hearts of other readers, it's a strong belief in humanity" (Pamuk, "Interview with Orhan Pamuk").

Pamuk's own words can frame a discussion that compares the universal theme of love in Dante and Pamuk: "My book is my attempt at being visionary through the experience of love. It has a tongue-in-cheek quality about the effect of love on one's spirit. The intensity of desire is so overwhelming that the narrator is in a new world, in a new life. It's about maturing through love, reaching a higher level of consciousness" (Pamuk, "Turkish Writer"). Students can be directed to the scene in *The New Life* in which Osman sees a photo of his beloved Janan in her parents' house after her disappearance:

> [B]ut seeing her framed photograph on the piano just as I took my leave, I regretted my decision. It was a picture of a nine-year-old Janan in pigtails, wearing a sweet angel's costume . . . whose every detail down to the tiny wings was appropriated from the West, standing between her parents and smiling slightly through the melancholy countenance of childhood. (35–36)

This scene recalls Dante's first vision of Beatrice in the *Vita Nuova*, brought to him by the angel of Love (God), wrapped in a crimson veil; God offers Beatrice the poet's heart for her to eat. There is a perfect symmetry with the Christian chronology that structures Dante's love story and their first meeting when Beatrice was nine. For Pamuk, the angel's costume is a metaphor for his dressing his Turkish love story in the clothing of Dante's story, a horizon of expectation familiar to Western readers. Reading the book later, Osman sees the little girl in the photo carried in the arms of Janan, whom he calls Love:

> [T]he chaotic images in my mind's eye cleared up, and Love became manifest in a halo of brilliant white, carrying a child in his arms. The child was the girl whose picture I had seen framed on the piano. The girl looked at me, smiling; she was perhaps about to say something but I had been unable to hear. I felt futile. I was in a painful agreement with an inner voice telling me that I would never be part of this beautiful picture. (36)

God, the angel of Love, and Dante's Beatrice are merged into Janan at several ages. But Pamuk is building on Borges as well. In "The Aleph," Borges's narrator returns (like Dante) to Beatriz's house every year on the anniversary of her death. Strikingly, on one such occasion he sees her photograph on the piano:

> Beside the flowerless vase atop the useless piano smiled the great faded photograph of Beatriz, not so much anachronistic as outside time. No one could see us; in a desperation of tenderness I approached the portrait:
>
> "Beatriz, Beatriz Elena, Beatriz Elena Viterbo," I said. "Beloved Beatriz, Beatriz lost forever—it's me, it's me, Borges." (281)

The superimposition of different faces or photographs of Beatrice/Beatriz becomes part of the superimposed totality of images that climaxes with Borges's narrator seeing the universe in a single point in space, Osman seeing his whole life in a dazzling light, and Dante seeing his whole book and universe in the eye of the Empyrean.

Finally, unlike the vast and open-ended global world, the global novel attempts to capture the whole world within a finite number of pages, and the book inevitably has to end with something close to a conclusion, even if a partial one. On the question of how much meaning global novels try to impose upon the postmodern, chaotic world, Calvino's conclusion to *If on a Winter's Night a Traveler* may be of help: "In ancient times a story could end only in two ways: having passed all tests, the hero and the heroine married, or else they died. The ultimate meaning to which all stories refer has two faces: the continuity of life, the inevitability of death" (259). Pamuk's description of how much distance and how much familiarity, how much localness and how much worldliness, one can expect from his practice of world literature can be summed up in class with his essay "My Father's Suitcase":

> But literature is never just a national concern. The writer who shuts himself up in a room and first goes on a journey inside himself will, over the years, discover literature's eternal rule: he must have the artistry to tell his own stories as if they were other people's stories, and to tell other people's stories as if they were his own, for this is what literature is. But we must first travel through other people's stories and books. . . . My world is a mixture of the local—the national—and the West.

This essay brings us full circle back to Casanova's cultural centers and peripheries and to the translatability of culturally rooted, existential experiences like love. Though the translation of cultural experiences is widely debated, in "My Father's Suitcase" Pamuk argues that the human transcends the cultural:

> My confidence comes from the belief that all human beings resemble each other, that others carry wounds like mine—that they will therefore under-

> stand. All true literature rises from this childish, hopeful certainty that all people resemble each other. When a writer shuts himself up in a room for years on end, with this gesture he suggests a single humanity, a world without a center.

Center and periphery, the local and the universal, the divine and the human, merge in the richly intertextual universe of *The New Life*.

NOTE

[1]This essay quotes from Güneli Gün's translation of *The New Life* published by Farrar, Straus, and Giroux in 1997.

Elective Asymmetries: Pamuk Teaching World Literature

David Gramling

> "Now it's as if everything I know about Islam is from *The Message*—you know, the film starring Anthony Quinn." Ka smiled. "It was showing not long ago on the Turkish channel in Germany—but, for some strange reason, in German."
>
> —Pamuk, *Snow*

Curricula have recently seen the rise of ambitious models for studying world literature, among them Itamar Even-Zohar's world systems–inflected approach, Franco Moretti's distant-reading calculus ("Conjectures"), the civic and cosmopolitical models of Pascale Casanova's *World Republic of Letters* and David Damrosch's *What Is World Literature?*, Emily Apter's notion of "nontranslation studies" (*Translation Zone*), and Pheng Cheah's call for a non-Mercatorian, temporal conception of world literature. Amid this methodological conjuncture, less emphasis has been placed on how literature selected as world literary may have already theorized itself from within. How, we may ask, has the latest global novel registered and refracted its putative selectability in the course of its own composition process? How does a world literary novel intratextually calibrate its linguistic, political, and formal positionality vis-à-vis its transnational adjudicators—whether the members of a Nobel committee, a Frankfurt Book Fair jury, or the translation rights bureau of a Bertelsmann subsidiary trade publisher? As Walter Benjamin once remarked in a similar vein, we might consider asking, How has (translated) world literature acquired the ability, power, and desire to read *us*—as its consumers (*Gesammelte Schriften* 1: 646–47)? Faced even in their preproduction stages with editors' strategic plans for marketing and circulation, with house translatability and style norms, and with translation-rights speculation schemes, twenty-first-century world literary texts are often inclined to critically textualize the very vetting procedures to which they were themselves subjected. While these may sound like problems for literary sociologists rather than for literary critics, the overtly metatextual novels of world literary authors such as Orhan Pamuk suggest that students of literature are on firm footing when close reading such phenomena. Whereas previous generations of students raised on postmodern thought may have delighted in pointing out that novelistic texts tend to deconstruct themselves self-reflexively from within, students of literature today are rather poised to ascertain how novels can intervene—on aesthetic, narrative, ethical, and intratextual levels—in precisely the global-circulatory logics that have brought them into being.

I first taught Pamuk's work in a University of Arizona graduate seminar entitled Translingual Modernities: Literature and Film on the German-Turkish Axis. I introduced Pamuk's self-described "political" novel *Snow* (2002) as a world literary text—but one that animates an uncanny asymmetrical affinity with Franz Kafka's *Castle* (1924), a submerged hypotext that is never named in *Snow* despite its protagonist's homophonic name, Ka. In presenting this structure of asymmetrical affinity as a critical problem, I assigned further readings: Even-Zohar on laws of literary interference, Roberto Schwarz on literary foreign debt, Meir Sternberg on polylingualism in the novel, and Sibel Erol ("Reading") on the doppelgänger trope as a heuristic for Occidentalism. To prime students about ongoing debates on world literature, I also assigned Tim Parks's polemical essay "The New Dull Global Novel" and Yaseen Noorani's essay "Hard and Soft Multilingualism." The participating students' home departments included Middle Eastern and North African studies, anthropology, and German studies; thus a third of the group would read both Pamuk and Kafka in English, a third in Turkish, and a third in German. No student commanded all three languages, so class discussions were consequently both translational, that is, concerned with the translated nature of the texts themselves, and translative, engaged in the processual practices of conveying meaning from one language to another (Pym 75). Though it may appear methodologically excessive, I insisted there was a strong historical justification for reading Pamuk in German and Kafka in Turkish. Pamuk's novel is partially set in Germany, a political landscape that has housed large-scale Turkish labor migration (1961–85) and religious-political refuge (1970–2000; 2013–present). Beginning in the late 1990s, German media and festival circuits have also hosted an intensified literary critical engagement with Turkey and Turkish literature in translation, as well as a belated rediscovery of the ongoing presence of Turkish-language literary production in German territory since before 1970. And Kafka's work was known to republican Turkey's intelligentsia, many members of which read him in German or English translation before Turkish translations were undertaken. Kafka's East-West parables and modernization farces then became a key figural repertoire in the large-scale, state-driven westernization campaigns that held sway from the 1940s to the1960s, during which Turkey's ministry of education commissioned translations of European modernist literature for appropriation and emulation in Turkish high schools. In a caprice of Occidentalism, Kafka's novel *The Castle*, which serves as a symbolic palimpsest in *Snow*, is titled in Turkish with the French loanword *Şato* in the translations by Kamuran Şipal and Şükrü Çorlu.

In preparing the seminar, I decided that these matters of circulation and translation would be primary categories of analysis, not just enriching extratextual contexts for understanding world literary history. Our close readings thus presumed a multidirectional and multilingual approach, in which Çorlu's and Şipal's Turkish translations of Kafka would enjoy no less primacy in our interpretive work than would Maureen Freely's English translation of Pamuk or Christoph Neumann's German translation (Pamuk, *Schnee*). However logical this principle of multilingual analysis seems when made explicit in this fashion, it conflicts routinely with literary-historical custom: Kafka reception since the early 1940s has been largely anglophone; and Turkish-German literature since the mid-1980s has been largely germanophone. These two contingencies of literary-sociological history—propelled in the first instance by National Socialism and exile, and in the second by the decline of labor internationalism in the Kohl-Reagan-Thatcher years—has cast a long shadow on the potential for collaborative, multilingual inquiry in these traditions.

Though our discussions of these two (or six) texts—indeed eight or nine, if we include each of the retranslations of Kafka in Turkish and English—were engaged on one level as translations of one another, the texts' variously multilingual entry points offered a prismatic touchstone for grasping the political and epistemological complexity in the stories themselves—how they cannot come to a satisfactory completion without one another. As a working translator, I wished to set a tone for the seminar that would not suppress questions of translation craft in favor of comparative critical philology. I also stressed, however, that the seminar was not a translation studies course as such, but a literature seminar where working affirmatively, not regretfully, with translations could constitute a new scholarly habit in philological training. In proposing this reorientation I discovered how rare it was for my students—as emerging philologists, literary scholars, anthropologists, comparatists, and indeed translators—to research multilingually in a sustained, institutionally mentored fashion. We did not merely work in several languages in the instrumental or occupational sense; rather, we engaged in the explicit, differential work of collaborative interpretation amid multiple languages, some of which would always be unknown to one or another collaborator present. In the following sections I suggest some reasons why the twenty-first-century modern language curriculum presents unprecedented opportunity, urgency, and relevance for such a commitment to researching multilingually and in (multiple) translation.

Teaching Pamuk in Multilingual Perspective

Perhaps more than other contemporary world literature personae, the narrators of Orhan Pamuk's novels—some of whom are named Orhan Pamuk—return again and again to questions of multilingual epistemology amid the pressures of market circulation and state censorship. Predominant in *Snow*, for instance, is a sustained concern for the pressurized political economy of publishable narratives amid European cultural consolidation and border patrolling. *Snow* itself was in part the result of sweeping European Union–oriented political reforms in Turkey at the turn of the century, which reformulated censorship statutes in such a fashion that allowed Pamuk to finally publish a novel about contemporary Turkish politics, highlighting—if not always by name—the Armenian Genocide, the ongoing state war against Kurds, domestic phone tapping and surveillance, the Turkish secret police bureaucracy, and the outsourcing of Islamist and Kurdish-nationalist militancy to West Germany since the 1970s. Pamuk sought legal counsel to examine the manuscript of *Snow* line by line to ensure the novel would pass muster with the Republic of Turkey's new, liberalized, EU-sanctioned censor (Pamuk, "Achte"). The resulting text is thus an utterly concrete artifact of post-Schengen European integration and forty years of EU-Turkey accession talks. Often overlooked in literary theory, such preproduction negotiations and their transnational, translingual discursive axes play a profound role in the twenty-first-century reemergence of what Schwarz calls "literary foreign debt" (50).

Snow presents students with a case study in the implications of literary—and otherwise symbolic—foreign debt precisely because it does not reduce the dynamics of the world literary system to simplistic notions of unidirectional imitation, lack, comparability, influence, or original-copy relations. In casting off the easy symbology of intercultural dialogue and comparativity so prevalent in Pamuk's previous novels like *The White Castle*, *Snow* becomes a highly stylized fiction about the preproduction discursive collusion between source language and target language literary politics and more broadly about accelerated paradigms of literary interference and translatability in the twenty-first century. With its anti-ironic, didactic narrative voice and Brechtian stylistics, *Snow* indeed suggests how its author may have grown to become, over his first two decades of publishing, a kind of *pícaro* of literary world-systems thinking. As if reckoning with the elaborate EU-oriented negotiations that preceded its publication, Pamuk seems to find ways to use the novel as an instrument to resist the orderly divide between published (translated) text and censored authorial activity—and to percuss against orthodox conceptions of authoriality and intentionality predominant in North Atlantic literary theory since New Criticism.

How can such a political economy of precaritized, censored, and nonetheless elite literary appearance be staged within a novel such as this? Like Kafka's K. in *The Castle*, Pamuk's protagonist dozes off in the novel at every available opportunity, leaving an opening for someone named Orhan Pamuk to hijack the story. Unlike in Kafka, whose narrators rarely stray—even in their sleepiest moments—from what Joseph Vogl calls Kafka's "fourth-person" point of view, the authorial Pamuk uses such liminal moments in his protagonist's consciousness to launch stealthy metaleptic authorial intrusions in his own name, for example, "[l]et us take advantage of this lull to whisper a few biographical details" (4).[1] Such flamboyant contaminations of the narrative field prompt us to wonder what function is fulfilled by the unauthorized, grandstanding presence of the cosmopolitan world literary star in his own texts? Is Pamuk joyriding through our world literary experience just for the fun of it?

Such moments of what we might consider a form of countertransference point students toward Pamuk's more meaningful epistemological project, one that has literary-theoretical and literary-didactic designs, not merely self-promotional ones. Pamuk's interpellations disrupt the readerly presupposition—promoted by most dust jackets, reviews, and prize press releases—that the novel exists primarily in order to disclose something representative about contemporary Turkey ("Nobel Prize"). Pamuk, of course, invites confusion and paradox on this point, seeming to imitate in the novel the generic habits of explanatory nonfiction, protocol literature, or New Journalism. Whereas Kafka assiduously cleansed his texts of all social deixis and local place-names, Pamuk dives headlong into an investigative forensics of an (apparently) local political landscape in Kars. Yet for every clause in *Snow* that describes local meanings in the northeastern Turkish border town where the novel takes place, another clause ruminates on how those local meanings have already been mediated and exchanged—often internationally—before they are circulated back in a legitimized, alienated form.

Snow's narrative thus dramatizes its own international, metatextual sojourn along global distribution pathways. For example, we learn how "[a] number of correspondents for French and German newspapers . . . did pick up on the item, and only after they had gone to [the city of] Batman and published stories in the European press did the Turkish press begin to take an interest: at this point, quite a few Turkish reporters paid visits to the city" (14). This account mimics the publication conditions and consequences of the novel itself, inducing a kind of *mise en abyme* of publishability, a conical structure at the center of which is nothing but "the silence of snow" (3)—the hypotextual "key term," in Raymond Williams's sense, of formal and semiotic erasure at the heart of the novel. In the opening pages of Kafka's *Castle*, snow is the negative principle ensuring the castle of Westwest its distinctive position, "free and light" above (7).

Demythologizing World Literature

Snow is clearly a work of literary-political didacticism—but to what end? And what bait for the neo-orientalist reader does the narrative lay out? It is certainly plausible to read or teach *Snow* as an auto-ethnography about the spectrum of secular-devout identities in Eastern Turkish cities; as an anti-allegory about class, regional animosities, and structural disenfranchisement in the shadow of westernization; as a bildungsroman about the reluctant atheist's unwitting experience of the divine; as a chronicle of the struggles of an exile poet, both privileged and entrapped by his own transnational mobility; or as a farce about the excesses of local nation-building pageantry in an age of globalization. Though one could lead a fruitful and comprehensive discussion on any of these themes, I propose that the novel teaches at the level of what Roland Barthes calls a "second-order signification" (*Mythologies* 235), a level that is less primarily interested in the experiential and thematic domains staged in the novel—secularity versus piety, provincial city versus megalopolis, East versus West, (Ottoman multicultural) imperiality versus (Turkish étatist) nationhood, journalism versus poetry, or even surveillance versus solitude. *Snow* deliberates above all about how these domains can be coercively arranged in relation to one another to produce a second-order sign for decontextualized translation and consumption abroad—what Barthes calls a "myth," a unity of signs drained of their primary-level meaning and conscripted for a subtle, but aggressive, ideological project. The material for myth can be religious, social, linguistic, experiential, or other, but the key criterion for mythmaking is that signs be harnessed for a communicative purpose that puts their local, vernacular, contextual, or experiential meanings "at a distance" (235). *Snow* uncovers how world literature is particularly susceptible to processes of mythologization—and often when an almost prurient realism appears to be afoot.

Snow thus offers students a compelling challenge: to analyze how themes of urgent contemporary topicality (theocracy, militancy, surveillance, insurgency, popular sovereignty, critiques of totalitarianism, military rule, coups, and so on) can easily become pressed into service of other subtle, modest, but deeply coercive purposes. In *Snow*, the elegant, second-order structure of mythic signification—what I regard as a kind of decoy—appears in the almost comical form of the snowflake, evoked on nearly every page of the novel. Pamuk's cartoon-like cosmological diagram of the snowflake—built upon three axes, twelve terminal poles, and nineteen thematic points along them—mythically arrests everything that has mattered in the novel thus far, from "The Chocolate Box" to "REASON" to "The Night of the Revolution" and "MEMORY" (261). Found in the poet Ka's notebook after his death, the reified, analytical snowflake seems at first to be a signature of both the creative and abstractive grandeur of the poet. Like Novalis's blue rose, Ka's snowflake is, however, also a diminutive, orderly, yet charismatic orientalist form, caricaturing the violent blizzard outside that conceals and cripples Kars and constitutes it as a potential literary-political site throughout the novel. The didactician Pamuk tempts readers—always pulled between orientalism and anti-orientalism—with an elegant, symmetrical symbol that offers heuristic foreclosure and a feeling of revelation at having uncovered the occult logic of the local. The Westerner's simultaneous affective embrace and epistemic totalization of the East—as embodied by everyone from Ka, to the grandiose intratextual Orhan Pamuk, to the novel's readers-in-translation—is, of course, a chief critical concern of Saidian thought, and Pamuk is certainly aware of how it constrains his "political" novel.

Asked to talk about East versus West in his work, Pamuk responds: "Here we come to the East-West question. Journalists are exceedingly fond of the term, but when I see the connotations it carries in some parts of the Western press, I'm inclined to think that it would be best not to speak of the East-West question at all. . . . There is . . . a strong suggestion that the culture, the way of life, and the politics of places like the one where I was raised provoke tiresome questions, and expectation that writers like me exist to offer solutions to the same tiresome questions" ("In Kars and Frankfurt").

In the spirit of this refutation, *Snow* aims to demythologize—in Barthes's sense—the syntax of the East-West relation and the epistemic negativity it generates. Upon arriving in Kars, Ka thinks, "It was as if he were in a place that the whole world had forgotten, as if it were snowing at the end of the world" (10). This outside observer in Kars is indeed a potential world literary writer, "accustomed to scanning for his name in literary journals" (27), one who had "first won the appreciation of the entire country with two collections entitled *Ashes and Tangerines* and *The Evening Papers*. Our young poet, who is also the winner of the Behçet Necatigil Prize, has come to Kars to cover the municipal elections for the *Republican*" (28). A bourgeois of Istanbul extraction, he is told that if he wishes to "see what Turkey was really like after his twelve-year absence [in political exile in Germany], he should think of going to Kars" (8).

Ka is thus always on the verge of committing all the neo-orientalist misdemeanors comparatists are warned against: poaching for authenticity, angling for nationalized representations, satisfying moral cravings to give voice to the silenced, and all the while surreptitiously seeking recognition for himself as an expert. John Zilcosky suspects that the word "vermessen" (to measure falsely) lies at the heart of Ka's literary forebear K.'s grand task as self-appointed land-surveyor in *The Castle* (49)—an ambition that Walter Sokel referred to as a "great fraud perpetuated against the reader" (59)—and this false measurement is potently reiterated in Ka's circuitous path of methodological, ethical, and affective folly at every turn.

In the Arizona seminar, we thus explored how *Snow* requires a reversal of critical attention, focusing on how and why Pamuk's text writes us as readers into regimes of comparativity in a radically uneven world, made even more uneven by new prerequisites of translatability in international trade publishing. *Snow*'s primary aim is to map out the epistemic conditions of twenty-first-century world literature and how texts themselves may offer teachers and students methodological instructions about these conditions. Even Ka's clandestine meeting with the militant Islamist ringleader Blue revolves around a retheorization of world literature selection criteria. Blue tells Ka:

> Once upon a time millions of people knew [the story of Firdevsi's *Shehname*] by heart—from Tabriz to Istanbul, from Bosnia to Trabzon—and when they

> recalled it they found the meaning in their lives. The story spoke to them in just the same way that Oedipus' murder of his father and Macbeth's obsession with power and death speak to people throughout the Western world. But now, because we've fallen under the spell of the West, we've forgotten our own stories. They've removed all the old stories from our children's textbooks. (78)

Blue characterizes the possibility of an alternative, hypotextual, or suppressed world literature as a kind of arms race against the leveling, "de-aestheticizing jaws of globalization" (Apter, *Against* 9). Blue's resigned intervention is in implicit dialogue with positions such as those expressed by Parks:

> Writing in the 1960's, intensely engaged with his own culture and its complex politics, Hugo Claus apparently did not care that his novels would require a special effort on the reader's and above all the translator's part if they were to be understood outside his native Belgium. In sharp contrast, contemporary authors like the Norwegian Per Petterson, the Dutch Gerbrand Bakker, or the Italian Alessandro Baricco offer us works that require no such knowledge or effort, nor offer the rewards that such effort will bring. More importantly the language is kept simple. Kazuo Ishiguro has spoken of the importance of avoiding word play and allusion to make things easy for the translator. Scandinavian writers I know tell me they avoid character names that would be difficult for an English reader. If culture-specific clutter and linguistic virtuosity have become impediments, other strategies are seen positively: the deployment of highly visible tropes immediately recognizable as "literary" and "imaginative," analogous to the wearisome lingua franca of special effects in contemporary cinema, and the foregrounding of a political sensibility that places the author among those "working for world peace."

Parks oversimplifies matters, of course. He pictures today's successful, globally mobile novel as little but a slick and passive delivery device, unburdened of its predecessors' (untranslatable) aesthetic and political ambitions and exempted from any commitment to leverage critique back toward the international reader-reviewer's gaze. Pamuk, for his part, seems poised to tell us about precisely these predicaments—not just in interviews and paratexts but in the novels themselves. *Snow* thus offers students of literature the opportunity to complicate the cynicism Parks presents, while acknowledging the economic and symbolic conditions that underlie Parks's concern about the structural attenuation of meaning in contemporary world literary circulation and translation.

Snow *as Globalization's Pathetic Fallacy*

Students will find a further critical resource in Pamuk's title, *Snow*, a substance and optical effect that, as a counterpoint symbolic form, allows Kafka's Castle of Westwest its position of distinction. While the omnipresent veil of a "silence of snow" in Pamuk intimates the constitutive absence of the city of Kars on any world literary map, snow also offers a kind of pathetic fallacy for the globalized gaze upon the local: "The weather office has announced that cold air coming straight from Siberia and the accompanying heavy snowfall will continue for three more days. And so for three days, the city of Kars will have to do as it used to do during the winters of old—stew in its own juices. This will offer us an opportunity to put our house in order" (30). Extraordinary conditions of blinding white compel the city to close in on itself, to give a momentarily deglobalized account of its homegrown attributes and political narratives, though many of these local particularities originate from a clandestine "elsewhere," whether Frankfurt, Istanbul, or Ankara. Getting stuck in Kars—a predicament faced by the novel's characters and its readers—could have been avoided altogether, we are told. On his way eastward, the ambitious author Ka, seeing the oncoming snow, "might have realized that he was traveling straight into a blizzard; he might have seen at the start that he was setting out on a journey that would change his life forever and chosen to turn back" (3–4). The comment may be another authorial index about the contingency of the novel itself—namely, the unlikelihood that it would ever have been written or published under ordinary circumstances of national sovereignty, that is, without the constant structuring pressures of EU-Turkey accession negotiations and the West Study Group's postmodern coup in 1997.

What, then, does this blinding whiteness in *Snow* intend to teach us about world literature in the adverse climates beyond cosmopolitan megalopolises like Istanbul? The formal effect of snow throughout the blizzard is negative: "Ka came to feel as if they had entered a shadow world. The rooms were so dark he could barely make out the shape of the furniture, so when he was compelled to look at the snow outside, it blinded him—it was as if a curtain of tulle had fallen before his eyes" (13). Snow is not merely a hindrance to visual perception; it is symbolically coded as the arbiter of publishability and mediation: "As the [electricity was cut and the] printing press whirred to a halt and the shop fell into an enchanted darkness, Ka was struck by the beautiful whiteness of the snow falling outside" (24). This whiteness of the snow outside the printing press indexes the attenuation of meaning present in the pattern of circulation that constitutes and reconstitutes the city of Kars in national-domestic and international-translated narrative.

Snow is a philosophical fiction about culture in the wake of what Noorani calls "soft multilingualism," where every local category of meaning is presumed to have an equivalent counterpart discourse in European languages and nation building histories. Pamuk hints at this early-twentieth-century transformation from hard to soft multilingualism in his historical accounts of Kars's colonial past:

> [T]he city was occupied by Armenian and Russian armies at different times and even, briefly, by the British. For a short time, when the Russian and Ottoman forces had left the city following the First World War, Kars was an independent state. . . . But when it came to renaming the five great Russian avenues, they couldn't think of enough great men from the city's history who weren't soldiers, so they ended up memorializing five great pashas. (20)

Snow offers students of literature a primer in the mechanics of world literary circulation under globalizing conditions. Neither cynical nor self-aggrandizing, each chapter prompts students with an entry point into a critique of world literature beyond mere comparativity, exportation, influence, and culturalism. The novel allows students to imagine the contingencies of narrative circulation, shaped by ever-evolving endeavors to monetize and securitize literary translation as a means of production, and to grasp the neo-orientalist implications for trade publishing amid that ongoing evolution.

NOTE

[1]This essay quotes from Maureen Freely's translation of *Snow* published by Alfred A. Knopf in 2004.

The Love Triangle in *Snow*

Bruce Robbins

> What does this murderer have that makes everyone fall for him?
>
> —Pamuk, *Snow*

"The 'hero' of a Scott novel," Georg Lukács writes in *The Historical Novel*, "is always a more or less mediocre, average English gentleman. He generally possesses a certain, though never outstanding, degree of practical intelligence, a certain moral fortitude and decency which even rises to a capacity for self-sacrifice, but which never grows into a sweeping human passion, is never the enraptured devotion to a great cause." In Lukács's view, the use of this "middling" hero is not "a symptom of Scott's mediocrity as an artist" but on the contrary "the clearest proof of Scott's exceptional and revolutionary epic gifts" (33). Indeed it enabled Scott to invent the genre of the historical novel. What the historical novel needs is a "neutral ground . . . on which the extreme, opposing social forces" of the day "can be brought into a human relationship with one another" (36). To put at the novel's center the "passionate partisans" of the respective sides, like the Robin Hood (Locksley) of Scott's *Ivanhoe* and the Napoleon of Tolstoy's *War and Peace*, would have been to create "a merely external picture of mutual destruction incapable of arousing the human sympathies and enthusiasms of the reader" (36). The reader, who probably comes from those "large sections of people who have always stood between the camps with fluctuating sympathies now for this side, now for the other," is less likely to identify with "the great figures of history" than with Scott's "middle-of-the-road heroes," who are less passionate and less committed (37). Thanks to such subdued, unimpassioned protagonists, dragged into a struggle they do not see as theirs, the historical crisis represented by the novel "is never abstract, the split into warring parties always runs through the center of the closest human relationships" (41). The mediocre hero produces a novelistic space for a "direct coming-to-grips of colliding opposites" in which readers can experience history as real (40).

When I teach Orhan Pamuk's novel *Snow*, sometimes in a lecture course and sometimes in a seminar that Pamuk and I coteach, I begin by laying out Lukács's account of Scott. I propose that Ka, the novel's protagonist, is a "mediocre hero." Even if *Snow* is less a historical novel and more a political one, this approach offers several benefits. First and foremost, it diverts attention away from Ka's personal characteristics—evaluation of a character's personality and likability being the default mode for undergraduates lacking advanced literary training—and refocuses it on his function: what the novel needs him for and does with him. Most obviously, in Ka's oscillating, uncommitted character the rival life philosophies and social energies of contemporary Turkey can cohabit, if only briefly. This humanizes such philosophies, softening the hard, propagandistic edges of attitudes that some would describe as terroristic, fundamentalist, or fascist and thus making them more comprehensible. Above all, thinking about Ka's function in the novel helps students recognize that the novel is about them rather than about Ka, despite the considerable time the reader spends inside Ka's subjectivity and the lack of contact with the inner thoughts and feelings of the "passionate partisans." For most students, shifting perspective from individual to social represents a major interpretive hurdle.

Lukács's scheme might seem to imply that *Snow* finally espouses a balanced, middle-of-the-road, or plague-on-both-your-houses position. In my experience many students are tempted by this view. For them, the morals of *Snow* are that all ideological investments are extreme, violent, and inappropriate and that the proper attitude toward them is one of withdrawal and critical detachment. My goal is to elicit a competing line of interpretation: the possibility that the novel doesn't celebrate the withdrawal into privacy and balanced impartiality but makes a subtle case for commitment to ideological causes—a commitment that is politically partisan and worthy of passion.

Students will likely want to discuss whether *Snow* is, for example, too uncritical of Islamism or too masculine in its treatment of the headscarf girls who commit suicide. Those are valuable and perhaps even necessary conversations. The detour through Lukács doesn't seek to avoid them, but it forces students to engage as well with the novel's form. The novel's most interesting ideological positions are given the shape of the love triangle. Formally speaking, Ka looks like a pale go-between shuttling between the vibrant, larger-than-life representatives of the novel's two major historical forces, authoritarian secularism and political Islam. Ka meets repeatedly with the secularist Sunay Zaim, the flamboyant actor-instigator of the anti-Islamic coup. Ka also has a series of searching, unpredictable dialogues with a charismatic underground leader of the political Islamists, Blue. Ka's role linking these ideologically committed characters, who never interact with each other directly, seems intended to create a balanced perspective, equidistant from both. Sunay and Blue both make persuasive statements regarding their ideological positions, but they both have obvious, even comic, flaws. However, the triangle is not symmetrical, for Sunay and Blue are not equal. There is only one hero in Pamuk's epic, and that is Blue.

Blue, the subject of Sunay's puzzled question in this essay's epigraph, is not the novel's protagonist. We are granted ample, repeated access to Ka's consciousness but not to Blue's. We follow Ka's movements but not Blue's. We see Blue—infrequently—as he is seen by others. He is presented as a fixed entity, as one who does not evolve. Lukács, who posits that the novelistic representation of world-historical figures will necessarily be limited in precisely these ways, is helpful in inducing students to accept a proposition they will probably find counterintuitive: that a character who commands so few of the novel's pages can nonetheless be central to its interpretation. Focusing on the love triangle can show Blue's centrality to *Snow*. The novel barely touches on Blue's Islamic beliefs, but it is organized around what can be called his sexiness. At the formal heart of the novel, I suggest, is the epigraph's apparently eccentric question of why so many people fall for Blue.

The love story may look like a distraction, a concession to vulgar readerly pleasures, even like a bit of casual camouflage designed to protect the novel from censorship. Censors tend not to scrutinize stories of personal relationships—or their authors—as carefully as those of religious assassinations and military coups. Students sometimes complain that the love story and especially its female object of desire are depicted in only the most desultory and conventional way. Ka is entranced by İpek's dazzling beauty; that cliché, repeated by the narrator, Orhan, sums up his desire. By contrast, the unhappy endings of the love triangle and of the novel, which are roughly simultaneous, are richly complex. Asked to explain the unhappy ending, students will likely answer that the key is Ka's sexual jealousy of Blue, which motivates him to betray his rival to the military. From this perspective, it is İpek's certainty of the betrayal that keeps her from leaving on the train with Ka. This is the first unhappy ending. The same certainty on the part of Blue's Islamist followers leads to Ka's assassination years later in Germany. That is the second unhappy ending. (The third is İpek's rejection of Orhan, himself jealous of Ka, Orhan's "more complex, passionate, authentic" original [455].)[1] The unhappy ending has in fact been decided before the putative betrayal and depends on something more elusive: not what Ka does but who he is in relation to Blue.

Politics aside, there are also personal factors that affect the relationship between Ka and İpek: Ka's mysterious melancholy, for example, which sends him to gaze sadly out the window at the falling snow only minutes after passionate lovemaking with İpek, and İpek's desire to stay close to her father and sister. But what actually kills the relationship is the revelation that until recently İpek had been Blue's lover. Ka and İpek both recognize instantly that this news is decisive: "Despite the loss they were suffering, they'd both relaxed—as people do when they realize they've run out of chances for happiness" (390). In a sense, Ka only learns that İpek is more honest about her emotions than he is—she knows that people do not actually fall in love so quickly. But the idea that İpek will come to love Ka in the future, in Germany, cannot offset the fact that now, in Kars, even without having seen Blue in months, İpek still insists that Blue loves her and not her sister (391). Her insistence opens up a painful admission: "'You only want me because you're trying to forget him!' said Ka. Looking into her face, he saw with horror that he had spoken the truth" (392).

Although İpek and Blue's affair has ended, Blue's love continues to matter enormously both to İpek and to the novel. In effect, it ruins Ka's chances of happiness well before the plot machinery has rumbled into motion. It decides the ending. Why does the novel give it so much weight? Blue's blue eyes cannot be the explanation. In a novel (where personal appearance in any case counts for less than in visual media) a love choice is really the choice of a vision of the world. What vision of the world, then?

For students who balk at the notion that a love triangle might be animated by something other than simple jealousy, it may be helpful to recall some notable literary triangles that pit a nationalist against a cosmopolitan. In Rabindranath Tagore's *The Home and the World* (1916), for example, the wife is seduced away from her cosmopolitan husband by a passionate anticolonial nationalist. The ending of James Joyce's story "The Dead" might be described as Gabriel Conroy's defeat in a competition for the affections of his wife, Greta—his rival being the long-dead suitor she suddenly remembers when Gabriel wants to be the one in her thoughts. While Gabriel imagines a passionate night, Greta reveals that she is filled with sad thoughts of a young man in Galway who died of love for her. This young man stands for Ireland's western, Gaelic-speaking heartland, whereas the husband is a Europe-oriented writer like Joyce himself. In the arena of the bedroom, when cosmopolitanism confronts the erotic or emotional power of the nation, the nation triumphs.

If we think of the ending of *Snow* as a competition for a woman's heart, certain things fall into place. As in Joyce's story, also set against a backdrop of falling snow, in *Snow* the mere memory of a former love is enough to defeat the protagonist. In stark terms, Blue represents the nation while Ka represents cosmopolitanism. But Ka is not a real cosmopolitan. He neither claims that Blue's version of local collectivity is immoral or constraining nor does he assert against it the higher standard of Istanbul or Germany or the welfare of humanity as a whole. Ka does not espouse democracy or women's rights. What he speaks up for is privacy, isolation, the right to be left alone. At the moment of his most strenuous outreach to political Islam, he discovers in himself a desire for poetic isolation. Arriving in a provincial, snow-enclosed Kars, he has found his dormant poetic gifts suddenly revived by contact with this artificially preserved corner of his homeland. To his surprise, he has also discovered God, whom he credits for his poems. In this mood, he visits a local religious leader. He is moved and he confesses. But in the act of confessing, he tells the sheikh, "I want a God who understands my need for solitude" (104). "I feel guilty about having refused all my life to believe in the same God as the uneducated," he continues. "But now I want to believe in that God who is making this beautiful snow fall from the sky . . . that God is not among you" (104–05).

If Ka's secularism is more accurately described as a yearning for solitude, it becomes more clear why he loses İpek to Blue. The only virtue of liberal democracy that Ka offers İpek is privacy—a Western value, but a privative one, a mere absence. What Blue really stands for, as opposed to what he seems to stand for, becomes, by contrast, a positive presence. Blue stands not for political Islam, Islam more generally, Turkish national identity (about which the novel grants him better lines), or the slogans that animate Blue's movement. The vision of the world with which Blue is most deeply associated centers on belonging—collectivity as such. Ka's invitation to İpek can be reduced to the proposition that private life flourishes when it is separated from public demands and engagements. Blue's counterproposition is that private life is indissociable from public life.

It's as if the novel wants to take Ka's side but can't quite manage to. And it isn't just Blue who makes the case against Ka. Both of the "passionate partisans" with whom Ka's unheroic wimpiness is contrasted, one officially representing religion and the other officially representing secularism, give Ka exactly the same advice: that he needs to belong. Ka's love of God, Blue says, "comes out of Western Romantic novels. . . . In a place like this, if you worship God as a European, you're bound to be a laughingstock. Then you cannot even believe you believe. You don't belong to this country; you're not even a Turk anymore. First try to be like everyone else. Then try to believe in God" (354). And when Ka, summoned to the headquarters of the coup, tells Sunay that he "may be starting to believe in God," Sunay responds that he is mistaken, but that in any case "it would make no sense to believe alone. You'd have to believe in him the same way the poor do; you'd have to become one of them" (219).

Believing the way the poor do, becoming one of the poor: here the reader's pursuit of the sources of Blue's erotic dominance again steps beyond the novel's array of political slogans. Ka, the educated, alienated exile, is trying to belong to something in Kars—but what? It's not religion. The crucial (and Dostoevskyan) chapter about the meeting at the Hotel Asia, in which all the anti-coup factions try to hammer out a common statement to be published in the West, is titled "We're Not Stupid, We're Just Poor!" (298). No faction claims this message, which keeps the focus on Turkey's subordination to the West but rules out political Islam's religious, cultural, identitarian view of it. Poverty doesn't confer an identity that anyone wants or needs to defend. It exists in the West as well as the East, though not equally. A secular fact, poverty is no more central to the platform of the secularists than to the religious party. Predictably, then, it doesn't figure in the final statement. Yet it hangs heavily over the dynamics of the love triangle that gives the novel its final shape and thus over the politics of the novel as a whole.

A few pages before the novel's end, Ka's friend and chronicler Orhan writes that "almost everyone I met on my walks around Kars was waiting for . . . a hero, some great man ready to make the large sacrifices that would deliver them all from poverty, unemployment, confusion, and murder" (458). Poverty is almost always the first word on such lists. Poverty and heroism are firmly linked: the suggestion is that one cannot be a hero without addressing poverty. Blue passes this test, even if he does so by speaking about religion and the nation rather than about poverty itself.

Of course, this sets a high bar for a hero. So high, in fact, that the novel is willing to entertain the notion that it would be a mistake for someone to try to be a hero. Although Orhan modestly goes on to explain how badly he himself disappointed Kars's desire for a hero, *Snow* can certainly be read as dismissing the aspiration itself as deluded, unrealistic, and provincial, like so much else that is believed in Kars. That is to say, one should know better than to ask for heroes. The hero stages coups and assassinations and gets innocent people killed. Better to stay a private person—even to be "mediocre." This line of interpretation gets a great deal of support: "'For me, it's very simple,' Necip said with pride. 'I want to marry Kadife, live in Istanbul, and become the world's first Islamist science-fiction writer'" (144). As individuals, even these supposed fanatics share the same private ambitions as a Western-educated metropolitan like Ka. Many Western-educated students will no doubt prefer this takeaway—that we are all Western individualists at heart.

No reader will have missed how consistently the novel represents the public domain as farcical. The coup, staged during a play, is a performance that won't last and doesn't even seem intended to. We know in advance that it will end when the curtain of snow is lifted, and when the end does come—with the ambiguous suicide or assassination of Sunay Zaim—that too happens on stage. In both cases the violence is largely, though of course not entirely, absurd. Bullets hit ornamental ceiling fixtures and sleeping grandfathers; one bullet is found buried in a hard-boiled egg. Prolepsis and analepsis redirect attention from the events themselves to predictions and then to reconstructions. As sites of individual investment, public projects seem destined to fail, on a par with the prospect that Sunay will get to play Atatürk or Mohammad. In such a world, what could possibly be done about poverty? There are no rich people in Kars—at any rate, no one rich enough to stand apart from Kars's pervasive misery, no one to stand for the machinery that divides the world into rich and poor. If such a machinery exists, the novel would oblige the reader to imagine it as invisible and most likely located in the West. Denouncing the West, as Blue does, is as close as the novel comes to showing a struggle against poverty—arguably, it's not close enough. Under these circumstances, it's no surprise that public action looks like farce.

In the light of how the novel represents public actions, students might well take the novel's moral meaning to be that expressed by Ka and repeated by Fazil: "I'm a typical atheist. I don't care about anything except love and happiness" (310). According to this view, the unheroic domain of private feelings is real. Public actions are unreliable and ungraspable; they lend themselves to postmodernism. The novel treats private actions in a mode of realism, in contrast to its treatment of public actions.

A plausible counterargument would have to establish that heroism—that is, public action—determines the private relations in the novel, which indeed the love triangle accomplishes. Blue's sexual charisma is of a piece with his Lukácsian role as a bearer of history. His ideas, which often seem misguided and even silly, do not define him. He lies about the number of those killed in the coup. At the meeting in the Hotel Asia, he confidently vouches for what we know to be a fiction, the invented journalist Hans Hansen who allegedly cares deeply about the plight of the Turks. Blue is nonetheless heroic because he possesses what Ka lacks: a personal life that is charged with public meaning. To Blue, history and politics aren't intrusions from elsewhere. There is no hint of hypocrisy, of an alternative self lurking behind his political self. Pamuk passes up all opportunities to present Blue as mean-spirited or self-interested when it counts most—for example, with regard to his personal safety or sexual pride. The novel does not indulge private cynicism toward the public hero that Lukács, borrowing from Hegel, calls the valet de chambre's view of history (47). Blue's unity of the private and public is what "makes everyone fall for him" and determines his victory in the love triangle.

Blue's sexual charm could of course be reduced to an uninteresting banality: the hero gets the girl (or all the girls). But the novel takes a detour through poverty to sidestep this banality. Necip, the young religious student who is about to be killed in the coup, lays out his argument for religion as follows: "If God does not exist, that means heaven does not exist either. And that means the world's poor, those millions who live in poverty and oppression, will never go to heaven. And if that is so, then how do you explain all the suffering of the poor? What are we here for, and why do we put up with so much unhappiness, if it's all for nothing?" (110). Of course, this is a secular theory of religion. The novel, to the extent that it takes sides on religion, embraces this secular view of political Islam as rooted in poverty. But the novel does not take Ka's side on religion. Ka doesn't give the old, yet still powerful, answers to Necip's questions: that expecting to go to heaven isn't the best way to confront poverty, that the poor should stop putting up with their unhappiness, that religion encourages them to do exactly that, and so on. "If I'm happy," Ka says, "that's all I care about."

It's a big if. Ka says that his happiness depends on two things: poetry and İpek's love. Being in Kars gives him poetry, but, by withdrawing from the cause of his countrymen, he denies himself İpek's love. When the plot makes this point, it endorses the opposing view of happiness that has been articulated by Blue. In Blue's prison cell, Ka has confessed his love for İpek and said that she is his one chance at happiness. Blue asks him to define happiness. Ka says, "Happiness is finding another world to live in, a world where you can forget all this poverty and tyranny. Happiness is holding someone in your arms and knowing you hold the whole world" (353). Responding to this vision of happiness and love as a means to escape from the world, Blue delivers his own judgment: "And know this: People who seek only happiness never find it" (379). Blue may be misguided on certain subjects, but the novel shows him to be right on this. Ka can't expect to find happiness by carrying off İpek and ignoring the "poverty and tyranny" suffered by his countrymen.

While Ka doesn't find happiness, Blue does. Blue seems to know that he will eventually be murdered by the military, but every time we see him he seems remarkably content. One might say that he finds happiness precisely because, unlike Ka, he seeks not only personal happiness but the happiness of the collective to which he belongs. And this is again why the scales of the love triangle tilt in his favor. In the formal tradition of Lukács's historical novel, *Snow* nurtures this unfashionable and often overlooked moral by letting it exert its subtle pressure from the margins.

The novel's artistry can be illustrated by several small elaborations on this organizing principle. One is the account of Turgut Bey, father of İpek and Kadife. A Ka of the previous generation, his (rather brilliant) portrayal in the novel exists in part to warn the protagonist of what he may become. Turgut Bey upsets the novel's apparent symmetry between the political passions of secularism and religion. He is a secularist, but he is also a former Communist who in his youth was tortured by the military. Like Ka, he can't be identified with the military coup any more than with the Islamists. He is counterbalanced, on the Islamist side, by his daughter Kadife, who is a kind of leader of the headscarf girls. Though she is Blue's mistress and ally, Kadife is also the closest thing the novel offers to an independent voice speaking on behalf of her gender. Like her father, she makes entirely secular arguments for what she does. Like the ubiquitous but shadowy Kurds, women don't fit neatly into the secular-religious divide. As major characters, both father and daughter suggest that the opposing slogans of political Islam and secular militarism may mask larger stakes that lie beneath and between the two movements.

Yet Pamuk keeps gently pushing the ideological power of the concept of poverty. Structurally speaking, Turgut Bey plays the role of the heavy father or blocking character. What stands between Ka and erotic satisfaction with İpek is Turgut Bey's fearful unwillingness to leave his hotel because "[t]he poverty of Kars ruins his mood" (255). Simply stated, the poverty of Kars prevents Ka's love story from reaching a successful conclusion.

There is perhaps something more in Ka's psychological resistance to his love story. The most mysterious aspect of Ka's character is his melancholy, which is also described as a fear of happiness. Fear of happiness seems to appear on its own irregular schedule, as if it existed in a purely psychological dimension that had nothing to do with the political plot. Yet, on reflection, its appearance makes a kind of sense. As Ka says, his desire for happiness is a desire to escape into a private, self-sufficient world of love and poetry where he can forget the misery of Kars. Fear of happiness would logically be a fear of succeeding to escape—Ka fears what he would become if he were to forget the poverty of Kars. The novel recognizes, if only obscurely, Ka's commitment to stay engaged in some way with the poverty of Kars when it represents him as afraid of private, individual happiness. Ka is not Blue, the hero whom everyone falls for, but Ka's form of heroism is good to have students meditate on.

NOTE

[1]This essay quotes from Maureen Freely's translation of *Snow* published by Vintage Books in 2005.

The Ekphrastic Detectives: Readers, Art, and Identity in *My Name Is Red*

Darcy Irvin

Who is the murderer in *My Name Is Red*? How might readers discover his or her identity? I open class discussion of this novel in my lower-division undergraduate course Literature as Art with these two seemingly simple questions. While the first question focuses on identity within the world of the novel, the second reminds students that their purported role as readers is to solve the whodunit through both textual and visual registers. These questions help us delve into the problems of identity in the novel—both the murderer's identity as an artist and character and the roles and identities that the text constructs for us as readers—by focusing on how the novel presents a supposed clash between what I will refer to as ideologies of sight and image production. These ideologies of sight consist of the religious and political beliefs the characters in the novel rely upon to define what they perceive to be correct and incorrect ways of literally and metaphorically viewing the world and the creation of images.We begin by discussing how the novel depicts what the characters refer to as Venetian art versus Ottoman art and the political and religious consequences of the artists' decisions about how to represent the world. We then turn our attention to the murderer, examining how Olive's conflicting artistic desires increasingly fracture his identity as a court miniaturist, an artist, and a Muslim. Finally, we explore how the novel constructs us as readers of verbal texts rather than as consumers of visual images. The class reflects on the ekphrastic nature of the novel, carefully considering how the novel both validates and disrupts conventional hierarchies of word and image by encouraging readers to visualize absent images through textual description alone. We conclude our class discussions by thinking through how the text positions readers not only as criminal detectives but also as aesthetic and ekphrastic detectives, joining discussions of art and identity with discussions of murder.

Visual Ideologies in My Name Is Red

My Name Is Red can be approached in numerous ways—as a detective story, as a postmodern novel, as an important work in Turkish national literature, and so on—but studying how Pamuk centers the plot on ideologies of seeing and image production is particularly rewarding. Pamuk's historicization of artistic developments does not entirely line up with scholarly views on the cultural exchanges of the period. Most notably, he has delayed Ottoman artists' contact with Western art in order to make that exposure more cataclysmic than it likely would have been in 1591, when the novel is set. As several scholars have noted, there was a great deal of mixing between Western and Ottoman artists well before the 1590s; Richard Ettinghausen, for instance, points out that the Ottoman court workshop in 1557 included at least two European painters (16). And while Pamuk's story focuses on Ottoman interest in European art, it does not give a full sense of the reciprocated European fascination with Ottoman art. For these reasons, I generally do not lecture comprehensively on Renaissance and Ottoman art of the sixteenth century. Instead, I ask students to identify passages from the novel where characters make assertions about differences between Venetian and Ottoman art. Then I provide historical examples of such artworks, which students can analyze in relation to the text.

The character Enishte is the novel's most notable proponent of the Venetian style. Enishte insists upon the power of images that visually reproduce the world in optically real ways even as he continues to value images produced in the emergent Ottoman style. Narrating his own fascination with Italian art, Enishte tells Black of his encounter with Venetian portraits, noting that the "Venetian virtuoso had made the nobleman's picture in such a way that you would immediately know which particular nobleman it was. If you'd never seen that man, if they told you to pick him out of a crowd of a thousand others, you'd be able to select the correct man with the help of that portrait" (27).[1] Although Enishte finds the portrait of a particular Venetian gentleman "bewildering," he also acknowledges its seductive influence: "I, too, wanted to be portrayed in this manner" (26). The portrait gains this power because it captures for eternity an individual's unique appearance so that "those who had never seen you alive, even years after your death, could come face-to-face with you as if you were standing before them" (27). These images appeal to Enishte in part because they freeze the past and effectively communicate it to a viewer in the future.

To illustrate the kind of art works that have captured Enishte's admiration, I introduce examples of sixteenth-century Venetian portraiture to the class. Tintoretto's *Sebastiano Venier at the Battle of Lepanto* (ca. 1571) is a good choice because it gives students a clear sense of how Italian portraits of the time relied on perspective and attempted to convey their subjects as specific individuals. The painting shows Sebastiano Venier, who was later elected Doge of Venice, wearing expensive armor and a sumptuous cape, which signifies his wealth. In the background is an optically realistic sea battle, indicating Venier's power and Venice's naval superiority. Titian's portrait of the art dealer Jacopo Strada (1567–68) similarly relies on sumptuous clothing to communicate the subject's status, which is also indicated by a marble statuette, ancient coins, a heavy gold chain, and books. While Enishte sees Western portraiture as a means of communicating an individual's wealth and power through the inclusion of significant possessions, such as his "clock, books, Time, Evil, Life, a calligraphy pen, a map, a compass" (26), the miniaturists praise other aspects of the Venetian style, in particular, the way it valorizes the individual artist, his vision, and identity and privileges an image's creator as much as its subject. When Black questions Master Osman in the workshop, for instance, the head illuminator defines the Venetian style as "an individual painting technique" practiced by artists who desire to "have a manner, an aspect distinct from others" (60). For Master Osman, specific techniques, such as perspective, are less significant than issues of "style" and "signature" (60).

The Ottoman style that developed in the workshop under Master Osman is in contrast with the Venetian style. Butterfly, Stork, and Olive all espouse the "old masters": they take pleasure in drawing purely from memory, venerate blindness as a means of achieving artistic transcendence, and insist upon visual representation's subordination to verbal representation. When asked to complete a picture of a horse for the Sultan's supposed contest, Butterfly first imagines how "Mir Musavvir [would] make this picture? How would Bihzad?" and then notes that "the beast entered my thoughts with such speed, that by the time I understood what it was, my damnable hand grabbed the brush and began to draw a miraculous horse beyond anyone's conception" (275). Butterfly's claim that his "hand grabbed the brush" before he was able to truly understand the image of the horse in his mind alludes to the miniaturists' validation of blindness as a means of escaping the oppressive visual reality of the physical world. As Olive tells Elegant:

> The old masters of Shiraz and Herat . . . claimed that a miniaturist would have to sketch horses unceasingly for fifty years to be able to truly depict the horse that Allah envisioned and desired. They claimed that the best picture of a horse should be drawn in the dark, since a true miniaturist would go blind working over that fifty-year period, but in the process, his hand would memorize the horse. (20)

According to the miniaturists, blindness frees the artist from the burden of seeing the world as it is rather than as the divine might see it. "Illustrating," Olive ironically informs Black, "was the miniaturist's search for Allah's vision of the earthly realm, and this unique perspective could only be attained through recollection after blindness descended" (80). Although each of the miniaturists willingly creates (or copies) an image for the Sultan's contest, some of them insist that paintings need to be part of a narrative, bound up in a book with other pages. Enishte tells Black that "[e]very picture serves to tell a story. . . . The images are the story's blossoming in color. But painting without its accompanying story is an impossibility" (25–26). Although Enishte at times admits to a fascination with Western-style portraiture, he nonetheless embraces the belief that pictures cannot stand alone but must be integrated with the narrative that they illustrate.

Perhaps most important, the miniaturists each distance themselves from the Venetian penchant for style. After hearing Butterfly's tales of the Khan, the Sultan, and the Shah, Black notes that the stories demonstrate "that 'signature and style' are but means of being brazenly and stupidly self-congratulatory about flawed work" (66). While the miniaturists are careful to present Black with crafted narratives that support the workshop's beliefs about seeing and painting, their chapters also challenge those ideological perspectives. Butterfly self-righteously tells Black that "as long as the number of worthless artists motivated by money and fame instead of the pleasure of seeing and a belief in their craft increases . . . we will continue to witness much more vulgarity and greed akin to this preoccupation with 'style' and 'signature'" (62). But to the reader he admits, "I made this introduction because this was the way it is done, not because I believed what I said" (62). Stork, perhaps the most openly experimental of the artists, acknowledges that he regularly departs from tradition: he does not "depict surprise, as it has been shown for centuries by hundreds of master miniaturists, as a figure with his index finger inserted into the circle of his mouth, but made the whole painting embody surprise" (74). And while Stork, as a member of the workshop, may believe that pictures are dependent upon the narratives they illustrate, he does not mind producing "a *Book of Costumes*" or a "collage album . . . for a Frankish traveler, scenes of fucking and other indecent pages . . . secretly dashed off for a pasha" (74). Stork's stories "reveal how time ends for the one who forsakes the perfect life and perfect illuminating," but Stork feels secure in making images outside the accepted bounds of the workshop's "perfect illuminating" (75). Stork and Butterfly, then, publicly follow the traditions of the old masters even as they secretly produce images that do not fit comfortably within those traditions, and they appear to readily dismiss the gap between what they say and what they believe.

Since some students may be unfamiliar with sixteenth-century Ottoman book art (or Ottoman art generally), it can be helpful to elucidate these passages by asking students to analyze examples from sixteenth-century manuscripts. Two especially rich images are "Muhammad Appearing at the Ka 'ba to Rid the Populace of an Unwanted Dragon" (Nakkaş Osman) and "Hunt" (Mīr 'Alī Shīr

Navā'ī). In "Muhammad Appearing at the Ka 'ba," students will immediately notice that Nakkaş Osman, the historical figure upon whom Master Osman is based, has indicated Muhammad's importance by making him the largest figure. In addition, the artist has covered the prophet's face in order to avoid depicting him, which can initiate a discussion about Islamic prohibitions against figural art alongside relevant passages from the novel. Students may also observe that the other figures in the painting tend to share similar facial characteristics and stylized hand gestures that are similar to those mentioned by the miniaturists in the novel. In "Hunt," students may note the idealized landscape in which the beautifully rendered horses appear to hover within a blue sky filled with flowering plants. Both images demonstrate the integration of image and text; boxes of written text are both part of the images and separated from them. Perhaps most remarkable in "Hunt" is the way in which the picture breaks through onto the page itself, suggesting a metaimage—an image that draws attention to itself as an image. A large tree seemingly grows out of the border surrounding the main picture, intertwined with flowers that both stand out from and mimic the golden swirls of blossoms and vines that make up the background of the page. Where, I ask the students, does the image or page begin or end? The tree breaking through to the page reminds students of moments in the novel when characters seem to break through the narrative and address the reader directly. These images, then, can serve multiple purposes in the classroom: as examples of sixteenth-century Ottoman book art and as aids to discussing the relation between image and text in the novel.

Once students feel comfortable identifying how the miniaturists repeatedly raise the specter of a crisis between conflicting visual ideologies, I ask them to consider how the text implies that this supposed crisis might simply be a problem of perception. All art, Enishte suggests, whether produced by Botticelli or Bihzad, is both imitation and innovation—a melding of the old and the new. "Nothing is pure," he tells his murderer, "in the realm of book arts, whenever a masterpiece is made . . . I can be certain of the following: Two styles heretofore never brought together have come together to create something new and wondrous. . . . To God belongs the East and the West. May He protect us from the will of the pure and unadulterated" (161). For Enishte, the problem with Ottoman art is not that it attempts to adhere to traditions—indeed, he celebrates the beauty and value of Ottoman art—but that its artists fail to recognize that their traditions are the result of innovation, integration, and adaptation. In discussing this passage, I have found it helpful to ask students to either support or challenge a reading of Enishte's claims. Does he believe what he says and does the novel, in a sense, agree with him? Instructors may wish to direct students' attention to the lengthy passage before Enishte's death in which he seems to foresee the decline of Ottoman art as a result of Western cultural hegemony (170–72). Students may point out that Enishte's is only one voice in a novel full of voices; others, however, may observe that Enishte's moderation ends up authorized through his meeting with a divine being he perceives as an "absolutely matchless red" (230). When Enishte asks this divine presence, whom he seems to regard as Allah, about the morality of his secret book, the response is "East and West belong to me," suggesting that the perceived aesthetic divisions between Venetian and Ottoman, Christian and Islamic, religious and secular, are human rather than divine (230). The response, moreover, echoes Enishte's own words that "to God belongs the East and the West" (161). This echoing of Enishte's words by Allah implicitly valorizes Enishte's assertions about the formation of aesthetic styles and the dangers of "the pure and unadulterated" (161). Through Enishte, therefore, the novel seems to embrace the inherent structural instability of any visual ideology.

Who Is the Murderer? Identity Production through Visual Art

While Stork and Butterfly remain fairly unaffected by the possibility of conflicting ideologies, for Olive the issue of image production results in the fragmentation of his character. Lacking the self-assurance of his fellow miniaturists, he worries constantly that he might sin by painting in new ways, confessing to Enishte that the criticisms about the secret book greatly weigh on him: "They say we've committed an unforgivable sin by daring to draw, from the perspective of a mangy street dog, a horsefly and a mosque as if they were the same size. . . . I cannot sleep for thinking about such things" (158). If the potential for blasphemy terrifies Olive—even to the point that he wonders if he could have committed "such an offense" unknowingly—the new style fascinates him as well (158). As he tells the reader, he visits Enishte not to kill him but because "I was so curious about that picture, not because of any sin I'd committed on its account—I genuinely wanted to see how it'd turned out" (163). For Olive, unlike for Butterfly, Stork, or Master Osman, the problem of style becomes a problem of identity: Who is Olive the artist? Olive the murderer? Is it possible for him to be both a faithful Muslim and a true miniaturist? A true miniaturist and interested in other artistic styles? Pamuk has tackled the topic of identity production in other novels, most notably in *The Black Book* and *Snow*. But in those novels identity is approached through verbal representation: in *The Black Book* Galip writes himself into being, while in *Snow* the narrator seeks Ka's identity through the poet's poems and letters. In *My Name Is Red*, Pamuk asks how one might use images to create a unified sense of self.

A useful exercise is to break students into groups and ask them to identify specific passages where Olive's increasingly fragmented sense of self becomes apparent. I point students to Olive's own assertions about his bifurcated self: "Now I am completely divided," he tells us, "just like those figures whose head and hands are drawn and painted by one master while their bodies and clothes are depicted by another" (97). Students seem especially drawn to the scenes before and during the murder of Enishte where, picking up the red inkpot, Olive remarks, "The hardworking miniaturist within me—that Master Osman had instilled in us all—was illustrating what I did and what I saw in distinct yet faded colors" (164). Students may also point to the scene where Olive, following Black through Istanbul, confuses his own identity with that of his rival's: "We were two men in love with the same woman; he was in front of me and completely unaware of my presence as we walked through the turning and twisting streets . . . and as we made ground, I felt I wasn't following him at all, but rather, that I was imitating him" (124). Although students may see this passage exclusively in terms of Olive's fragmented identity and his desire to find himself in others, the mention of imitation reminds us that the murderer's central crisis is not a love triangle involving himself, Black, and Shekure but an ideological struggle between different ways of producing art. The questions Olive asks himself are, Should he imitate others, and if so, whom? If he fails to imitate the old masters or the Venetian artists "correctly," is he inept or is he innovative?

Eventually, Olive wholly conflates style and identity, perhaps hoping that in producing a self-portrait he will produce a unified sense of self. He describes his attempts at self-portraiture in heart-rending terms:

> When I could see my face in the mirror from where I sat, I attempted to draw my portrait in charcoal. I drew for a long time, patiently. Much later, when I saw that once again the face on the page didn't resemble my face in the mirror, I was filled with such misery that tears welled in my eyes. How did the Venetian painters that Enishte described with such flourish do it? I then imagined myself to be one of them, thinking that if I illustrated in that state of mind, I could perhaps make a convincing self-portrait. (283)

Olive's identity has become so fragmented that he must imagine himself as another person entirely in order to paint his own portrait. The clash of ideology that Enishte sees as potentially fruitful initially appears to require Olive to become a completely different person and artist. By the end of the novel, however, Olive asserts that in producing a new style he has rediscovered himself. Despite confessing that the self-portrait causes him loneliness and guilt, he proudly displays it to his fellow miniaturists: "I felt unbridled elation because the picture . . . situated me at the center of a vast world. . . . I was both the center of everything, like a sultan or a king, and, at the same time, myself" (398).

Ekphrasis: The Visual versus the Verbal

Various character-narrators in the novel insist that readers should uncover the identity of the murderer. But how? The novel has made it difficult by depicting identity as something that is unknowable: How can reader-detectives possibly uncover the identity of a murderer-artist who cannot even identify himself? What, exactly, does it mean to identify Olive? And how can we, readers external to the world of the story, identify him? The story asserts that the murderer's identity can be discovered in the illuminated manuscripts of the Sultan's treasury, but readers can access the illuminations only through ekphrasis, "the verbal representation of visual representation" (Heffernan 3). We are dependent on the descriptions by Black and Master Osman as they pore over volume after volume, searching for the stylized horse nostrils that appear on the sheet of horse images left behind on Elegant's corpse (yet another set of images we cannot see). The chapters devoted to the treasury collect together the lost images described by Enishte just moments before his death, when he offers to Olive and the reader a lengthy catalogue of ways in which "our methods will die out, our colors will fade," concluding with "your dying shahs, your prisoners of war, your infidel galleons and your rival cities, your shiny dark nights that glimmer as if night itself had flowed from your pen, your stars, your ghostlike cypresses, your red-tinted pictures of love and death, yours and all the rest, all of it will vanish . . ." (172). Enishte suggests that Western culture will inevitably dominate, yet he simultaneously celebrates art forms that may otherwise become forgotten. Most important, this passage implies that while the artworks themselves may be lost to our sight, they can continue to exist in some ghostly form through verbal representation. The novel, then, becomes an ekphrastic archive and readers the ekphrastic detectives who must search this archive for a description of an image that will identify the murderer.

Readers are obliged to attend closely to ekphrasis because of its prominence in the novel: the artists tell stories about specific paintings, various characters describe their actions as though they are part of a painting, and the novel concludes with Shekure's assertion that she desires two portraits of herself, which she describes in detail for the reader. Verbal representation, moreover, is an integral element of the artistic process. In the *Book of Festivities* and in Enishte's pages, images are conceived through verbal forms, either as the narrative written by the Sultan's master calligrapher or as a set of instructions given to the artist. As the murderer bemoans to Elegant before killing him, "They commission paintings from us, ordering us to arrange a ship, an antelope or a sultan within the borders of a particular frame, demanding a certain style of bird, a certain type of figure, take this particular scene from the story, forget about such-and-such" (20). Only when Olive completes the final pages of the secret book, drawing his own portrait rather than that of the Sultan, does his art become liberated from language: Olive has not been ordered by anyone to draw this portrait and no story exists upon which he can base his image. Instead, he relies solely on the sight of his image reflected in a mirror. Readers, of course, have only ekphrastic access to this image. "Try to discover who I am," the murderer challenges in his first chapter, "from my choice of words and colors, as attentive people like yourselves might examine footprints to catch a thief" (17). Despite our ability to read the story from the perspectives of multiple characters, we lack the vision of the conventional detective who can directly examine visual evidence, like the footprints of a thief.

Writing Assignments

Below are writing assignments that I have found to be successful in teaching *My Name Is Red.*

Ekphrastic writing. Ask students to select an image from the Italian Renaissance and another from a sixteenth-century Ottoman manuscript and to write an ekphrastic description of each image. What do they notice about each image as they write? What choices do they make—do they write as though the image itself can speak, for instance? Have students read one another's ekphrastic writings. Can they identify (or even draw) the image described?

Tweeting as characters. Ask students to select one or two characters from the novel and to write a series of microtexts on any given topic. What might the characters choose to address in a series of tweets? How do students replicate or change the style, voice, or identity of their chosen characters? Do they use images in their tweets and if so, how and why? A short reflection on their decisions can foster additional discussion. This assignment can be an especially fun way to help students think about the unique voices of these characters and their beliefs and values.

Textual annotations. Assign students to produce a short annotation for a reference in the text and ask them to present it to the class. This helps build common knowledge about unfamiliar topics, such as the artists, books, images, or historical events that the characters mention.

Image selection. Divide students into small groups and ask them to locate (in a digital library such as *Artstor*) images of Venetian or Ottoman art from the 1580s and 1590s. They can then present their images to the class, alongside applicable passages from the text.This exercise clarifies how different characters view the two styles of art.

Book review. Assign John Updike's review of the novel ("Murder in Miniature") and ask students to respond to Updike or write a review of their own.

Art theft narrative. Partway through the novel Olive steals the pages of the secret book and finishes them on his own, altering the book's function and worth. Ask students to "steal" a work of local, publicly available art and to write at least 1,300 words (in any form of their choosing) about how the theft defines and changes the value of the work of art. This is an enormously popular assignment and students have produced wonderful responses, creating songs, fake newspaper articles, photographic essays, original works of visual art, and even a computer program (with the essay appearing in the code).

NOTE

[1] This essay quotes from Erdağ Göknar's translation of *My Name Is Red* published by Alfred A. Knopf in 2001.

Illuminating *My Name Is Red* and *The Museum of Innocence*

Nhora Lucía Serrano

> We are in the epoch of simultaneity: we are in the epoch of juxtaposition, the epoch of near and far, of the side-by-side, of the dispersed. . . . [O]ur experience of the world is . . . that of a network that connects points and intersects with its own skein.
>
> —Michel Foucault, "Of Other Spaces"

Visual Introductions and Textual Visuality

How can students learn firsthand about Western and Turkish notions of iconography and representation, be introduced to theoretical notions of intertextuality and mimesis, and reconceptualize medieval illuminated manuscripts and modern museum catalogs as visual literary forms? Put another way, how does one teach literature and art comparatively, in a global context, across time periods and cultures, and in an interdisciplinary format? Orhan Pamuk's *My Name Is Red* and *The Museum of Innocence* encourage a visual studies approach that addresses these concerns and engages students' interest in world literature.

In world literature survey lectures, in upper-level, discussion-based undergraduate courses, and in introductory graduate comparative literature seminars (from courses that survey twentieth-century world literature and art to those that focus on special topics), *My Name Is Red* and *The Museum of Innocence* lend themselves naturally to the interdisciplinary and critical methodology of visual studies. Whether based in a comparative literature or literature department, my visual studies courses frame Pamuk's novels alongside other literary works in translation by diverse authors such as Lewis Carroll, Edgar Allan Poe, Rebecca Harding Davis, Carlos Fuentes, Adolfo Bioy Casares, Franz Kafka, Nikolai Gogol, Jorge Luis Borges, James Joyce, Kazuo Ishiguro, Slavenka Drakulić, and Alice Munro, among others. These courses draw students from studio arts, history of art and architecture, and philosophy and literature departments alike. In all these courses, I discuss the literary works as exemplary models of a special type of visual discourse, which I dub *textual visuality*. Drawn from Lynda Nead's idea of visual discourse in *Myths of Sexuality*, which construes art in the modern era as a discourse because it extends beyond mere visual images to the practices, institutions, and knowledge of art itself (4), textual visuality emphasizes the intertextuality between the text and image and their praxes. It also puts the critical spotlight on both the text and the image as discursive formations.

Put simply, textual visuality underscores the use of ekphrasis and mimesis in order to shape how diverse worlds are understood through contrasting and often contradictory lenses.

At the beginning of any visual studies course I assign selections from Michel Foucault's *The Archaeology of Knowledge* (21–40) in order to introduce students to the concepts of discourse and discursive formation. I then offer an introductory lecture on visuality and vision from literary and cultural studies perspectives. Students become familiar with Hal Foster's idea of visuality and his emphasis on how various forms of vision—how we see, how we are allowed or made to see—are also fragmented, distorted cultural productions (ix). In a subsequent discussion that draws from cultural studies, we review Stuart Hall's definition of culture, in which the production and exchange of ideas and their ensuing practices are considered a construct (2). Integral to this discussion for advanced undergraduate and graduate students is the French film critic Christian Metz's notion of a scopic regime, where vision is understood not as a universal, singular undertaking but as multifarious, distinctive ways of seeing, each of which is a manifestation of culture (61). With exposure to visual studies terminology that is related to cultural production, discourse, and power, students acquire the foundational tools that allow them to more readily grasp Pamuk's interlacing narratives, his myriad of crafty narrators, and his own textual visuality. These introductory readings are moreover imperative for the later discussion of Pamuk's use of ethos, ekphrasis, mimesis, metaphor, and metonymy.

Throughout the introductory lectures and discussions I emphasize how Pamuk's novels hinge on Western concepts of representation and a sense of textual visuality in order to manipulate literary conventions as well as to introduce the world of each novel to Western readers. My first class on Pamuk is always dedicated to a comparative analysis; I begin by explaining that, similar to the postmodern style of Borges, Pamuk employs metafictional techniques that at once draw readers into the story and lend the narrators an awareness of their fictionality. However, I stress that this type of postmodern narrative—where isolation, distortion, dislocation, and the disfigurement of metanarratives predominate—is equally understood through the lens of textual visuality.

Before turning to any literal image or object related to the novels, it is crucial that students appreciate how Pamuk's characters are imbued with a classical visual ethos. In an upper-level undergraduate or graduate course, I build upon an earlier class discussion on Aristotle's *Ars Rhetorica*, demonstrating how Pamuk borrows from Aristotelian thought to create his textual visuality. For example, I mention how Aristotle considers poetry and the visual arts as equals in respect to characterization and the ethical influence upon the audience. For Aristotle, as for Pamuk, pictorial narratives should depict the subjects and their actions in a manner that conveys their ethical characters and moral choices. Pamuk's objective, I demonstrate, is to depict a character's visual ethos in language (mimesis) in order to appeal to the audience (pathos) and support the character's reasoned and verbal discourse (logos).

In subsequent classes where we discuss Pamuk's use of ekphrasis and mimesis, questions of intertextuality within and across cultural lines also naturally arise. In order to teach students about the vast history and the numerous theoretical approaches to these rhetorical devices, I assign selected readings from primary sources: Erich Auerbach's *Mimesis*, W. J. T. Mitchell's *Picture Theory*, Françoise Meltzer's *Salome and the Dance of Writing*, Hans Belting's *Likeness and Presence*, and Michael Ann Holly's *Past Looking*. In an upper-level undergraduate or graduate class on ekphrasis and mimesis I assign Michel Foucault's "Of Other Spaces," in which the author discusses how space can be perceived to be a virtual, versatile place that brings together objects and ideas of diverse geographies and chronologies. The narrative structures of *My Name Is Red* and *The Museum of Innocence* can be shown to be reminiscent of Foucault's approach to the encyclopedic collection. Pamuk himself employs a paradigmatic approach when he juxtaposes Western notions of representational art and mimesis with non-Western ones. For this reason, I frame the discussion of ekphrasis and mimesis comparatively, as contrasting aesthetics.

The success of teaching Pamuk's textual visuality also depends on the organization of the syllabi as comparative. First, it is vital that his novels are paired with Western and other non-Western counterparts as well as with supplemental readings that are grounded in art historical and philosophical discourses. After all, if the course outcomes specify that students will develop and hone skills in literary analysis through the broad sampling of literary works and modes of visual texts from around the world, then Pamuk's novels must too be introduced comparatively. I discovered that Pamuk's novels thrive under the critical visual lens when taught midway through the semester and when coupled with literary works such as Poe's "The Oval Portrait" (151–54), Gogol's "The Portrait" (340–93), Harding Davis's *Life in the Iron Mills*, Borges's "The Library of Babel" (*Collected Fictions* 51–58), Fuentes's *Aura*, Umberto Eco's *The Name of the Rose*, Ishiguro's *An Artist of the Floating World*, Drakulić's *A Guided Tour through the Museum of Communism*, or Lawrence Weschler's *Mr. Wilson's Cabinet of Wonder*.

An in-class group exercise has students creatively interrogate the use of metonymy and ekphrasis in Poe's narrative and in *My Name Is Red* and *The Museum of Innocence*. First, students sketch side by side the main portrait from each story. Second, as a group they examine how well the written description guided them in their sketches. Last, the entire class discusses the extent to which they used their imagination to fill in missing information and complete their visual rendering. After the exercise students analyze how the portrait is a metonym for vision, the artist, imagination, and divergent notions of representation. To compare the portrayals of social class, gender, and daily life one can juxtapose *My Name Is Red* with illuminations, such as those from the *Très*

Riches Heures du Duc de Berry ("Très Riches Heures"). I have students describe in a ten-minute writing exercise one of these Western illuminations from the perspective of one of Pamuk's characters: Black, Red, or Kemal. Through this exercise students quickly glean the importance of ekphrasis in illuminated manuscripts. Together with specific interdisciplinary assignments, the course organization stresses that Pamuk's narrative scopic regime is cross-cultural. In this manner, students see how Pamuk's textual visuality feeds on a variety of intertextual discourses and become novice practitioners of visuality themselves. Moreover, students learn from Pamuk's novels that images and visual literacy are essential to their humanities education. By the end of the semester, through a combination of *PowerPoint* presentations, museum and library visits, and visually centered assignments and workshops, students acquire the critical skills to discuss intertextuality, ekphrasis, and mimesis in Pamuk's novels through theory, philosophy, literature, art, and practice.

My Name Is Red ***and the Illuminated Manuscript***

> Soon after we can see, we are aware that we can also be seen. The eye of the other combines with our own eye to make it fully credible that we are part of the visible world.
>
> —John Berger, *Ways of Seeing*

Set in late-sixteenth-century Istanbul during nine days of the reign of the Ottoman Sultan Murat III, *My Name Is Red* is a metafictional novel that recounts the story of a murdered miniaturist and the relation of the crime to the making of a secret book and its Venetian-influenced illustrations. Interwoven with this main storyline is the courtly love story of Black and Shekure, which is in itself a reworking of Nizami's twelfth-century Persian tragic romance *Hüsrev and Shirin*. A potpourri of genres—detective, historical, and romance—*My Name Is Red* also incorporates differing attitudes from the West and East about decorative border ornamentation and representational art in order to question if art is idolatrous. With richly descriptive passages (which can serve as a primer for in-class ekphrastic exercises), allusions to the Western European style of illuminations, and references to non-Western illuminated manuscripts—such as Ibn Qayyim Al-Jawziyya's *Book of the Soul*, Suriname-i Hümayun's *Book of Festivities*, Firdawsi's *Shahnameh* ("Book of Kings"), and Nizami's *Hüsrev and Shirin*—Pamuk's novel is a perfect example of textual visuality.

In preparation for a class discussion that centers on the artists Black, Olive, Enishte, Butterfly, Master Osman, Stork, and Elegant, students are assigned selections from John Berger's *Ways of Seeing*. According to Berger, sight always exists before the written word, and knowledge is thus gained from drawing connections between what we see and the sense of ourselves in this world. Pamuk's novel presents various opportunities for students to directly interrogate Berger's ideas in the light of Metz's scopic regime. For an in-class exercise, divide the class into groups and assign each group a different miniaturist. Groups then discuss three questions from their character's point of view: Does Enishte's book embrace idolatrous art? Does the character prefer to work on book projects that situate art as conceptual or as representational? In the character's opinion, what is blindness? Students listen to the other groups' responses and begin to comprehend the various ways of seeing. This assignment works equally well for formal group projects in which students prepare *PowerPoint* presentations to illustrate their character's perspective and engage with Metz's scopic regime.

My Name Is Red portrays sixteenth-century Venice as a place where individual artistic styles flourished. While reading the novel, students should be exposed to Western medieval and Renaissance illuminated manuscripts—through *PowerPoint* presentations, a museum visit, or a class meeting at the campus library's special collections—so that they may visualize how an illuminated manuscript is written and decorated by hand. In contrast, the novel depicts sixteenth-century Istanbul (standing in for all of the Ottoman Empire) as a place where collective artistic style is prized and individual styles and signatures are considered flaws. In early modern Ottoman art, illustrations are meant to illuminate the manuscripts, not the artists themselves. To allow students to distinguish between Western and Eastern illuminations and their respective bookmaking processes, I conduct an illuminated manuscript workshop day with a colleague from the Fine Arts Department. Students appreciate learning about how manuscripts are made, from the paper to the layout to the calligraphy. During this special practicum class, the students work in groups much like in a medieval guild and in Master Osman's book arts workshop, with each student performing a unique role—patron, scribe, illuminator, gilder, and so on—and working on a specific part of the page—marginalia, historiated letter, text, sketching, illumination. In this exercise students are encouraged to illuminate a passage from either the titular chapter 31, "My Name Is Red," or from chapter 32, "I, Shekure." In chapter 31 the pigment red narrates its importance to vision through a parable of two blind artists who argue what it means to be a color. Students are told that the words *miniature* and *miniaturist* are derived from the Latin word *minium*, which also, coincidentally, signifies the red pigment of paint. The practicum exercise offers students hands-on engagement with illumination and the debate of conceptual versus representational art. In contrast, in illuminating chapter 32, which has a female narrator, students explore the idea of courtly love, figuration, and whether there is a gender component to illumination and representation in Western or Eastern art. This practicum component demystifies the final project in which students independently create their own illuminations.

Back in our traditional classroom setting, students readily discuss manuscript making as a metaphor for the novel and the clash of perspectives between the

Sultan and Enishte. Enishte seeks to incorporate Venetian-style portrait of the Sultan within a book intended to celebrate the thousandth year of the Muslim calendar, Hijra. However, the Sultan only agrees to the concealment of the portrait, a decision that sets into motion the murder and the novel's frenzied debate on art. Especially in the light of the practicum component, I discuss the Sultan's decision within the context of an ancient type of manuscript creation, the palimpsest, where a parchment page is scraped of its original writing in order to be used anew. The notion of a palimpsest can build upon earlier discussions of intertextuality: one can make an analogy that in the novel Eastern art is gradually disappearing in favor of Western art—like a palimpsest, Eastern art will become a faded remnant under the new, dominant Western style.

Students immensely enjoyed the visual exercises, and their critical research, analytical discussion, and writing skills improved exponentially after a hands-on visual assignment about textual visuality.

Sample Textual-Visuality Final Project: Illumination and Ekphrasis

Students participate in a workshop class in which they learn the basic elements of illumination. I ask students to bring a set of colored pencils, watercolors, or crayons.

In the practicum component related to the unit on illuminated manuscripts, the student will create (write and draw) an illuminated page for a final project. The student will depict one scene of the student's choice from one of the semester's literary texts. The illuminated page must include one large frontispiece with a decorated letter in the style reminiscent of either Western or Eastern art. The page must include text as well as the appropriate embellishment and marginalia.

The second component of the final project is a two-page response paper that accompanies the illumination. The response will either discuss the process of making the illuminated page, such as decisions regarding color, layout, choice of scene, and so on, or describe the illuminated page to a blind person.

The Museum of Innocence *and the Cabinet of Curiosity*

> O bliss of the collector, bliss of the man of leisure!
>
> —Walter Benjamin, "Unpacking My Library"

Set in 1970s Istanbul, and akin in plot to Gabriel García Márquez's *Love in the Time of Cholera*, Pamuk's *The Museum of Innocence* is a tragic story that introduces students to the incompatibility of modern and traditional notions of love and to the desire to collect personal mementos related to forbidden, sexual love. With a non-Western city in flux as its backdrop, and the impulse for collecting in its foreground, Pamuk's novel juxtaposes divergent visualities toward the material object and memory. In other words, the scopic regimes in the novel are in conflict with one another regarding what is appropriate to show and display and what needs to be concealed. In a visual studies course where the praxis of exhibition and spectatorship is studied, this novel offers another way to critically, interdisciplinarily interrogate concepts of ekphrasis, metaphor, metonymy, and intertextuality.

In an introductory seminar class at either the undergraduate or graduate level, I find that it takes two weekly class sessions to cover the multitude of visual concepts and themes in *The Museum of Innocence* and its companion piece, *The Innocence of Objects*, the catalog of the physical Museum of Innocence in Istanbul. During our first meeting I argue that Pamuk's novel acts like a textual museum in which the narrator Kemal, the fictional Orhan, and Pamuk the writer are its three paradigmatic curators. I assign Walter Benjamin's "The Task of the Translator" to frame my interpretation and guide the ensuing class discussion. Since the novel asks to be read alongside the museum catalog, I suggest that Pamuk gestures to Benjamin and that the two texts are translations of each other. For Pamuk, the inscribed Benjaminian messages in which the catalog re-creates the novel's experience of forbidden love—for example, Kemal's obsession with Füsun and his re-creation from memory of their physical encounters—are not only carried from one text to another and transferred as seemingly quotidian objects to an imagined museum; they are also re-created and revalued through the reader's experience of the objects in a new location, through reimagining history, and through the texts' use of synecdoche, chiasmus, and metaphor. I conclude with the suggestion that the novel is an exemplary mimetic object of textual visuality because it proposes itself as a museum guidebook, that is, one that serves as a replacement for the actual catalog. Put simply, the *Museum of Innocence* is a prose guide to the objects found in Kemal's museum of memory and experience.

At the second class meeting we discuss the supplementary reading, selections from Marcel Proust's *In Search of Lost Time*. My objective is for students to interrogate the seemingly contradictory and visually narrative frames of memory and time. The class discusses the first narrative frame in *The Museum of Innocence*, the star-crossed lovers: Kemal, a wealthy member of elite Turkish Islamic society, and Füsun, a poor, working-class shop girl and long-lost relative of Kemal's. Their haphazard encounter sets the novel's cataclysmic events and protracted narration in motion. In order to demonstrate Pamuk's borrowing of the Proustian sense of memory and time, we do close readings of passages from early in the novel that encapsulate Kemal's introspective narration ([Alfred A. Knopf] 3–7, 14–20, 27–31, 49–60, 176–84). I then suggest that these passages work much in the same vein as a discursive formation because Kemal's first-person narration represents memory as an involuntary impulse that shapes how the reader perceives time passing and the changing city of Istanbul, and, ultimately, objectifies Füsun as an artist's muse. From Kemal's account of his love for the young Füsun to the detailed descriptions of the particular settings and objects related to their rendezvous, the first-person narration is one of a besotted and lovelorn protagonist. Kemal's narration is an exemplary performance of ekphrasis, describing the memory of forbidden love as if it were a portrait upon which the reader gazes.

Pamuk's homage to French writers does not end with Proust. Kemal's narration resembles Baudelairean narration, and Kemal, strolling through the streets of Istanbul, recalls the literary archetype of the flâneur. To elucidate this point, I hand out the opening pages to Émile Zola's *The Masterpiece*, and we discuss the relation between introspective narration, point of view, and urban description. For those students interested in a modern approach to the flâneur, I further recommend de Certeau's *The Practice of Everyday Life*, which suggests that a flâneur reappropriates streets and their objects. Kemal as flâneur consumes and creates daily objects to subvert traditional notions of love and desire. As a fun exercise to conclude this class, I ask students to jot down, in five to ten minutes, their walk to class that day to enact the role of the literary flâneur. In a course where I require a class blog, I recommend that students post their flâneries accompanied by a photo or an image that represents their stroll. This exercise has students experiment with descriptive language and embrace textual visuality.

In the second seminar meeting on *The Museum of Innocence*, I make the suggestion that Pamuk's novel could be read as a metaphor for the museum catalog as well as for a cabinet of curiosity, both of which are literal manifestations of textual visuality. I assign the first ten pages from Denis Diderot's *Salon of 1765* to compare Diderot's ekphrastic sketch of the Salon paintings to Pamuk's description of objects related to Füsun. As students analyze Kemal's obsession with Füsun through the materiality of objects, the class quickly grasps the rhetorical kinship the museum catalog shares with literature. To further this idea, I hand out photocopied pages of museum catalogs from around the world. As students compare the Louvre's description of Leonardo da Vinci's *Mona Lisa* with the campus museum's catalog and Pamuk's narratives, they begin to explore the concepts of appropriation, display, and objectification as well as the logic and organization of a museum catalog.

The class discussion then turns to the cabinet of curiosity and the Renaissance *Wunderkammer*. In a brief lecture with a *PowerPoint* presentation, I show the Neapolitan Ferrante Imperato's 1599 engraving from *Dell'Historia Naturale*, which illustrated Ferrante's own collection (Imperato). The engraving shows the *Wunderkammer* as a private room (*studiolo*) with bookshelves where early modern collections were organized and displayed. After the class discusses this engraving's relevance to Pamuk's work, I show an image of the Theodore Roosevelt Rotunda from the American Museum of Natural History in New York and pose the question, What's the difference between a museum that houses dinosaur bones and Pamuk's museum? Students readily jump from declaring that museums are cultural constructions to recognizing them as sites where death, nostalgia, and the bliss of collecting are exhibited. This discussion facilitates another crucial line of inquiry that correlates the romance of Kemal and Füsun with Pamuk's romantic attachment for a long-lost Istanbul. For those students interested in pursuing this topic further for a comparative research paper, I recommend Weschler's thought-provoking account of the odd exhibits at the Museum of Jurassic Technology in Los Angeles. Like Pamuk's novel, Weschler's book is a sentimental recollection of a person's possessions; both books validate the historical, cultural relevance of their respective collections. Weschler's first-person narration is similar to Kemal's introspective flâneur style, and both authors seek to describe peculiar, everyday objects that are connected to a single person.

As an in-class visual exercise that closes the discussion on Pamuk, I recommend that students take five to ten minutes to create a postcard with magazine images. Then, I ask them to address it to a friend and write about an object or person that caught their attention during the day. In a course where I require a blog, I recommend that they post their writings accompanied by a photo of their postcard. In this exercise students experiment with descriptive language, explore commercial and aesthetic associations of the postcard's text and image, and embrace textual visuality from the vantage point of the creator of the message.

As a conclusion to the subject, I offer students the option to complete a final visual project that builds upon the concept of textual visuality and its relation to the museum catalog and the cabinet of curiosity. Students handcraft their own cabinets and write the accompanying catalogs. If possible, and with student consent, I secure a case in either the campus museum, library, or college office where I display these projects; much like a special exhibition, I leave a guestbook for comments. The guestbook entries make evident that students and colleagues alike enjoy seeing interdisciplinary Pamukian work on display. From a visual studies perspective *The Museum of Innocence* is a manifestation of a scopic regime in its own right as well as a literal manifestation of textual visuality where intertextuality, ekphrasis, and rhetorical devices intersect with taxonomy, the flâneur, collecting, and the museum.

Sample Textual-Visuality Final Project: Cabinet of Curiosity

In lieu of a final research paper, students may choose to create a three-dimensional cabinet of curiosity made up of objects related to school life. I limit the final product to eight to twelve shelves, to pocket-sized objects—photographs of objects are acceptable—and to a portable cabinet. As part of this assignment students are required to produce a catalog of the collection: each object must be described and discussed in no more than two double-spaced pages. A cover page describing the collection overall must be included with the catalog, but the inclusion of images is optional.

The Novel as Museum, the Museum as Novel: Teaching *The Museum of Innocence*

Yin Xing

Teaching Orhan Pamuk's *The Museum of Innocence* is a peculiar and intriguing experience: peculiar because it is rare to teach literature both as a book and as a museum and intriguing because the teacher has to create a museum while teaching the course. Pamuk originally conceived the novel as taking the form of a museum catalog for the private museum created by his hero, Kemal, in memory of Kemal's lost love, Füsun; the fictional museum assembled everyday objects that had belonged to Füsun or that were associated with their love affair. As Pamuk planned and wrote the novel, he renovated an old building in his Istanbul neighborhood to serve as the physical manifestation of his story. In the end, the novel took on a more conventional narrative form, and once the museum opened, Pamuk wrote a catalog for it, entitled *The Innocence of Objects*. Both in the novel and in the catalog, the distinction between writing and collecting is blurred and the border between fiction and reality is crossed, in the sense that the novelistic fiction is turned into a physical reality in the form of things collected, exhibited, and cataloged in a museum. In this way, reading becomes a form of collecting and collecting in turn becomes writing, and teachers and students play multiple roles as readers, collectors, and writers.

The roles become all the more complicated outside Istanbul, especially when students' cultural history differs from Pamuk's and they initially know little about the circumstances under which the novel was written and the museum built. My experiences teaching in China can help teachers outside Istanbul address these complications. Classes that cannot visit the museum can nonetheless study Pamuk's catalog *The Innocence of Objects*, arranged according to the narrative structure of the novel. The catalog describes and photographically represents seventy-four exhibits, each of which is displayed in a glass-fronted vitrine of polished wood and corresponds to a chapter in the novel (a few of the novel's eighty-three chapters aren't represented in the catalog because the corresponding exhibits hadn't been finalized in the museum's display by spring 2012, when the catalog was published, three years after the novel). In explaining the relation among the novel, the museum, and the catalog, Pamuk makes it clear that "the museum is not an illustration of the novel, and the novel is not an explanation of the museum" (*Innocence* 18).

Comparing the novel with the catalog yields unexpected results. Reading the novel without looking at the vitrine that Pamuk "is particularly fond of" (*Innocence* 100), we learn about the heroine Füsun's "catalogue of the 'other men' who had enjoyed her kisses, and . . . those who had failed to compel her to go further" (*Museum* 60).[1] We are told of the experiences (and nightmares) of "all presentable Istanbul girls," who are haunted from a young age by the "dark specters" that accost them on the streets; as they grow up, these girls, like Füsun, gain profound knowledge of "Istanbul's streets, bridges, hills, cinemas, buses, crowded squares, and isolated corners," which are "filled with these shadowy Uncles Sleaze, Shithead, and Ugly." Istanbul is "never short of men finding imaginative new ways to touch" Füsun or to "pinch her, squeeze her or brush her from behind" (56–57). These references to the shameless uncles and the innocent girls are among many perverse aspects of modern life that are concretized in the everyday objects collected by Kemal, including in one display a Kütahya ashtray, a teacup, a glass, a seashell, and a girl's hair clip. All these objects remind readers of the place and the time or of the "heavy, draining, crushing atmosphere" that Kemal describes (55). In the novel these objects lead directly into the narrative. But it is also possible to consider the vitrine displays in the museum and catalog—in the context of a foreign classroom, the catalog stands in for the museum—without knowledge of how they relate to the novel.

For instance, Box 14 in the catalog (*Innocence* 100–01) shows a surrealist picture with a seashell hanging in the middle of the left side, a cup of red tea under it, and on the right a suspended pack of cigarettes with the Kütahya ashtray beneath it. In the foreground, between the teacup and the ashtray, is the hair clip. Besides these objects, there is half of a broken bracelet in the left front corner, and a crab-like sea creature just behind the ashtray, seemingly crawling toward a red car right behind the hair clip. Just to the right of the teacup there is a miniature lamppost, identical to those standing in the black-and-white background, a photograph of the Dolmabahçe pier that Pamuk obtained from a junk dealer. The position of the lamppost visually connects these objects in the foreground with the cityscape in the background photograph, and so something personal merges with the collective, and an individual's memories with those of the city.

A more careful comparison of Box 14 with the original pier picture, also provided in the catalog (102–03), reveals that there is a group of idle people standing on the pier. In the vitrine these figures are obscured by the teacup. In the display a woman in a red blouse and a white skirt walks toward the red car, which was gray in the original photograph. The woman and the car, located where the black-and-white photograph borders the colorful world in which Füsun's objects exist, evidently belong to the colorful world. If the group of people standing on the pier in the picture signify something of the time and place when the picture was taken, then their omission must mean something. Does it point to modernity replacing history? Does the looming background of the city indicate that the colorful present is haunted by the monochrome past? Or has a collective past given way to a more individual present?

The addition of the woman and the changing of the car's color may support these questions or serve as the ideological underpinnings of the story. You can ask students to delineate the differences between the vitrine in the museum and the chapter in the novel as well as the differences between the picture of the box in the catalog and the picture that serves as the background in the box. Evidently the picture of the box is surreal in the sense that it represents neither the story told in the novel nor the objects displayed in the museum. Across different spans of time and different frames of space, the picture locates a personal past within a collective past and a personal love story within the story of a modern city, suggesting "the whims of uncalculated beauty," the "beauty where neither the mind conceived of nor the hand intended any" (*Innocence* 100, 103).

Classes should explore the ways in which *The Museum of Innocence* is a story about the past that describes many objects as mementos, such as the lover's earrings, torn ticket stubs, cigarette butts, and a quince grinder. These objects were collected by Pamuk for the writing of the novel: he would hunt for objects to illustrate a chapter or come across a chance find in an antique shop that would inspire an episode. Writing the novel and collecting the objects share the same objective, the preservation of a half-forgotten era of the nation's cultural history. On a literal level, the novel is written in memory of Füsun, cousin and lover of the would-be curator of the museum, whose name seems to echo the Turkish word *hüzün*, meaning "melancholic introspection," or simply "melancholy," to which Pamuk devoted a whole chapter in *Istanbul: Memories and the City*. This echo may lead students to think about the deep structure of the story, which invites "the willing participation of the reader's imagination," as Pamuk put it in his Norton lectures at Harvard, later published as *The Naive and the Sentimental Novelist* (123).

Pamuk elaborated in his Norton lectures that writing the novel included "finding, studying, and describing objects that inspired me," and "gradually filling up my studio with old medicine bottles, bags of buttons, National Lottery tickets, playing cards, clothes, and kitchen utensils . . . a dress in a bright fabric with orange roses and green leaves on it . . . just right for Füsun," and "a black-and-white photo from the 1930s." The objects, which triggered "situations, moments, and scenes" in the writer's imagination, were intended to enable readers to "channel the story through the objects" (121–22). A literature class that studies the novel alongside the catalog can do exactly that.

What is the story behind the stories of all these objects? What is the picture within the picture in Box 14? What exactly was the purpose of writing the novel, building the museum, and cataloging the vitrines of the exhibition? By studying each object displayed in the museum or its catalog, we can imagine the story behind it and associate the object with other objects. For instance, the Kütahya ashtray in Box 14 can be associated with the wall-size display of the cigarette butts in Box 68 (*Innocence* 226–27), which correspond to the 4,213 cigarette stubs described in chapter 68 of the novel. These stubs, reddened by Füsun's lovely lipstick, "bore the unique impress of her lips at some moment whose memory was laden with anguish or bliss, making these stubs artifacts of singular intimacy" (*Museum* 393). These artifacts, which turn out to be the objects that "correspond most truly to Aristotle's moments," "moments belonging to the past," tell more than the story of Füsun, of how the cigarettes "touched her rosy lips and entered her mouth" (397). The cigarettes are her brand of Samsuns, for which Kemal says that "I gave up Marlboro"—an imitation of the American brand smuggled into Turkey. Behind these cigarette butts is a message about modernity in Turkey: how Western products, including fake Marlboros, champagne, designer handbags, transistor radios, and electric blenders, became popular among young consumers desiring a modern lifestyle.

Amid this consumerist zeal and Western aspiration, tradition lingered in "rituals that allowed families to act 'as if' they were respecting tradition, even as they broke it" (*Museum* 394). The detailed description of how Füsun smoked—"half trying to hide from her father," "covering her cigarette with the curved hand," and turning her head to the right to exhale, "directing the fast cloud of dark blue smoke to a point far from the table" (394)—along with descriptions of other everyday rituals shows a culture in which, with the advent of rapid modernization and urbanization, things treasured in the past are soon forgotten. They become the "unpalatable anthropological truths" that will be left to shimmer with a quiet beauty in a sentimental museum (61).

A valuable essay to assign as secondary reading is Ackbar Abbas's "Walter Benjamin's Collector," which expounds Benjamin's profound insight into things past, tracing the experience of modernity in the figure of the collector. The essay prepares students to think theoretically and critically about collecting and collectors. Benjamin examines the ambivalent modern social space, divided into exterior and interior, and defines the modern collector as the *étui*-man, or "case-man," "the true inhabitant of the interior." To oppose the destructive character of modern life, the *étui*-man collects and preserves objects in velvet-lined cases (appropriately for our context, *étui* can also mean "cigarette case"). He is closely connected with objects in the interior: he "hides behind" them, "glorifies them, fetishizes them," and succumbs to the "phantasmagoria of the interior," the concretization of "the problem of commodity fetishism." Yet the *étui*-man resists the problem of the age, stripping objects of their commodity character or use value by possessing them and hording them in the interior, by turning them into art, and, in the process, by turning artworks into "mere objects of contemplation" (220).

Building on Benjamin, Abbas identifies collectors and writers. Both try "to make something out of the rubbish heaps of history, turning compositions out of compost" (222), and "under certain conditions, the experience of possession could be transformed into the possession of experience" (231). Pamuk—either the writer as collector or the other way around—compiles his museum collection while writing his novel, confronting, not avoiding, the experience of modernity. Modernity, especially the ruination of old cityscapes, as Pamuk relates in various texts, threatens the past and the memories of the past: "First we lose a memory, but we know we've lost it and we want it back. Then we forget we have forgotten it, and the city can no longer remember its own past. The ruins that cause us such pain and open the road to forgetfulness become, in the end, the lots on which others can found new dreams" (*Other Colors* 69).[2] What are these new dreams? On what ruins are they built? What memory of the past has been lost? Students can explore these questions through Pamuk's novel and its catalog. More important, they can reflect on their own national culture and its global setting.

My students in China can consider the history of modernization and westernization in China and Turkey, reflecting on the parallels and the differences. North American classrooms today often have students of foreign birth or recent descent; these students can compare what Pamuk writes about Turkey with what they know of their own family's points of origin. Such comparisons can help them relate to the novel's rich portrayal of the ambiguous attractions of Western material culture in the Turkey of Pamuk's youth. The objects described in the novel and exhibited in the museum reveal a particular picture of Turkey between 1970 and 1983. It is the Turkey fascinated by Western commodities for the first time, even as its material world remained immersed in the traditional patriarchy, political repression, and cultural loss that had accelerated with the Kemalist reforms of the 1920s. It is the Turkey that, on the one hand, confronted the influx of foreign objects such as electric razors, can openers, designer handbags, and Chevrolets, and on the other, felt the loss of such "things that gave the city its exotic allure," including "dervish lodges, fires, the beauty of cemeteries, the palace and its harem, the beggars, the packs of roaming dogs, the prohibition against drinking, the seclusion of women, the city's air of mystery, the Bosphorus tour, and the beauty of the skyline" (*Istanbul* 237).[3] These lost things—things that made Turkey exotic and mysterious to Westerners in the nineteenth century—belonged to the Ottoman Empire. By the 1970s they had been replaced by Western things and the commodity fetishism of Western capitalism.

Pamuk's hero, Kemal, enters this commodified world by way of a fake designer handbag, sold in a shop where Füsun is working as a salesgirl and signaling the flirtatious and ostentatious allure of the Western commodity. In returning the bag to the shop, Kemal comes to know Füsun, his lost and found love object, and initiates a love-and-hate relationship with her, which ends with Füsun's tragic death. The death can be blamed not only on Kemal's irresponsibility but also on a long history of women's oppression under Turkish patriarchy, heightened by post-Ottoman cultural insecurity. After he loses Füsun, Kemal wanders through the streets of Istanbul, which "was now a galaxy of signs that reminded me of her," and realizes "how much Füsun's fragility reflected the bashfulness of the Turkish people" (*Museum* 167). Here we see the link between Füsun and the Turkish people, between Kemal the collector and his collected objects, and between the personal history and memory of Pamuk's heroine and those of the nation as a whole.

Beyond specific cultural or national comparisons, *The Museum of Innocence* can prompt discussion about memory. What memories of the past should be preserved, and how do we preserve them? What are the consequences of the loss of historical memory to personal or national histories? In our contemporary consumer society, are memories themselves reduced to collectibles? How do we distinguish collecting from hoarding, aesthetic appreciation from commodity fetishism?

Studying the novel together with selections from the museum catalog, students observe that the young Turks who have grown up under the influence of westernization desire modern identities and experiences but also possess a strong attachment to things. This attachment will first become a passion for ownership and "under certain conditions, the passion for possession could be transformed into the possession of experience" (Abbas 230). For Pamuk, this passion has created a huge number of strange hoarders or "sick" collectors, "eternally patient guardians of a community's sacred relics," whose attachment to objects "stemmed from their personal heartbreak and sorrowful life histories, but they remained honestly convinced of the importance of their contribution to the very society that mocked them" (*Innocence* 49). But whether they are "sick" collectors, mad hoarders, or sacred guardians, the collections they create will evoke similar sentiments "of how at one point in the past, some people had lived in a given street, neighborhood, or city; and of how they had then departed, leaving behind old newspapers, masses of paper and objects, pictures, photographs, and furniture" (*Innocence* 51).

This perspective opens up exciting pedagogical opportunities. The class can visit a local museum and investigate the ways in which it tells a story—and perhaps conceals other possible stories—through its choice of objects and their arrangement. Either in person or by visiting museum Web sites, the class can work in small groups to look at a range of kinds of museums—house museums devoted to famous writers or political figures, museums of popular culture or folk art, art museums—and together assemble a kind of virtual collection of collections. In such an exercise students ask who the "patient guardians" of the collection are, consider what sentiments the collections arouse, and contemplate what the collections mean for the community as a whole.

Pamuk focuses on ordinary, everyday objects and the person who patiently picks them up, accumulates them, collects and catalogs them. This collector is a version of Baudelaire's rag-picker, who "combines the attitude of writer and collector to cultural history" (Abbas 231). An assignment related to the collecting of everyday objects can have students bring in an object from their neighborhood (or a photograph of it) and discuss its relation to the city's collective memory; or, students can bring in objects from their own households or dormitories that preserve the memory of family or community members or events. For Pamuk, such everyday objects communicate with people and with one another:

> The more I looked at the objects on my desk next to my notebook—rusty keys, candy boxes, pliers, and lighters—the more I felt as if they were communicating with one another. Their ending up in this place after being uprooted from the places they used to belong to and separated from the people whose lives they were once part of—their loneliness, in a word—aroused in me the shamanic belief that objects too have spirits. (*Innocence* 52)

These spirits inspire the writer—he impulsively buys certain objects and weaves them into his story in a seemingly endless process of rag-picking, cataloging, and collecting. In creating the museum and writing the novel Pamuk experiences moments of seeing new beauty in things past or in things vanishing. Students can be asked to try the same thing by writing the (true or imagined) stories of objects they find. Storytelling is a way of transmitting experience through language, while collecting is a way of transmitting experience through objects. Both are modes of discourse opened up to interpretation, and both require a language with which the experience of history and of modernity can be articulated.

Thinking about Pamuk's objects and those in their own lives as storytelling assemblages, students can further explore the relation between life and work in *The Museum of Innocence*, where the author as creator begins to merge with the creation itself. Similarly, in *Istanbul* Pamuk's personal history and the history of the city are illustrated with photographs whose functions are evidently the same as illustrations of the museum exhibits in *The Innocence of Objects*. Studying these books together, students can shuttle back and forth through the stories, the objects, and the pictures, in order to explore how Pamuk recomposed everyday observations, revealed "the deeper meaning of life," and constructed "the core defining quality of a novel" (*Naive* 131).

In a course on the modern novel, instructors can discuss how *The Museum of Innocence* differs from the work of writers such as James Joyce and Marcel Proust, in which memories are represented as involuntary and objects serve as triggers for remembering the past. Pamuk's work is indebted to both of these modernists, as well to the postmodernism of writers such as Jorge Luis Borges and Italo Calvino, both of whom Pamuk praises in *The Naive and the Sentimental Novelist* for enhancing the novel's authenticity and persuasiveness by consolidating "the tradition of thinking via the medium of the novel" (135). For all his literary debts, Pamuk's ultimate purpose is "preservation, conservation and the resistance to being forgotten" (135). Preservation resists forgetting, but it may also compensate for loss, as when Kemal starts to collect everything connected to Füsun and the experience he desperately longed to perpetuate. To explore these ideas, have students collect a number of things that would perpetually remind them of past experiences they wish to preserve and then write a short story as an aid in preserving the memory.

Writing and collecting become opportunities for Pamuk, like Kemal, to relive moments of joy, sadness, and shame; students too can delve into significant moments from their lives through writing and collecting. For Pamuk these moments are never strictly personal: his work crosses multiple forms and media and blurs the distinctions between novels and museums, imagination and reality, subjects and objects, and the author-collector and his social milieu. As Irmak Ertuna argues, "it is by dissolving the boundaries between Kemal and his social milieu and by embedding his story within the social history of Turkish modernization that Pamuk can achieve such an anthropological materialism . . . and hence imply a radically different relationship between subject and the object" (109). Kemal's story is best interpreted within the cultural history embodied in the objects through which he reconstructs his experience; conversely, the culmination of Pamuk's years of omnivorous collecting for the museum is best appreciated through the story of the lovelorn Kemal in Pamuk's beloved Istanbul.

In reading the novel together with the catalog, students observe the novelist-collector drawing out the humble objects with sharply observed stories of everyday life and preserving the experience of a pivotal period of modernity. One final task for students is to make connections between literature and history, whether collective or personal; between reality and imagination; and between things collected in a museum and things depicted in writing. And in filling the gap between individual story and collective history, past and present, Istanbul and Beijing (or their own corner of the world), students will become what Benjamin calls "the physiognomists of the world of objects" and "interpreters of fate" (*Illuminations* 60–61), aesthetically and socially aware observers for whom experience is not just an immediate response to the ever-changing truth of the world but a "profane illumination that perceives the everyday as impenetrable, the impenetrable as everyday" (*Reflections* 190).

NOTES

[1] This essay quotes from Maureen Freely's translation of *The Museum of Innocence* published by Alfred A. Knopf in 2009.

[2] This essay quotes from Maureen Freely's translation of *Other Colors* published by Alfred A. Knopf in 2007.

[3] This essay quotes from Maureen Freely's translation of *Istanbul: Memories and the City* published by Vintage Books in 2006.

NOTES ON CONTRIBUTORS

Hülya Adak is associate professor of comparative literature at Sabancı University and a visiting professor at the Freie Universität Berlin and Universität Potsdam. She is the author of *Halide Edib and Political Violence: The Armenian Genocide, Dictatorships and Nonviolence* (2016). She is the editor, with Erika Glassen, of *Hundert Jahre Türkei: Zeitzeugen erzaehlen*. Her articles have appeared in the journals *PMLA*, *South Atlantic Quarterly*, *Journal of Genocide Research*, *Journal of Middle East Women's Studies*, and *New Perspectives on Turkey*.

Barish Ali is associate professor of English at State University of New York, Buffalo State College. He is the author of articles on Alan Moore and Eddie Campbell's *From Hell*, on Lawrence Durrell's *Bitter Lemons*, on Orhan Pamuk's *My Name Is Red*, and on David Bowie.

Bernt Brendemoen is a professor of Turcology at Oslo University. His work has focused on Turkish dialectology and historical linguistics. He is the author of *The Turkish Dialects of Trabzon: Their Phonology and Historical Development* (2002). He has translated five of Orhan Pamuk's novels into Norwegian and has written several articles on Pamuk's authorship.

David Damrosch is Ernest Bernbaum Professor of Comparative Literature at Harvard University. His books include *What Is World Literature?* (2003), *The Buried Book: The Loss and Rediscovery of the Great Epic of Gilgamesh* (2007), and *How to Read World Literature* (2nd ed., 2017). He is the general editor of the six-volume *Longman Anthology of World Literature*; coeditor of *The Princeton Sourcebook in Comparative Literature* (2009), of *The Routledge Companion to World Literature* (2011), and of *Crime Fiction as World Literature* (2017); and editor of *Teaching World Literature* (2009) and of *World Literature in Theory* (2014). He is the founder and director of Harvard's Institute for World Literature.

Gloria Fisk is associate professor of English at Queens College, City University of New York. Her essays have appeared in *The American Reader*, *Comparative Literature*, *Contemporary Literature*, *n+1*, and *New Literary History*. Her first book is *Orhan Pamuk and the Good of World Literature* (2017).

Carolyn McCue Goffman is senior instructor in the Department of English at DePaul University. She is the author of "From Religious to American Proselytism: Mary Mills Patrick and the 'Sanctification of the Intellect,'" in *American Missionaries and the Middle East: Foundational Encounters* (2011) and of other publications on women and missionaries in the Ottoman Empire.

Erdağ Göknar is best known for his award-winning translation of Pamuk's *My Name Is Red* (2001), which marked Pamuk's emergence as an author of world literature, leading to Pamuk's Nobel selection in 2006. Göknar is also the translator of A. H. Tanpınar's *A Mind at Peace*. He is associate professor of Turkish and Middle Eastern studies at Duke

University and the director of the Duke Middle East Studies Center. His translations have earned him the International IMPAC Dublin Literary Award and two NEA translation fellowship grants. He is the author of a work of literary criticism on Pamuk, *Orhan Pamuk, Secularism, and Blasphemy: The Politics of The Turkish Novel* (2013); and of a poetry collection, *Nomadologies* (2017).

David Gramling is associate professor of German studies at the University of Arizona. He is the author of *The Invention of Monolingualism* (2016) and various publications on multilingualism and translation, Turkish-German literature, and LGBT studies. With Chantelle Warner, he edits the journal *Critical Multilingualism Studies*. He is coinvestigator on the AHRC grant Researching Multilingually, based in Glasgow, Scotland.

Didem Havlioğlu is a teaching fellow at Duke University. She has published articles, in Turkish and in English, on gender and intellectual history in Turkish literature. She is the author of *Mihrî Hatun: Performance, Gender-Bending, and Subversion in Ottoman Intellectual History* (2017).

Darcy Irvin is a visiting assistant professor at the University of Puget Sound. Her research explores how British authors and readers adapted to nineteenth-century developments in visual print culture and is focused especially on the works of Charles Dickens, George Eliot, Charlotte Brontë, H. Rider Haggard, and Arthur Conan Doyle.

Djelal Kadir is Edwin Erle Sparks Professor Emeritus of Comparative Literature at Pennsylvania State University and Distinguished Visiting Professor at the Scuola di dottorato in Scienze dell'interpretazione e della produzione culturale, Università di Roma, "La Sapienza." He is the founding president of the International American Studies Association and former editor of the international quarterly *World Literature Today*. Among other works, he is the author of *The Other Writing: Postcolonial Essays in Latin America's Writing Culture* (1993) and *Memos from the Besieged City: Lifelines for Cultural Sustainability* (2011) and the coeditor of the six-volume *Longman Anthology of World Literature* (2004) and *The Routledge Companion to World Literature* (2011).

E. Khayyat is assistant professor of comparative literature and of African, Middle Eastern, and South Asian languages and literatures at Rutgers University. A former editor in chief of the Istanbul journal *Cogito*, he has written numerous articles on literary theory, philosophy, and Turkish literature and edited *Dunya Edebiyati Deyince* ("The Stakes of a World Literature"; 2009). He is completing a book on nineteenth- and twentieth-century Turkish literature and culture.

John Limon is John J. Gibson Professor of English at Williams College. He is the author of *The Place of Fiction in the Time of Science: A Disciplinary History of American Writing* (1990), *Writing after War: American War Fiction from Realism to Postmodernism* (1994), *Stand-Up Comedy in Theory; or, Abjection in America* (2000), and *Death's Following: Mediocrity, Dirtiness, Adulthood, Literature* (2012).

Jennifer Malia is assistant professor of English at Norfolk State University and was formerly assistant professor of writing studies at the American University of Sharjah in the United Arab Emirates. Her work has appeared in *Women's Studies*, *The Conradian*, *Extrapolation*,

Pacific Coast Philology, *Academic Exchange Quarterly*, *Critical Approaches to Joseph Conrad*, and *Fan Phenomena: Jane Austen*. She is currently writing a book on satirical fiction on terrorism and sensational media responses to political violence in the late nineteenth and early twentieth centuries.

B. Venkat Mani is professor of German at the University of Wisconsin, Madison. He is the author of *Cosmopolitical Claims: Turkish-German Literatures from Nadolny to Pamuk* (2007) and of *Recoding World Literature: Libraries, Print Cultures, and Germany's Pact with Books* (2017). He is the editor of several collected volumes on cosmopolitanism and world literature.

Bruce Robbins is Old Dominion Foundation Professor in the Humanities in the Department of English and Comparative Literature at Columbia University. He is the author of *Perpetual War: Cosmopolitanism from the Viewpoint of Violence* (2012). A companion volume, *The Beneficiary*, is forthcoming. He is a coeditor of *Cosmopolitics: Thinking and Feeling Beyond the Nation* (1998), of *Cosmopolitanisms* (2017), and of *The Longman Anthology of World Literature*.

Esra Mirze Santesso is associate professor in the Department of English at the University of Georgia. She is the author of *Disorientation: Muslim Identity in Contemporary Anglophone Literature* (2013) and the coeditor of a collection titled *Islam and Postcolonial Discourse* (2017). Her essays have appeared in various journals, including *Recherche Littéraire / Literary Research*, *The Comparatist*, and *Postcolonial Text*. Her 2008 interview with Orhan Pamuk was published in *PMLA*.

Nhora Lucía Serrano is a visiting assistant professor of comparative literature at Hamilton College. She is the coeditor of *Curious Collectors, Collected Curiosities* (2011) and has written several articles and essays that focus on visual studies and medieval and Renaissance studies. She is the 2014 recipient of the Smithsonian National Postal Museum and the Washington 2006 World Philatelic Exhibition Scholarship.

Sevinç Türkkan teaches modern Turkish literature and intellectual history at the University of Rochester. Her work has appeared or is forthcoming in *Translation and Literature*; *Orhan Pamuk: Critical Esays on a Novelist between Worlds*; *Türkisch-deutsche Studien Jahrbuch*; *Teaching Translation*; *Global Perspectives on Orhan Pamuk*; *Post-1960 Novelists in Turkey, Making Connections: Interdisciplinary Approaches to Cultural Diversity*; *International Journal of the Humanities*; *Crossing Borders with Foreign Language Films*; and the *Encyclopedia of Literary and Cultural Theory*. Her translations from Turkish and German have appeared in the *Best European Fiction* and *K1N: Journal of Literary Translation*. Her translation of Aslı Erdoğan's *The Stone Building and Other Places* is forthcoming (2017).

Delia Ungureanu is assistant director of Harvard's Institute for World Literature and assistant professor of literary theory at the University of Bucharest. She is the author of *From Paris to Tlön: Surrealism as World Literature* (2017) and of *Poetica Apocalipsei: Războiul cultural în revistele literare românesti, 1944–1947* (2012). She has published essays on canon formation, modem poetry, and poetics and is coediting *Romanian Literature for the*

World: Circulation and Exchange on the International Market, a special issue of the *Journal of World Literature.*

Yin Xing is associate professor of English at Renmin University of China in Beijing. She is the author of *Women Writing the City: Studies on Experience of Modernity in Twentieth-Century British Women's Fiction* (published in Chinese) and other journal articles in Chinese and in English on Pamuk and other modern writers.

SURVEY PARTICIPANTS

Beyazıt Akman, *State University of New York, Geneseo College*
Barish Ali, *State University of New York, Buffalo State College*
Esra Almas, *Doğus University and University of Amsterdam*
Rula Baalbaki, *American University of Beirut*
Katarzyna Bartoszynska, *Bilkent University*
Pelin Başcı, *Portland State University*
Petra de Bruijn, *Leiden University*
David M. Buyze, *University of Vermont*
Iclal Cetin, *State University of New York, Fredonia State College*
Nancy Dayton, *Taylor University*
Eda Dedebaş, *Boğaziçi University*
Alicia Ellis, *University of Chicago*
Esim Erdim, *University of Mississippi*
Gloria Fisk, Queens College, *City University of New York*
Carolyn McCue Goffman, *DePaul University*
Erdağ Göknar, *Duke University*
David Gramling, *University of Arizona*
Didem Havlioğlu, *Istanbul Şehir University*
Trevor Hope, *Yaşar University*
Elizabeth Horan, *Arizona State University*
Gunvald Ims, *University of Osla*
Darcy Irvin, *University of Puget Sound*
Sibel Irzık, *Sabanci University*
Khalida Kareemi, *De Anza College*
Persis Karim, *San Jose State University*
Christopher Larkosh, *University of Massachusetts, Dartmouth*
Jennifer Malia, *American University of Sharjah*
Laci Mattison, *Florida State University*
Michael McGaha, *Pomona College*
Brian Mello, *Muhlenberg College*
Gaura Shankar Narayan, *State University of New York, Purchase College*
Loisa Nygaard, *University of California, Santa Cruz*
Jeannette Okur, *University of Texas, Austin*
Maya Ombasic, *University of Montréal*
Almila Ozdek, *University of Maryland, College Park*
Jale Parla, *Istanbul Bilgi University*
Frances Restuccia, *Boston College*
S. I. Salamensky, *University of California, Los Angeles*
Esra Mirze Santesso, *University of Georgia*
Nhora Lucía Serrano, *Hamilton College*
Michelle B. Slater, *Sacred Heart University*
Lisa Udel, *Illinois College*
Joya Uraizee, *Saint Louis University*

WORKS CITED

Abbas, Ackbar. "Walter Benjamin's Collector: The Fate of Modern Experience." *New Literary History*, vol. 20, no. 1, 1988, pp. 217–37.

Adak, Hülya. "Gendering Denial Narratives of the Decade of Terror (1975–1985): The Case of Samiha Ayverdi / Neşide Kerem Demir and Hatun Sebilciyan / Sabiha Gökçen." *Journal of Genocide Research*, vol. 17, no. 3, 2015, pp. 327–43.

———. *Pamuk's Encyclopedia: A Structural and Cultural Analysis of the Encyclopedic Novel*. 1994. U of Chicago, MA thesis.

Afridi, Mehnaz M., and David M. Buyze, editors. *Global Perspectives on Orhan Pamuk: Existentialism and Politics*. Palgrave Macmillan, 2012.

Ahmad, Aijaz. "Jameson's Rhetoric of Otherness and the 'National Allegory.'" *Social Text*, no. 17, Autumn 1987, pp. 3–25.

Ahmet Mithat Efendi. "İkram-ı Aklam." 1897. *Klasikler Tartismasi, Baslangic Dönemi*, edited by R. Kaplan, Atatürk Kültür Merkezi, 1998, pp. 65–69.

Algan, Bülent. "The Brand New Version of Article 301 of Turkish Penal Code and the Future of Freedom of Expression Cases in Turkey." *German Law Journal*, vol. 9, no. 12, 2008, pp. 2237–51.

Ali, Barish, and Caroline Hagood. "Heteroglossic Sprees and Murderous Viewpoints in Orhan Pamuk's *My Name Is Red*." *Texas Studies in Literature and Language*, vol. 54, no. 4, 2012, pp. 505–29.

Almond, Ian. "Borges the Post-orientalist: Images of Islam from the Edge of the West." *Modern Fiction Studies*, vol. 50, no. 2, 2004, pp. 435–59.

———. "Islam, Melancholy, and Sad, Concrete Minarets: The Futility of Narratives in Orhan Pamuk's *The Black Book*." *New Literary History*, vol. 34, no. 1, 2003, pp. 75–90.

———. *Sufism and Deconstruction: A Comparative Study of Derrida and Ibn 'Arabi*. Routledge, 2010.

Alpay, Necmiye. *Dilimiz, Dillerimiz: Uygulama Üzerine Yazılar*. Metis, 2004.

———. "Kar kışkırtıcı." *Milliyet Kitap*, 8 Mar. 2002, www.milliyet.com.tr/ozel/kitap/020308/kimne.html. Accessed 27 Feb. 2016.

Anadolu-Okur, Nilgün, editor. *Essays Interpreting the Writings of Novelist Orhan Pamuk: The Turkish Winner of the Nobel Prize in Literature*. Edwin Mellen Press, 2009.

Andrews, Walter G. "*The Black Book* and Black Boxes: Orhan Pamuk's *Kara Kitap*." *Edebiyat*: *Journal of Middle Eastern Literatures*, vol. 11, no. 1, 2000, pp. 105–29.

Annaud, Jean-Jacques, director. *The Name of the Rose*. Twentieth Century Fox, 1986.

"Applause for Pamuk's Political Remarks at Frankfurt Awards Ceremony." *Hürriyet*, 24 Oct. 2005, www.hurriyet.com.tr/applause-for-pamuks-political-remarks-at-frankfurt-awards-ceremony-3429945.

Apter, Emily S. *Against World Literature: On the Politics of Untranslatability*. Verso, 2013.

———. *The Translation Zone: A New Comparative Literature.* Princeton UP, 2005.

The Arabian Nights. Edited by Mahdi Muhsin, translated by Husain Haddawy, W. W. Norton, 2008.

Aristotle. *The Art of Rhetoric.* Edited and translated by Hugh Lawson-Tancred, Penguin Books, 1992.

Asad, Talal. "The Concept of Cultural Translation in British Social Anthropology." *Writing Culture: The Poetics and Politics of Ethnography*, edited by James Clifford and George E. Marcus, U of California P, 1986, pp. 141–64.

Attâr, Farid ud-Din. *The Conference of the Birds.* Translated by Afkham Darbandi and Dick Davis, Penguin Books, 1984.

Atwood, Margaret. "Headscarves to Die For." *The New York Times*, 15 Aug. 2004, www.nytimes.com/2004/08/15/books/headscarves-to-die-for.html.

Auerbach, Erich. "Figura." Translated by Ralph Manheim and Catherine Garvin. *Scenes from the Drama of European Literature*, U of Minnesota P, 1985, pp. 11–78.

———. *Mimesis.* 1953. Translated by Willard R. Trask, Princeton UP, 1974.

Avatar. Directed by James Cameron, Twentieth-Century Fox, 2009.

"Avoiding EU Condemnation: Turkey Drops Orhan Pamuk Trial." *Spiegel Online International*, 23 Jan. 2006, www.spiegel.de/international/avoiding-eu-condemnation-turkey-drops-orhan-pamuk-trial-a-396786.html.

The Axis of Evil Comedy Tour. Performance by Maz Jobrani, Ahmed Ahmed, Aron Kader, and Dean Obeidallah, Levity, 2006. DVD.

Bakhtin, M. M. *The Dialogic Imagination.* Translated by Caryl Emerson and Michael Holquist, edited by Holquist, U of Texas P, 1981.

———. *"Speech Genres" and Other Late Essays.* Translated by Vern W. McGee, edited by Caryl Emerson and Michael Holquist, U of Texas P, 1986.

Barthes, Roland. *Mythologies.* Translated by Richard Howard and Annette Lavers, Hill and Wang, 2012.

———. *The Pleasure of the Text.* Translated by Richard Miller, Hill and Wang, 1975.

Bayrakçeken, Aylin, and Don Randall. "Meetings of East and West: Orhan Pamuk's Istanbulite Perspective." *Critique*, vol. 46, no. 3, 2005, pp. 191–204.

Behrens-Abouseif, Doris. *Beauty in Arabic Culture.* Markus Weiner Publishers, 1999.

Belge, Murat. *Edebiyat Üzerine Yazılar.* 1994. İletişim, 1998.

———. "Love Me or Leave Me? The Strange Case of Orhan Pamuk." *openDemocracy*, 18 Oct. 2005, www.opendemocracy.net/arts-turkey/orhan_pamuk_2935.jsp. Accessed 22 Mar. 2015.

[Bellini, Gentile]. *A Seated Scribe.* 1479–81. *Isabella Stewart Gardner Museum*, www.gardnermuseum.org/collection/browse?filter=artist:3157.

Belting, Hans. *Likeness and Presence: A History of the Image before the Era of Art.* U of Chicago P, 1994.

Benjamin, Walter. *Gesammelte Schriften.* Edited by Rolf Tiedemann and Hermann Schweppenhäuser, Suhrkamp, 1972–89. 7 vols.

———. *Illuminations*. Edited by Hannah Arendt, translated by Harry Zohn, Schocken Books, 2007.

———. *Reflections*. Edited by Peter Demetz, translated by Edmund Jephcott, Random House, 1995.

———. "The Task of the Translator." *Illuminations*, translated by Harry Zohn, edited by Hannah Arendt, Schocken Books, 1968, pp. 69–82.

Berger, John. *Ways of Seeing*. 1972. British Broadcasting Corporation and Penguin Books, 1991.

Berman, Marshall. "Orhan Pamuk and Modernist Liberalism." *Dissent*, no. 56, Spring 2009, pp. 113–18.

Berman, Paul. "Young Turk." *The New Republic*, 9 Sept. 1991, pp. 36–38.

Borges, Jorge Luis. "The Argentine Writer and Tradition." Translated by Esther Allen. *Selected Nonfictions*, edited by Eliot Weinberger, Penguin Books, 1999, pp. 420–27.

———. *Collected Fictions*. Translated by Andrew Hurley, Viking, 1998.

Boyd, Brian. *Vladimir Nabokov: The American Years*. Princeton UP, 1991.

Bozdoğan, Sibel, and Reşat Kasaba, editors. *Rethinking Modernity and National Identity in Turkey*. U of Washington P, 1997.

Brendemoen, Bernt. "Orhan Pamuk—bir Türkçe sözdizimi yenilikçisi." Esen, *Kara Kitap*, pp. 144–58.

———. "The Turkish Language Reform and Language Policy in Turkey." *Handbuch der türkischen Sprachwissenschaft*, Harrassowitz Verlag, 1990, pp. 454–92.

Burkett, Molly. "Twelve Nobel Laureates in Literature Who Have Been Banned, Censored, or Exiled in the Past Twenty Years." *Sampsonia Way: An Online Magazine for Literature, Free Speech, and Social Justice*, 1 Nov. 2011, www.sampsoniaway.org/blog/2011/11/01/12-nobel-laureates-in-literature-who-have-been-banned-censored-or-exiled/. Accessed 1 Sept. 2014.

Calvino, Italo. *If on a Winter's Night a Traveler*. Translated by William Weaver, Lester and Orpen Dennys, 1995.

Can, Taner, et al., editors. *Orhan Pamuk: Critical Essays on a Novelist between Worlds*. Ibidem Press, 2017.

Carver, Robert. "Let Constantinople in Tiber Melt." *Orhan Pamuk Site*, İletişim, www.orhanpamuk.net/popup.aspx?id=58&lng=eng.

Casanova, Pascale. "Literature as a World." *New Left Review*, vol. 31, Jan.–Feb. 2005, pp. 71–90.

———. *The World Republic of Letters*. Translated by M. B. DeBevoise, Harvard UP, 2004.

Certeau, Michel de. *The Practice of Everyday Life*. Translated by Steven F. Rendall, U of California P, 1984.

Cheah, Pheng. "World against Globe: Toward a Normative Conception of World Literature." *New Literary History*, vol. 45, no. 3, Summer 2014, pp. 303–29.

Çiçekçioğlu, Feride. "Difference, Visual Narration, and Point of View in *My Name Is Red*." *Journal of Aesthetic Education*, vol. 37, no. 4, Winter 2003, pp. 124–37.

———. "A Pedagogy of Two Ways of Seeing: A Confrontation of 'Word and Image' in *My Name Is Red*." *Journal of Aesthetic Education*, vol. 37, no. 3, Fall 2003, pp. 1–20.

Clark, Hilary. *The Fictional Encyclopedia*. Garland Publishing, 1990.

Clemens, Colleen Ann Lutz. "'Suicide Girls': Orhan Pamuk's *Snow* and the Politics of Resistance in Contemporary Turkey." *Feminist Formations*, vol. 23, no. 1, 2011, pp. 138–54.

Cooke, Miriam. "Deploying the Muslimwoman." *Journal of Feminist Studies in Religion*, vol. 24, no. 1, 2008, pp. 91–99.

Cooppan, Vilashini. "World Literature and Global Theory: Comparative Literature for the New Millennium." *Globalism and Theory*, special issue of *Symplokē*, vol. 9, no. 1–2, 2001, pp. 15–43.

Damrosch, David. *How to Read World Literature*. Wiley-Blackwell, 2009.

———. *What Is World Literature?* Princeton UP, 2003.

Damrosch, David, and Gayatri Chakravorty Spivak. "Comparative Literature / World Literature: A Discussion with David Damrosch and Gayatri Spivak." *Comparative Literature Studies*, vol. 48, no. 4, 2011, pp. 455–85. *JSTOR*, www.jstor.org/stable/pdf/10.5325/complitstudies.48.4.0455.pdf.

Danforth, Nick. "A Less Familiar Faith." *Today's Zaman*, 29 May 2013, www.todayszaman.com/op-ed_a-less-familiar-fatihby-nick-danforth-_316860.html.

Dante. *The Divine Comedy: Paradise*. Translated by Mark Musa, Penguin Books, 1986.

———. *Inferno*. Edited and translated by Robert M. Durling, Oxford UP, 1996. Vol. 1 of *The Divine Comedy of Dante Alighieri*.

———. *The New Life*. Translated by Dante Gabriel Rossetti, New York Review Books, 2002.

Darnton, Robert. "What Is the History of Books?" *The Case for Books: Past, Present, and Future*, PublicAffairs, 2009, pp. 175–206.

Deckard, Sharae, et al. *Combined and Uneven Development: Towards a New Theory of World-Literature*. Liverpool UP, 2015.

Demir, Neşide K. (Sâmiha Ayverdi). *The Armenian Question in Turkey: History's Revelations to the Mother of a Martyr*. Kuşak Ofset, 1980.

———. *Türkiye'nin Ermeni Meselesi*. Kubbealtı Neşriyatı, 1976.

Derrida, Jacques. *Monolingualism of the Other; or, The Prosthesis of Origin*. Translated by Patrick Mensah, Stanford UP, 1998.

Derviş, Pelin, et al., eds. *Becoming Istanbul: An Encyclopedia*. Garanti Galeri, 2008.

"Diagnosis." *Oxford English Dictionary*, Oxford UP, 2015, www.oed.com.ezaccess.libraries.psu.edu/view/Entry/51836?.

Diderot, Denis. *"Salon of 1765" and "Notes on Painting."* Translated by Jean Seznec and Jean Adhémar, Clarendon Press, 1975.

Doyle, Laura, and Laura Winkiel, editors. *Geomodernisms: Race, Modernism, Modernity*. Indiana UP, 2005.

Draaisma, Douwe. *Metaphors of Memory: A History of Ideas about the Mind*. Cambridge UP, 2000.

Drakulić, Slavenka. *A Guided Tour through the Museum of Communism*. Penguin Books, 2011.

Ecevit, Yıldız. *Orhan Pamuk'u Okumak: Kafası Karışmış Okur ve Modern Roman*. İletişim, 2004.

Eckermann, Johann Peter. *Conversations with Goethe*. Translated by Gisela C. O'Brien, Ungar, 1964.

Eco, Umberto. *The Name of the Rose*. Harcourt Brace Jovanovich, 1983.

———. *Six Walks in the Fictional Woods*. Harvard UP, 1994.

Edib, Halide Adivar. *Memoirs of Halide Edib*. 1926. Introduction by Hülya Adak, Gorgias Press, 2004.

Ekrem, Selma. *Unveiled: The Autobiography of a Turkish Girl*. 1930. Introduction by Carolyn Goffman, Gorgias Press, 2005.

Erguvanlı, Eser E. *The Function of Word Order in Turkish Grammar*. U of California P, 1984.

Erickson, Edward J. *Ordered to Die: A History of the Ottoman Army in the First World War*. Greenwood Press, 2001.

Erol, Sibel. "The Chronotope of Istanbul in Orhan Pamuk's Memoir *Istanbul*." *International Journal of Middle East Studies*, vol. 43, no. 4, 2011, pp. 655–76.

———. Introduction. *House with Wisteria: Memoirs of Turkey Old and New*, by Halide Edib. 1926. Transaction Publishers, 2009, pp. vii–xxxv.

———. "Reading Orhan Pamuk's *Snow* as Parody: Difference as Sameness." *Comparative Critical Studies*, vol. 4, no. 3, 2007, pp. 403–32.

Eronat, Canan Yücel, editor. *Tanpınar'dan Hasan-Ali Yücel'e Mektuplar*. Yapı Kredi, 1997.

Ertuna, Irmak. "The Mystery of the Object and Anthropological Materialism: Orhan Pamuk's *Museum of Innocence* and André Breton's *Nadja*." *Journal of Modern Literature*, vol. 33, no. 3, 2010, pp. 99–111.

Ertürk, Nergis, "Those outside the Scene: *Snow* in the World Republic of Letters." *New Literary History*, vol. 41, no. 3, 2010, pp. 633–51.

Esen, Nüket, editor. *Kara Kitap Üzerine Yazılar*. Can Yayınları, 1992.

———. Preface. Esen, *Kara Kitap*, pp. 7–11.

Esen, Nüket, and Engin Kılıç, editors. *Orhan Pamuk'un Edebi Dünyası*. İletişim, 2008.

Esmer, Pelin. *Ten to Eleven*. Sinefilm, 2009.

Ettinghausen, Richard. *Turkish Miniatures from the Thirteenth to Eighteenth Centuries*. UNESCO, 1965.

Even-Zohar, Itamar. "Laws of Literary Interference." *Poetics Today*, vol. 11, no. 1, 1990, pp. 53–72.

Evin, Ahmet. *Origins and Development of the Turkish Novel*. Bibliotheca Islamica, 1983.

"Ezra, Codex Amiatinus." *Wikimedia Commons*, upload.wikimedia.org/wikipedia/commons/4/44/CodxAmiatinusFolio5rEzra.jpg.

Farred, Grant. "'To Dig a Well with a Needle': Orhan Pamuk's Poem of Comparative Globalization." *The Global South*, vol. 1, nos. 1–2, 2007, pp. 81–99.

Faulkner, William. *As I Lay Dying*. Vintage Books, 1990.

———. *Light in August*. Vintage Books, 1990.

———. *The Sound and the Fury*. Vintage Books, 1990.

Findley, Carter V. *Turkey, Islam, Nationalism, and Modernity: A History, 1789–2007*. Yale UP, 2010.

Finn, Robert P. *The Early Turkish Novel, 1872–1900*. Isis, 1984.

Flaubert, Gustave. *Madame Bovary*. Translated by Eleanor Marx Aveling, W. W. Norton, 2004.

———. *Madame Bovary*. Translated by Lydia Davis, Penguin Books, 2011.

Flood, Alison. "Frankfurt Book Fair: Orhan Pamuk Denounces Turkish Oppression." *The Guardian*, 15 Oct. 2008, www.theguardian.com/books/2008/oct/15/orhan-pamuk-turkey-oppression. Accessed 1 Sept. 2014.

———. "Turkey and Twitter: Major Authors Join PEN International Appeal to End Ban." *The Guardian*, 27 Mar. 2014, www.theguardian.com/books/2014/mar/28/zadie-smith-rushdie-pamuk-pen-international-letter-turkey-twitter-ban.

Foster, Hal. *Vision and Visuality*. Bay Press, 1988.

Foucault, Michel. *Archaeology of Knowledge*. Translated by A. M. Sheridan Smith, Routledge, 2002.

———. "Of Other Spaces." Translated by Jay Miskowiec. *Diacritics*, vol. 16, no. 1, Spring 1986, pp. 22–27.

"Friedenspreis für Pamuk: Türkische Reaktionen." *Der Tagesspeigel*, 25 Oct. 2005, www.tagesspiegel.de/kultur/friedenspreis-fuer-pamuk-tuerkische-reaktionen/653348.html.

"Friedenspreis für Schriftsteller Orhan Pamuk." *Frankfurter Allgemeine Zeitung*, 22 June 2005, www.faz.net/aktuell/feuilleton/auszeichnung-friedenspreis-fuer-schriftsteller-orhan-pamuk-1236446.html.

Frost, Robert. *Robert Frost on Writing*. Rutgers UP, 1973.

Fuentes, Carlos. *Aura*. [Farrar, Straus, and Giroux], 1975.

Galip, Şeyh. *Beauty and Love*. Translated by Victoria Rowe Holbrook, Modern Language Association of America, 2005.

———. *Hüsn ü Aşk*. Edited by Victoria Rowe Holbrook, Modern Language Association of America, 2005.

Genette, Gérard. *Paratexts: Thresholds of Interpretation*. Translated by J. Lewin, Cambridge UP, 1997.

Göçek, Fatma Müge. *Denial of Violence: Ottoman Past, Turkish Present, and Collective Violence against the Armenians, 1789–2009*. Oxford UP, 2015.

Gogol, Nikolaĭ Vasil'evich, Richard Pevear, and Larissa Volokhonsky. *The Collected Tales of Nikolai Gogol*. Vintage Books, 1999.

Gökalp, Ziya. *Yeni Hayat*. İkbal Kitabevi, 1941.

Göknar, Erdağ. "The Novel in Turkish: Narrative Tradition to Nobel Prize." *Turkey in the Modern World*, edited by R. Kasaba, Cambridge UP, 2008, pp. 472–503. Vol. 4 of *The Cambridge History of Turkey*.

———. "Occulted Texts: Pamuk's Untraslated Novels." Afridi and Buyze, pp. 177–98.

———. *Orhan Pamuk, Secularism, and Blasphemy: The Politics of the Turkish Novel.* Routledge, 2013.

———. "The Ottoman Legacy and the *White Castle.*" *Journal of Turkish Literature*, no. 7, 2010, pp. 123–39.

Güler, Ara. *Ara Güler's İstanbul: Forty Years of Photographs.* Thames and Hudson, 2009.

Gülsoy, Murat. "Orhan Pamuk." *Açık Şehir: Özel*, TRT Türk, 28 Sept. 2011. *YouTube*, www.youtube.com/watch?v=6tSWZ3qZq5g.

Gürbilek, Nurdan. "Dandies and Originals: Authenticity, Belatedness, and the Turkish Novel." *South Atlantic Quarterly*, vol. 102, no. 2–3, 2003, pp. 599–628.

Gürçağlar, Şehnaz Tahir. *The Politics and Poetics of Translation in Turkey (1923–1960).* Editions Rodopi, 2008.

Hall, Stuart, editor. *Representation: Cultural Representations and Signifying Practices.* SAGE Publications, 1997.

Halman, Talât S., and Jayne L. Warner. *A Millennium of Turkish Literature: A Concise History.* Syracuse UP, 2011.

(Harding) Davis, Rebecca, and Tillie Olsen. *Life in the Iron Mills: Or, the Korl Woman.* Feminist Press, 1972.

Heffernan, James A. W. *The Museum of Words: The Poetics of Ekphrasis from Homer to Ashbery.* U of Chicago P, 1993.

Heidegger, Martin. *Being and Time.* Translated by Joan Stambaugh, Harper and Row, 1962.

Hergé. *Les aventures de Tintin: Tintin au Congo.* 1931. Casterman, 1982.

Hickman, Bill, translator. The Story of Joseph: *A Fourteenth-Century Turkish Morality Play by Sheyyad Hamza.* Syracuse UP, 2014.

Hile, Rachel E. "'The Spanish Tragedy' as Intertext for Orhan Pamuk's *Kar* (*Snow*)." *Mediterranean Studies*, no. 18, 2009, pp. 143–67.

Hitchins, Keith. "World Literature in Review: Turkish." *World Literature Today*, vol. 65, no. 4, 1991, p. 764.

Hodgson, Marshall. *The Classical Age of Islam.* U of Chicago P, 2009. Vol. 1 of *The Venture of Islam.*

Holbrook, Victoria. *The Unreadable Shores of Love: Turkish Modernity and Mystic Romance.* U of Texas P, 1994.

Holly, Michael Ann. *Past Looking: Historical Imagination and the Rhetoric of the Image.* Cornell UP, 1996.

Huntington, Samuel P. "The Clash of Civilizations?" *Foreign Affairs*, vol. 72, no. 3, 1993, pp. 22–49. *JSTOR*, www.jstor.org/stable/20045621.

Hutcheon, Linda. *The Politics of Postmodernism.* Routledge, 1990.

Imperato, Ferrante. *Dell'Historia Naturale.* Naples, 1599. *Wikipedia*, en.wikipedia.org/wiki/Ferrante_Imperato#/media/File:RitrattoMuseoFerranteImperato.jpg.

Inception. Directed by Christopher Nolan, Warner Brothers, 2010.

"Index Translationum: Bibliographic Search." *UNESCO*, www.unesco.org/xtrans/. Accessed 8 Dec. 2014.

İrdelmen, Erol. "Kar'ın Eleştirisi." *Milliyet blog*, 3 Dec. 2012, blog.milliyet.com.tr/kar-in-elestirisi/Blog/?BlogNo=390657. Accessed 27 Feb. 2016.

Irzık, Sibel. "Orhan Pamuk's *Snow*: Re-imagining the Boundaries between East and West, Art and Politics." *Europe and Its Boundaries*, edited by Andrew Davison and Himadeep Muppidi, Lexington Books, 2009, pp. 189–202.

Iser, Wolfgang. *The Act of Reading: A Theory of Aesthetic Response*. Johns Hopkins UP, 1978.

Ishiguro, Kazuo. *An Artist of the Floating World*. Putnam, 1986.

James, Henry. *The Figure in the Carpet*. Cosmpolis, 1896.

Jameson, Fredric. "Third-World Literature in the Era of Multinational Capitalism." *Social Text*, no. 15, Fall 1986, pp. 65–88.

Jauss, Hans Robert. *Aesthetic Experience and Literary Hermeneutics*. Translated by Michael Shaw, U of Minnesota P, 1982.

Johanson, Lars. "Bestimmtheit und Mitteiungsperspektive im Türkischen Satz." *Zeitschrift der Deutschen Morgenländischen Gesellschaft*, supplement 3, part 2, Steiner, 1977, pp. 1186–203.

Kadir, Djelal. "The Siege of Baghdad: Rashiduddin Fazlullah, Orhan Pamuk, and the Commissions of History." *Memos from the Besieged City: Lifelines for Cultural Sustainability*, Stanford UP, 2011, pp. 41–60.

Kafka, Franz. *The Castle*. Translated by Mark Harman, Schocken Books, 1998.

———. *Şato*. Translated by Şükrü Çorlu, Ithaki, 2006.

———. *Şato*. Translated by Kamuran Şipal, Cem Yayınevi, 1982.

Karabaşoğlu, İsa İlkay. "Hafiye Galip İşbaşında: *Kara Kitap*'ın bir polisiye roman olarak okunması." *Dergah*, no. 282, August 2013, pp. 5–25.

Karakaş, Abdullah. "*Kara Kitap*'ta Toplumdan Bireye Kimlik." *Fraktal*, no. 1, Dec.-Jan.-Feb. 2013–14, pp. 6–10.

Karnaydağ, Arslan. "Türkiye'de Yayıncılığın Gelişmesi ve Sorunları." *Cumhuriyet Dönemi Türkiye Ansiklopedisi* [Encyclopedia of Turkey in the Republican Period], vol. 10, İletişim, 1985, pp. 2823–36.

Kayra, Osman K. "Pamuk'un romanına 'üslup' eleştirisi." *Zaman*, 22 July 2008, www.zaman.com.tr/gundem_pamukun-romanina-uslup-elestirisi_717123.html. Accessed 27 Feb. 2016.

Kellman, Steven G. "The White Castle." *Magill Book Review*, Nov. 1991, connection.ebscohost.com/c/book-reviews/9111187082/white-castle. Accessed 21 Feb. 2017.

Kietzman, Mary Jo. "Speaking 'to All Humanity': Renaissance Drama in Orhan Pamuk's *Snow*." *Texas Studies in Literature and Language*, vol. 52, no. 3, 2010, pp. 324–53.

Kılıç, Engin, editor. *Orhan Pamuk'u Anlamak*. İletişim, 1999.

Kilito, Abdelfattah. *Thou Shalt Not Speak My Language*. Translated by W. Hassan, Syracuse UP, 2008.

Kim, Sooyong. "Master and Disciple: Sufi Mysticism as an Interpretive Framework for Orhan Pamuk's *Kara Kitap*." *Turkish Studies Association Bulletin*, no. 17, Fall 1993, pp. 23–42.

———. "Mürşid ile mürid: *Kara Kitap*'ı bir yorumlama çerçevesi olarak Tasavvuf." Esen, *Kara Kitap*, pp. 233–56.

Kincaid, Jamaica. "On Seeing England for the First Time." *Transition*, no. 51, 1991, pp. 32–40.

"Koç University Mission Statement." Koç University, www.ku.edu.tr/en/mission. Accessed 18 Sept. 2014.

"The Koran: Joseph." *The Norton Anthology of World Masterpieces*, edited by Maynard Mack et al., vol. 1, W. W. Norton, 1997, pp. 874–80.

Lehman-Haupt, Christopher. "Turkish Novel as Antidote for East-West Despair." *The New York Times*, 19 Apr. 1991, www.nytimes.com/1991/04/29/books/books-of-the-times-turkish-novel-as-antidote-for-east-west-despair.html.

Lewis, Geoffrey. *The Turkish Language Reform: A Catastrophic Success*. Oxford UP, 1999.

Lewis, Pericles. *Religious Experience and the Modernist Novel*. Cambridge UP, 2010.

Lloyd, David. *Nationalism and Minor Literature: James Clarence Mangan and the Emergence of Irish Cultural Nationalism*. U of California P, 1987.

Lukács, Georg. *The Historical Novel*. Translated by Hannah Mitchell and Stanley Mitchell, U of Nebraska P, 1983.

———. *The Meaning of Contemporary Realism*. Merlin Press, 1963.

Mani, B. Venkat. "Breaking Down the Walls: The European Library Project." *The German Wall: Fallout in Europe*, edited by Marc Silberman, Palgrave Macmillan, 2011, pp. 205–25.

———. *Recoding World Literature: Libraries, Print Culture, and Germany's Pact with Books*. Fordham UP, 2016.

———. "Turkish-German Reattachments: Orhan Pamuk's *The New Life*." *Cosmopolitical Claims: Turkish-German Literatures from Nadolny to Pamuk*, by Mani, U of Iowa P, 2007, pp. 146–82.

Mann, Thomas. *Buddenbrooks: Verfall Einer Familie*. Fischer, 1930.

Marien, Mary Warner. "Catch a Turkish Story Star." *Christian Science Monitor*, 12 Apr. 1991.

Marx, Karl, and Friedrich Engels. "The Manifesto of the Communist Party." *Political Writings*, edited by David Fernbach, vol. 1, Vintage Books, 1974, pp. 62–98.

Massignon, Louis. *Hallaj: Mystic and Martyr*. Edited and translated by Herbert Mason, Princeton UP, 1994.

Mattar, Karim. "Orhan Pamuk and the Limits of Translation: Foreignizing *The Black Book* for World Literature." *Translation and Literature*, vol. 23, no. 1, 2014, pp. 42–67.

McGaha, Michael D. *Autobiographies of Orhan Pamuk: The Writer and His Novels*. U of Utah P, 2008.

McGoldrick, Dominic. *Human Rights and Religion: The Islamic Headscarf Debate in Europe*. Hart Publishing, 2006.

McGrath, Charles. "A Grab of Postmodern Literary Devices Helps Shape Orhan Pamuk's Career." *The New York Times*, 13 Oct. 2006, www.nytimes.com/2006/10/13/books/13pamu.html?_r=0.

McKeon, Michael. *The Origins of the English Novel, 1600–1740*. Johns Hopkins UP, 1987.

Meltzer, Françoise. *Salome and the Dance of Writing: Portraits of Mimesis in Literature*. U of Chicago P, 1987.

Metz, Christian. *The Imaginary Signifier: Psychoanalysis and the Cinema*. Indiana UP, 1982.

Mīr 'Alī Shīr Navā'ī. "Hunt." Circa 1530. *The Topkapı Saray Museum: The Albums and Illustrated Manuscripts*, edited by J. M. Rogers, Little, Brown, 1986, plate 133.

Mirze, Z. Esra. "Silence, Secularism and Fundamentalism in *Snow*." Afridi and Buyze, pp. 157–76.

Mitchell, W. J. T. *Picture Theory*. U of Chicago P, 1994.

Mohanty, Chandra Talpade. "Under Western Eyes: Feminist Scholarship and Colonial Discourses." *Third World Women and the Politics of Feminism*, edited by Mohanty et al., Indiana UP, 1991, pp. 51–80.

Moran, Berna. *Türk Romanına Eleştirel Bir Bakış*. İletişim, 1983.

———. "Üstkurmaca olarak *Kara Kitap*." Esen, *Kara Kitap*, pp. 80–91.

Moretti, Franco. "Conjectures on World Literature." *New Left Review*, vol. 1, no. 1, 2000, pp. 54–68.

———. *Modern Epic: The World System from Goethe to García Márquez*. Translated by Quintin Hoare, Verso Books, 1996.

Mufti, Aamir. "Orientalism and the Institution of World Literatures." *Critical Inquiry*, vol. 36, Spring 2010, pp. 458–93.

"Museum of Innocence in the Formation Process." *Hürriyet Daily News*, 25 Aug. 2009, www.hurriyetdailynews.com/museum-of-innocence-in-the-formation-process.aspx?pageID=438&n=museum-of-innocence-on-the-formation-process-2009-08-25. Accessed 27 Feb. 2016.

"Museum of Innocence: Turkish Museum Is European Museum of the Year 2014." *European Museum Forum*, www.europeanmuseumforum.info/emya/history/121-2014-tallinn-estonia.html.

Nakkaş Osman, "Muhammad Appearing at the Ka 'ba to Rid the Populace of an Unwanted Dragon." 1594. *The Topkapı Saray Museum: The Albums and Illustrated Manuscripts*, edited by J. M. Rogers, Little, Brown, 1986, plate 165.

Nead, Lynda. *Myths of Sexuality: Representations of Women in Victorian Britain*. Blackwell, 1988.

Nielson, Paula. "The White Castle." *Library Journal*, 15 Feb. 1991, pp. 222–23.

"The Nobel Prize in Literature 2006—Press Release." *Nobelprize.org*, Nobel Media AB, 12 Oct. 2006, www.nobelprize.org/nobel_prizes/literature/laureates/2006/press.html.

"The Nominees: 2003—*My Name Is Red*." *International Dublin Literary Award*, 2002, www.dublinliteraryaward.ie/nominees/my-name-is-red/.

Noorani, Yaseen. "Hard and Soft Multilingualism." *Critical Multilingualism Studies*, vol. 1, no. 2, 2013, pp. 7–28.

Öktem, Kerem. *Angry Nation: Turkey since 1989.* Zed Books, 2011.

"The Old Testament: The Story of Joseph." *The Norton Anthology of World Masterpieces*, edited by Maynard Mack et al., vol. 1, 1997, pp. 60–71.

"Orhan Pamuk davası düştü." *Radikal*, 23 Jan. 2006, www.radikal.com.tr/politika/orhan-pamuk-davasi-dustu-769636/.

"Orhan Pamuk hakkında suç duyurusu." *Hürriyet*, 18 Feb. 2005, www.hurriyet.com.tr/orhan-pamuk-hakkinda-suc-duyurusu-297614.

Ortiz, Fernando. *Cuban Counterpoint: Tobacco and Sugar.* 1940. Translated by Harriet de Onís. Duke UP, 2003.

Özkırımlı, Atilla. "Biçimin işlevi yerine getiremediği roman: *Sessiz Ev*." *Cumhuriyet*, 23 Feb. 1984, www.cumhuriyetarsivi.com/katalog/192/sayfa/1984/2/23/5.xhtml.

Özyürek, Dursun. "*Kara Kitap*'ta İslami edebiyatların izleri." *Dergah*, no. 288, 2014, pp. 9–10.

Paker, Saliha. "Reading Turkish Novelists and Poets in English Translation: 2000–2004." *Translation Review*, no. 68, 2005, pp. 6–14.

Paker, Saliha, and Melike Yılmaz. "A Chronological Bibliography of Turkish Literature in English Translation: 1949–2004." *Translation Review*, no. 68, 2005, pp. 15–18.

Pamuk, Orhan. "Achte auf die Details des Lebens: Ein Interview mit Orhan Pamuk." Interview by Jürg Lau. *Die Zeit Online*, 14 April 2005, www.zeit.de/2005/16/InterviewPamuk.

———. "The Anger of the Damned." Translated by Mary Isin. *The New York Review of Books*, 18 Oct. 2001, www.nybooks.com/articles/2001/11/15/the-anger-of-the-damned/.

———. "Author in the Classroom: An Interview with Orhan Pamuk." Interview by Pınar Batur. *Middle East Studies Association Bulletin*, no. 41, June 2007, pp. 8–15.

———. *Benim Adım Kırmızı.* İletişim, 1998.

———. *Beyaz Kale.* İletişim, 2000.

———. "Big Think Interview with Orhan Pamuk." *The Big Think*, bigthink.com/videos/big-think-interview-with-orhan-pamuk.

———. *The Black Book.* Translated by Maureen Freely, Vintage Books, 2006.

———. *The Black Book.* Translated by Güneli Gün, Farrar, Straus, and Giroux, 1994.

———. *Cevdet Bey ve Oğulları.* Karacan, 1982.

———. *Cevdet Bey ve Oğulları.* 1982. İletişim, 1996.

———. "Controversial Turkish Novelist Wins Nobel Prize in Literature." Interview by Jeffrey Brown. *PBS NewsHour*, 12 Oct. 2006, www.pbs.org/newshour/bb/entertainment-july-dec06-pamuk_10–12/.

———. "Conversation: Nobel Laureate Orhan Pamuk." Interview by Jeffrey Brown. *PBS NewsHour*, 26 Feb. 2010, www.pbs.org/newshour/art/conversation-orhan-pamuk/.

———. "Conversations with History—Orhan Pamuk: Finding an Authentic Voice." Hosted by Harry Kreisler, 6 Nov. 2009. Institute of International Studies, U of California, Berkeley. *YouTube*, www.youtube.com/watch?v=zy62YqDeE0c&t=19s.

———. "An Evening with Orhan Pamuk." Interview for University of California Television, 19 Oct. 2007, U of California, Santa Barbara, Arts and Lectures, Campbell Hall. *YouTube*, www.youtube.com/watch?v=OUPGV1u9bds&t=77s.

———. "Freedom to Write." Translated by Maureen Freely. *The New York Review of Books*, 25 May 2006, www.nybooks.com/articles/2006/05/25/freedom-to-write/.

———. *Gizli Yüz: Senaryo.* With Ömer Kavur, İletişim, 1998.

———. "Granta Conversation with Orhan Pamuk." Interview by John Freeman. *Vimeo*, vimeo.com/8577736.

———. "Implementing Disform: An Interview with Orhan Pamuk." Interview by Z. Esra Mirze. *PMLA*, vol. 123, no. 1, 2008, pp. 176–80.

———. "In Kars and Frankfurt." Translated by Maureen Freely, *Friedenpreis des Deutschen Buchhandels*, 2005, www.friedenspreis-des-deutschen-buchhandels.de/sixcms/media.php/1290/Orhan%20Pamuk%20Acceptance%20speech%202005.pdf. Accessed 15 Feb. 2017.

———. *The Innocence of Objects.* Translated by Ekin Oklap, Abrams, 2012.

———. Interview by Charlie Rose. *Charlie Rose*, 24 Jan. 2008, charlierose.com/videos/27641.

———. Interview by Charlie Rose. *Charlie Rose*, 28 Dec. 2009, charlierose.com/videos/13590.

———. Interview by Charlie Rose. *Charlie Rose*, 13 May 2011, charlierose.com/videos/18601.

———. Interview by Charlie Rose. *Charlie Rose*, 29 Oct. 2012, charlierose.com/videos/21178.

———. "Interview: Orhan Pamuk; 'I Was Not a Political Person.'" Interview by Alexander Star. *The New York Times*, 15 Aug. 2004, www.nytimes.com/2004/08/15/books/interview-orhan-pamuk-i-was-not-a-political-person.html.

———. "Interview with Orhan Pamuk." Interview by Horace Engdahl. *Nobelprize.org*, Nobel Media AB, 6 Dec. 2006, www.nobelprize.org/mediaplayer/index.php?id=106&view=2. Accessed 11 Oct. 2014.

———. *İstanbul: Hatıralar Ve Şehir.* Yapı Kredi, 2003.

———. *Istanbul: Memories and the City.* Translated by Maureen Freely, Vintage Books, 2004.

———. *Istanbul: Memories and the City.* Translated by Maureen Freely, Alfred A. Knopf, 2006.

———. *Istanbul: Memories and the City.* Translated by Maureen Freely, Vintage Books, 2006.

———. *Kafamda Bir Tuhaflık.* Yapı Kredi Yayınları, 2014.

———. *Kar.* İletişim, 2002.

———. *Kara Kitap.* Can Yayınları, 1990.

———. Kara Kitap*'ın Sırları: Orhan Pamuk'un Yazı ve Resimleriyle.* With Darmin Hadzibegovic, Yapı Kredi Yayınları, 2013.

———. "Karaosmanoğlu (mis)translation?" E-mail message received by Sevinç Türkkan, Aug. 2014.

———. *Kırmızı Saçlı Kadın*. Yapı Kredi Yayınları, 2016.

———. "Love, Death, and Storytelling." *New Statesman*, vol. 135, no. 4823–25, 18 Dec. 2006, pp. 434–36.

———. *La maison du silence*. Translated by Münevver Andaç, Gallimard, 1988.

———. *Masumiyet Müzesi*. İletişim, 2008.

———. "Meine Großmutter stiftete zehn Lira." Interview by Iris Alanyalı. *Die Welt*, 20 Oct. 2005, www.welt.de/kultur/article172021/Meine-Grossmutter-stiftete-zehn-Lira.html. Accessed 15 May 2015.

———. "Memories of a Public Square." Translated by Ekin Oklap. *The New Yorker*, 5 June 2013, www.newyorker.com/books/page-turner/memories-of -a-public -square.

———. *The Museum of Innocence*. Translated by Maureen Freely, Alfred A. Knopf, 2009.

———. *The Museum of Innocence*. Translated by Maureen Freely, Faber and Faber, 2009.

———. "The Museum of Innocence: From the Novel to the Museum." University of Verona, 11 Apr. 2014. *YouTube*, www.youtube.com/watch?v=WtzJVX 20OXQ&t=7s.

———. "My Father's Suitcase." 2006. *Nobelprize.org*, Nobel Media AB, 11 Oct 2014, www.nobelprize.org/nobel_prizes/literature/laureates/2006/pamuk-lecture_en.html.

———. "My First Passport: What Does It Mean to Belong to a Country?" Translated by Maureen Freely, *The New Yorker*, 16 Apr. 2007, www.newyorker.com/magazine/2007/04/16/my-first-passport.

———. *My Name Is Red*. Translated by Erdağ M. Göknar, Alfred A. Knopf, 2001.

———. *My Name Is Red*. Translated by Erdağ M. Göknar, Faber and Faber, 2001.

———. *My Name Is Red*. Translated by Erdağ M. Göknar, Vintage Books, 2002.

———. *My Name Is Red*. Translated by Erdağ M. Göknar, Alfred A. Knopf, 2010. Everyman's Library Contemporary Classics.

———. "My Turkish Library." Translated by Maureen Freely, *The New York Review of Books*, 18 Dec. 2008, www.nybooks.com/articles/2008/12/18/my-turkish-library/.

———. *The Naive and the Sentimental Novelist*. Translated by Nazım Dikbaş, Harvard UP, 2010.

———. *The New Life*. Translated by Güneli Gün, Farrar, Straus, and Giroux, 1997.

———. *The New Life*. Translated by Güneli Gün, Vintage Books, 1998.

———. "On Trial." Translated by Maureen Freely, *The New Yorker*, 19 Dec. 2005, www .newyorker.com/magazine/2005/12/19/on-trial.

———. "Orhan Pamuk: Bridging Two Worlds." Interview by Elizabeth Farnsworth. *PBS NewsHour*, 20 Nov. 2002, www.pbs.org/newshour/bb/entertainment-july-dec02 -pamuk_11–20/.

———. "Orhan Pamuk on Taksim Square, the Effects of *Breaking Bad*, and Why the Future of the Novel Is in the East." Interview by Pankaj Mishra. *New Republic*,

29 July 2013, newrepublic.com/article/113948/orhan-pamuk-interview-taksim-square-erdogan-literature.

———. "Orhan Pamuk: The Art of Fiction No. 187." Interview by Ángel Gurría-Quintana. *The Paris Review*, no. 175, Fall-Winter 2005, www.theparisreview.org/interviews/5587/the-art-of-fiction-no-187-orhan-pamuk.

———. "Orhan Pamuk: Un écrivain turc à succès." *Blue Blanc Turc*, www.bleublancturc.com/TurcsconnusFR/Orhan_Pamuk.htm. Accessed 15 Feb. 2017.

———. *Öteki Renkler: Seçme Yazılar ve Bir Hikaye*. İletişim, 1999.

———. *Other Colors: Essays and a Story*. Translated by Maureen Freely, Alfred A. Knopf, 2007.

———. *Other Colors: Essays and a Story*. Translated by Maureen Freely, Vintage Books, 2007.

———. "A Private Reading of André Gide's Public *Journal*. Translated by Mary Isin. *Social Research*, vol. 71, no. 3, Fall 2014, pp. 679–90.

———. *The Red-Haired Woman*. Translated by Ekin Oklap, Alfred A. Knopf, 2017.

———. "A Religious Conversation." *Granta*, translated by Maureen Freely, no. 85, 2002, pp. 64–66.

———. *Saf ve Düşünceli Romancı*. İletişim, 2011.

———. "Salaam Bombay!" *Times Literary Supplement*, no. 4823, 8 Sept. 1995, p. 3.

———. *Schnee*. Translated by Christoph K. Neumann, Fischer Taschenbuch Verlag, 2009.

———. *Sessiz Ev*. Can Yayınları, 1983.

———. *Şeylerin Masumiyeti: Masumiyet Müzesi, İstanbul*. İletişim, 2012.

———. *Silent House*. Translated by Robert P. Finn, Alfred A. Knopf, 2012.

———. *Snow*. Translated by Maureen Freely, Alfred A. Knopf, 2004.

———. *Snow*. Translated by Maureen Freely, Faber and Faber, 2004.

———. *Snow*. Translated by Maureen Freely, Vintage Books, 2005.

———. *A Strangeness in My Mind: A Novel*. Translated by Ekin Oklap, Alfred A. Knopf, 2015.

———. "A Taste of Death: Patricia Highsmith's Crime Time." Translated by Murat Seçkin in collaboration with the author, *The Village Voice*, no. 37, 17 Nov. 1992, pp. 107–08.

———. "To Look out the Window." *The Norton Anthology of World Literature*, edited by Martin Puchner, 3rd ed., vol. F, W. W. Norton, 2012, pp. 1275–92.

———. "Turkey's Divided Character." *New Perspectives Quarterly*, vol. 17, no. 2, Spring 2000, pp. 20–22.

———. "The Turkish Trauma." Interview by Jörg Lau. *Sign and Sight*, 18 Apr. 2005, www.signandsight.com/features/115.html.

———. "Turkish Writer Captures the Intensity of Desire." Interview by Judy Stone. *The San Francisco Chronicle*, 27 Apr. 1997, www.sfgate.com/books/article/author-interview-Turkish-Writer-Captures-the-2842721.php. Accessed 24 Feb. 2016.

———. "University Lecture: A Discussion with Orhan Pamuk." Hosted by Lee C. Bollinger and John H. Coatsworth, 21 Dec. 2012, Columbia U. *YouTube*, www.youtube.com/watch?v=1D88ODerQN0&t=142s.

———. *The White Castle.* Translated by Victoria Holbrook, Carcanet, 1990.

———. *The White Castle.* Translated by Victoria Holbrook, George Braziller, 1990.

———. *Yeni Hayat.* İletişim, 1994.

"Pamuk Alman basınında." *Hürriyet*, 24 Oct. 2005, www.hurriyet.com.tr/panuk-alman-basininda-3431045.

"Pamuk Receives Award." *Hürriyet Daily News*, 16 Aug. 2012, www.hurriyetdailynews.com/pamuk-receives-award-from-chinese-platform.aspx?pageID=238&nID=27875&NewsCatID=386.

Parini, Jay. "Pirates, Pashas, and the Imperial Astrologer." *The New York Times Book Review*, 19 May 1991, p. 3.

Parks, Tim. "The New Dull Global Novel." *The New York Review of Books*, 9 Feb. 2010, www.nybooks.com/daily/2010/02/09/the-dull-new-global-novel/.

Parla, Jale. *Babalar ve Oğullar: Tanzimat Romanının Epistemolojik Temelleri.* İletişim, 1990.

———. "Dark Knowledge Befits Dark Colors: Turkish Novelists Interrogate the Ideology of Light." *New Perspectives on Turkey*, no. 41, 2009, pp. 9–42.

———. "From Allegory to Parable: Inscriptions of Anatolia in the Turkish Novel." *New Perspectives on Turkey*, no. 36, 2007, pp. 11–26.

Pizer, John. "Goethe's 'World Literature' Paradigm and Contemporary Cultural Globalization." *Comparative Literature*, vol. 52, no. 3, 2000, pp. 213–27.

Plett, Heinrich, editor. *Intertextuality.* De Gruyter, 1991.

Poe, Edgar Allan, and Philip Van Doren Stern. *Edgar Allan Poe.* Penguin Books, 1977.

Porter, Yves. "From the 'Theory of the Two Qalams' to the 'Seven Principles of Painting': Theory, Terminology, and Practice in Persian Classical Painting." *Muqarnas*, no. 17, 2000, pp. 109–18.

Pratt, Mary Louise. "Art of the Contact Zone." *Profession*, 1991, pp. 30–40. *JSTOR*, www.jstor.org/stable/25595469.

Proust, Marcel. *Swann's Way.* Translated by C. K. Scott Moncrieff, Modern Library, 1992.

Pym, Anthony. *Methods in Translation History.* Routledge, 2014.

Quataert, Donald. "Ottoman History Writing and Changing Attitudes towards the Notion of 'Decline.'" *History Compass*, no. 1, 2003, pp. 1–10.

Rilke, Rainer M. *Duino Elegies: Bilingual Edition.* Translated by Edward A. Snow, North Point Press, 2000.

Rossetti, Dante Gabriel. *Paolo and Francesca da Rimini. Tate*, www.tate.org.uk/art/artworks/rossetti-paolo-and-francesca-da-rimini-n03056.

Rûmî, Jalal al-Dīn. *The Masnavi.* Translated by J. A. Mojaddedi, Oxford UP, 2004.

———. *Rumi: Swallowing the Sun.* Translated by Franklin D. Lewis, Oneworld, 2007.

Rushdie, Salman. *Imaginary Homelands: Essays and Criticism, 1981–1991.* Penguin Books, 1992.

Said, Edward W. *Orientalism*. Vintage Books, 1979.

Sample, Mark. "Investigation (Oscar Wao)." *21st Century Literature*, 14 Oct. 2012, samplereality.com/gmu/442/course-guidelines/investigation-oscar-wao/. Accessed 14 Sept. 2014.

Savaş, Elif. *Coup/Darbe: A Documentary History of the Turkish Military Interventions*. MM Films, 2000.

Schiller, Friedrich. *On Naive and Sentimental Poetry*. 1800. Translated by William F. Wertz, Schiller Institute, 2005, www.schillerinstitute.org/transl/schiller_essays/naive_sentimental-1.html. Accessed 31 Aug. 2014.

Schleiermacher, Friedrich. "On the Different Methods of Translating." Translated by S. Bernofsky. *The Translation Studies Reader*, edited by Lawrence Venuti, 3rd ed., Routledge, 2012, pp. 43–63.

Schwarz, Roberto. "The Importing of the Novel to Brazil and Its Contradictions in the Work of Roberto Alencar." *Misplaced Ideas: Essays on Brazilian Culture*, edited by John Gledson, Verso Books, 1992, pp. 41–77.

Sells, Michael Anthony. *Early Islamic Mysticism: Sufi, Qur'an, Mi'raj, Poetic, and Theological Writings*. Paulist Press, 1996.

Seyfeddin, Ömer. "Sanatı İdrak." 1918. *Doğumunun 100. Yılında Ömer Seyfeddin*, Marmara University Press, 1984, pp. 292–95.

Seyhan, Azade. *Tales of Crossed Destinies: The Modern Turkish Novel in a Comparative Context*. Modern Language Association of America, 2008.

Shaw, Yan Overfield. "Orhan Pamuk." *Turkish Novelists since 1960*, edited and introduced by Burcu Alkan and Günay-Erkol Çimen, Gale, 2014, pp. 243–68. *Dictionary of Literary Biography*, vol. 373.

Smith, Wendy. "Orhan Pamuk: Outspoken Turk." *Publishers Weekly*, vol. 251, no. 34, 23 Aug. 2004, www.publishersweekly.com/pw/print/20040823/29671-outspoken-turk.html.

Sokel, Walter Herbert. *The Myth of Power and the Self: Essays on Franz Kafka*. Wayne State UP, 2002.

Steinberg, S. "Forecasts: Fiction." *Publishers Weekly*, vol. 238, no. 10, 22 Feb. 1991, p. 212.

Steinhart, Eric. "The Master-Slave Dialectic." Unpublished manuscript. William Patterson U, 1998.

Sternberg, Meir. "Polylingualism as Reality and Translation as Mimesis." *Poetics Today*, vol. 2, no. 4, 1981, pp. 221–39.

Stone, Leonard. "Minarets and Plastic Bags: The Social and Global Relations of Orhan Pamuk." *Turkish Studies*, vol. 7, no. 2, 2006, pp. 191–201.

Tanpınar, Ahmet Hamdi. *Beş Sehir* [Five Cities]. 13th ed., Dergah, 1999.

———. *Edebiyat Üzerine Makaleler*. M. E. B. Devlet Kitapları, 1969.

———. *A Mind at Peace*. 1949. Translated by Erdağ M. Göknar, Archipelago, 2011.

———. *The Time Regulation Institute*. 1954. Translated by Ender Gürol, Turko-Tatar Press, 2002.

———. *XIX. Asır Türk Edebiyatı* [Nineteenth-Century Turkish Literature].1949. Yapı Kredi Yayınları, 2006.

Teltscher, Kate. "Reading Orientalism in Istanbul: Edward Said and Orhan Pamuk." *Edward Said and the Literary, Social, and Political World*, edited by R. Ghosh, Routledge, 2009, pp. 137–49.

Thomas, D. M. "The New Life." *The New York Times*, 6 Apr. 1997, www.nytimes.com/1997/04/06/books/pamuk-life.html.

Tintoretto. *Sebastiano Venier at the Battle of Lepanto*. 1571. *Kunsthistoriches Museum Wien*, www.khm.at/objektdb/detail/1570/.

Titian. *Jacopo Strada*. 1567–68. *Kunsthistoriches Museum Wien*, www.khm.at/objektdb/detail/1949/.

Tolstoy, Leo. *Anna Karenina*. 1877. Translated by Constance Garnett. *Project Gutenberg*, www.gutenberg.org/files/1399/1399-h/1399-h.htm. Accessed 2 Sept. 2014.

"Les Très Riches Heures du duc de Berry Janvier." *Wikimedia Commons*, commons.wikimedia.org/wiki/File:Les_Tr%C3%A8s_Riches_Heures_du_duc_de_Berry_Janvier.jpg.

Turgenev, Ivan S. *Fathers and Sons*. Translated by Richard Freeborn, Oxford UP, 1998.

Türkkan, Sevinç. "Orhan Pamuk's *Kara Kitap*: (British) Reception vs. (American) Translation." *Making Connections: Interdisciplinary Approaches to Cultural Diversity*, vol. 11, no. 2, 2010, pp. 39–58.

———. "Orhan Pamuk's *Kara Kitap* (*The Black Book*): A Double Life in English." Afridi and Buyze, pp. 159–76.

———. "Pamuk, the Storyteller: Elements of *The Thousand and One Nights* in *The Black Book*." Can et al., pp. 83–109.

Updike, John. "Anatolian Arabesque." *The New Yorker*, 30 Aug. 2004, www.newyorker.com/magazine/2004/08/30/anatolian-arabesques.

———. "Murder in Miniature." *The New Yorker*, 3 Sept. 2001, www.newyorker.com/magazine/2001/09/03/murder-in-miniature.

———. "Vagueness on Wheels, Dust on a Skirt." *The New Yorker*, 19 Sept. 1991, pp. 103–05.

Vaisman, Daria. "Orhan Pamuk and Turkey's Future." *openDemocracy*, 1 Dec. 2006, www.opendemocracy.net/arts-Literature/pamuk_exile_4147.jsp. Accessed 11 Sept. 2014.

Vanilla Sky. Directed by Cameron Crowe, Paramount Pictures, 2001.

Venuti, Lawrence. "How to Read a Translation." *Words without Borders*, www.wordswithoutborders.org/article/how-to-read-a-translation. Accessed 12 Dec. 2012.

———. *The Translator's Invisibility: A History of Translation*. 2nd ed., Routledge, 2008.

Vogl, Joseph. "Vierte Person. Kafkas Erzählstimme." *Deutsche Vierteljahresschrift*, no. 68, 1994, pp. 745–56.

Welles, Orson, director. *The Trial*. Astor Pictures Corporation, 1962.

"Die Welt mit westlichen Augen betrachten." *Die Zeit Online*, 6 Oct. 2005, www.zeit.de/zuender/2005/42/pamuk.

Weschler, Lawrence. *Mr. Wilson's Cabinet of Wonder*. Pantheon Books, 1995.

White, Hayden V. *Tropics of Discourse: Essays in Cultural Criticism*. Johns Hopkins UP, 1978.

Williams, Raymond. *Keywords: A Vocabulary of Culture and Society*. Oxford UP, 1976.

Yücel, Tahsin. "Kara Kitap." *Dipnot Kitap Kulübü*, dipnotkitap.net/DENEME/Kara_Kitap_Tahsin_Yucel.htm. Originally published in *Hürriyet Gösteri*, no. 120, Nov. 1990, pp. 45–48.

Zilcosky, John. *Kafka's Travels: Exoticism, Colonialism, and the Traffic of Writing*. Palgrave Macmillan, 2003.

Ziya Paşa. "Şiir ve inşa." *Hürriyet*, no. 11, 7 Sept. 1868, pp. 3–4.

Zola, Émile. *The Masterpiece*. Translated by Thomas Walton and Roger Pearson, Oxford UP, 2008.

INDEX